Dropouts in America

Dropouts in America

Confronting the Graduation Rate Crisis

Edited by
GARY ORFIELD

Harvard Education Press
Cambridge, Massachusetts

Library of Congress Control Number 2004108772

Paperback Edition: 1-891792-53-9
Library Edition: 1-891792-54-7

Published by Harvard Education Press,
an imprint of the Harvard Education Publishing Group

Harvard Education Press
8 Story Street
Cambridge, MA 02138

Cover Design: Alyssa Morris
Cover Photo: Corbis
Typesetting: Sheila Walsh

The typefaces used in this book are Adobe Garamond for text and Adobe Garamond and Stone Sans for display.

*This book is dedicated to those who labor to
reconnect the educational pipeline and to give hope and
tools to students who are in serious danger of losing their future.
They help keep alive the possibility of a fair chance for Latino,
African American, and American Indian students,
who so often go to schools where few find success
and too many are without hope.*

Contents

Acknowledgments

This book would have been impossible without the collaboration of many people. The conference that initiated this work grew out of a close cooperation with Robert Schwartz and Achieve, Inc., and the excellent staff work of Elizabeth DeBray, now on the faculty of the University of Georgia. Support from Blenda Wilson and the Nellie Mae Foundation were crucial in launching the conference. The editing of the initial papers by Robert Rothman moved us a long step forward. Dan Losen of The Civil Rights Project staff played a major role in helping organize the conferences, where new insights were developed in collaboration with researchers, policymakers, educators, and activists, as well as Jobs for the Future, Teachers College, Dean Eugene Garcia and Teresa Huerta at Arizona State University, Jack Wuest and the Alternative Schools Network, Northwestern University, and the numerous other universities and education and civil rights groups that cosponsored conferences with us.

All of our authors were willing to answer hard questions, deal with severe space limitations, and do a great deal to make their research more useful to citizens and leaders across the country. Funding from the Mott and Carnegie foundations, among others, made this work possible. Finally, the book simply would not have been completed in a timely fashion were it not for the deep dedication, the organizational skills and consistent attention of Jennifer Blatz, the fine editing work of Carolyn Peelle, the attention to detail that Himabindu Kolli demonstrated in the final stages of the manuscript production, and strong prodding from the Harvard Education Press, particularly Caroline Chauncey and Dody Riggs.

Losing Our Future:
Minority Youth Left Out

GARY ORFIELD

Every year, across the United States, a dangerously high percentage of students —mostly poor and minority—disappear from the educational pipeline before graduating from high school. Nationally, only about two-thirds of all students—and only half of all blacks, Latinos,[1] and Native Americans—who enter ninth grade graduate with regular diplomas four years later. For minority males, these figures are far lower. The implications of these high dropout rates are far reaching and devastating for individuals, communities, and the economic vitality of this country. Yet, because of misleading and inaccurate reporting of dropout and graduation rates, the public remains largely unaware of this educational and civil rights crisis. Very little energy has been put into addressing this problem, or even into producing accurate statistics on graduation levels.

Dropping out often leads to economic and social tragedy. High school dropouts are far more likely than graduates to be unemployed, in prison, unmarried or divorced, and living in poverty. A 2002 U.S. Census Bureau report, for example, shows that the mean earnings of young adult Latinos who finish high school are 43 percent higher than those of Latinos who drop out.[2] A 2003 study based on U.S. Justice Department data reports that two-thirds of prison inmates are dropouts, and that an incredible 52 percent of all African American male dropouts in their early thirties have prison records.[3] A 2003 report on the Chicago job market shows that more than half of young adult male African American dropouts in that city have no jobs at all.[4]

In 2002, the average annual earnings of an adult high school dropout were $18,800, down by about a tenth in real terms since 1975. The good jobs that in generations past allowed unionized workers without an education to earn a family wage and achieve economic security are largely gone. The industrial work force has shrunk by 2.3 million jobs since 1991.[5] Even full-time workers can often expect only a succession of dead-end jobs paying not much above the minimum wage, with few or no benefits, and real wages that will decline steadily over time.

The social costs of the dropout crisis are tremendous in scope and duration. Many high school dropouts are not able to provide the essentials for their families, and studies indicate that the economic and societal effects of dropouts' lost earnings and taxes persist for many years. Moreover, children of dropouts are far more likely to be in weak schools, perform badly, and drop out themselves, thus creating powerful intergenerational social problems. When an entire racial or ethnic group experiences consistently high dropout rates, these problems can deeply damage the community, its families,[6] its social structure, and its institutions.

More and more of our future workers are from racial and ethnic groups whose young people are having severe difficulty finishing high school. About one-sixth of American students are African American, and slightly more are Latino. The proportion of students of color in our nation's schools is rising; by mid-century, whites are likely to make up only two-fifths of the total school-age population. Black and Latino students are highly segregated by both race and poverty, and for many Latinos the separation is intensified by linguistic isolation. The schools where these students are increasingly concentrated have low achievement levels, often lack qualified teachers, and tend to lose most of their students as dropouts. When students begin to have the problems that are strongly predictive of dropping out, no one does anything. Often no one even notices. In the worst cases, these students are encouraged to leave. No one cares enough to make an honest report on how many students are lost, how many lives are ruined.

These students are the future of many of our cities and rural communities. If we write them off, they will find ways to live—ways that will often be destructive to the core values of our communities. The reality today is that we are ignoring the issue because of misleading data, of prejudice against poor and nonwhite adolescents, and because there are no simple answers to these tough questions. But we are dealing with the devastating consequences of family destruction, community decline, and incredibly costly and largely unsuccessful intervention through the criminal justice system, without thinking about how to use some of those resources to instead change young people's lives for the better. This disconnection is inexcusable, especially in a society where education is so central to an individual's life chances.

The goal of this book is to raise public awareness of this issue, and to make improving high school graduation rates a central component of national educational reform efforts. Understanding why this is a basic civil rights issue in contemporary society requires focusing on the severe racial disparities in high school graduation rates that exist at the school and district levels.

A CATASTROPHE IGNORED

Most Americans think that if you add the number of dropouts to the number of graduates, you get 100 percent of the students in a school. If you didn't drop out, then you must have graduated. This is almost never true in official statistics. In some districts it is just assumed that a missing student enrolled somewhere else, so many students aren't counted as either dropouts or graduates. As a result, the data that state and local officials release suggest a much higher completion rate. These statistics sound good and make the school officials look good, but are often off by several orders of magnitude. Texas and California, for example, are among the states that report very low dropout rates but have a great many students who do not receive diplomas.

National statistics are equally misleading. In June 2004, for example, the U.S. Census Bureau released a report claiming that "high school graduation rates reach all-time high," based on a national survey.[7] Yet studies we present in this book report that these data are seriously inaccurate, particularly for minority students, and do not begin to describe the conditions in the nation's large urban centers and in the rural South.

Most state and local dropout statistics are flawed to the point of being worthless, yet little federal or state money is devoted to getting accurate numbers. Phillip Kaufman, who prepared many federal dropout reports and analyzed the strengths and weaknesses of the major data sources (ch. 5), commented at a 2001 conference, "The federal government spends over $40 million on the National Assessment of Educational Progress [testing a national sample of students]. It probably spends less than $1 million on dropout statistics."[8]

We put great pressure on our schools to raise test scores and very little to ensure that students graduate. Congress took a first step in recognizing the severity of the dropout problem by including graduation rate accountability provisions in the 2001 No Child Left Behind Act (NCLB). Unfortunately, the requirements of that part of the law are being widely ignored (see ch. 2): The Department of Education subsequently issued regulations that allow schools, districts, and states to all but eliminate graduation rate accountability, and not even to report graduation data for minority subgroups. In contrast, annual improvements on test scores for all racial groups are required. Most state and local dropout statistics are worthless and misleading in reporting this disaster. Very little federal or state money is devoted to dropout prevention or even getting accurate numbers. The result is that a school or school district can be honored and praised for raising its test scores even when it is pushing low-achieving students out of school in order to raise average scores.

WHY DON'T WE EVEN KNOW THE NUMBERS?

The lack of accurate data on high school completion rates in part reflects the fact that we really do not have very good data on most aspects of schooling, except for enrollment, attendance, and free-lunch status, all of which are required for state and federal funding. The major exception is test scores, which in the past two decades of test-driven accountability plans have become the most highly valued outcome of public education. Under the NCLB, annual gains on standardized math and reading test scores determine the fate of a school. It's ironic that school officials are held strictly accountable for assuring that students take these kinds of tests, but no one is held accountable if half the students from a school simply disappear from the records.

In fact, no one knows exactly how many students drop out of American high schools because the vast majority of states do not follow individual students over time, but merely report annual enrollments. State and local dropout reports rely on decisions of school principals and staffs about how to classify and report students' lack of attendance. There are often a number of categories in which students are not counted as dropouts, even if they never graduated. One state counts students who go to jail as transfer students, for example. More commonly, students receiving or studying for a GED are not counted as dropouts, though they have left school and are pursuing a different and much less valuable credential. Schools often have little or no information about what has happened to a student who disappears, and they tend to make optimistic guesses. Neither the state nor the federal statistical offices check the data. Under these circumstances, underreporting is extremely common. It's not unusual for a school to report a 10 percent dropout rate when the number of graduates is 70 percent lower than the number of ninth graders enrolled four years earlier.

To know exact graduation rates, we would have to give each student a single lifetime education ID number and follow them individually through all the grades, wherever they moved, and then find out where and whether each of them actually received a regular diploma. Without such information, we will never know exactly what happens to students. A handful of states are building such systems, but it will be years before they produce good data. To implement and monitor such efforts nationwide would require a major federal effort.

In this book, we present reports by scholars who use several different methods of estimating dropout rates to support their conclusions. Each concedes serious weaknesses in the data; none claims that the datasets used are without problems. Until better systems are created, however, more accurate estimates can only be obtained through more careful analysis of existing data elements. Our analysis places central emphasis on methods closely related to the approach recommended by Congress in the No Child Left Behind Act: following cohorts of students through schools and districts, and comparing the number of graduates with the number of students from that age group enrolled four years earlier. (A similar method was used during the Reagan administration by the Department of Education.)

A related approach is used by Christopher Swanson of the Urban Institute (ch. 1), who uses a Cumulative Promotion Index (CPI) to calculate the probability that a student entering the ninth grade will complete high school on time with a regular diploma. His computations draw on enrollment information from the Department of Education's annual Common Core of Data, rather than dropout statistics. Because the CPI only requires data from two consecutive years, it can quickly estimate current educational conditions for all groups.

Following a graduating class from ninth to twelfth grade is also a useful and quick analytic tool for detecting low graduation rates. Researchers from Johns Hopkins term this enrollment comparison the *promotion power* of a school. When they examined enrollment data in urban schools from the 100 largest school districts in the country (ch. 3), their research showed that the twelfth-grade class had shrunk by more than half in 317 of the 661 schools sampled. Only approximately 42 percent of all the freshmen made it to grade 12 in schools where 90 percent or more of the students were children of color. While comparing enrollment data is not a foolproof method for calculating graduation rates, it offers an extremely straightforward and simple way to detect large problems.

Robert Hauser's research (ch. 4) offers an excellent and thorough analysis of the trends in the most commonly cited dropout data, the Census Bureau's Current Population Survey (CPS). Since this is the source of the most widely reported national data, it is important to understand what it tells us and what its limitations are. For instance, the survey relies not on actual degrees but on self-reporting from a large household sample survey that excludes the military and institutionalized population. It has a poor record of counting some other groups, particularly young minority males. Thus, the sample is not drawn in a way to track accurately the populations of special interest to our civil rights work. In fact, according to enrollment and degree data gathered by the National Center for Education Statistics (NCES) and the Office for Civil Rights, the CPS data suggest that more minority students had graduated from high school than were even enrolled in twelfth grade!

Balfanz's and Swanson's analyses of the NCES enrollment data, using two different but related statistical procedures, break down the numbers by race, gender, state, district, and school. Where the CPS data show low dropout rates for all groups except Latinos, analyses based on the NCES enrollment data show exceptionally low graduation levels for blacks, Latinos, and Native Americans. In addition, Balfanz's results allow us to locate the crisis in particular kinds of schools, such as segregated high-poverty urban high schools, many of which appear to graduate far fewer than half of their students. Similar statistics have recently been produced by the conservative Manhattan Institute and by The Education Trust, a strong supporter of high-stakes testing policies. There is growing consensus across ideological lines that this general approach is the best available technique for estimating graduation rates. Accordingly, we believe that the Balfanz and Swanson analyses yield the most compelling data for policy purposes.

CAUSES AND CURES

Given that this problem is severe and deeply threatening to many communities, the immediate questions that arise are what causes it, and what can we do about it? These questions are the focus of the second half of this book. Rumberger's analysis of the research on the causes of dropping out (ch. 6) shows that there are many, both in school and in family and community life. Addressing each of these can help reduce the loss of talent.

In the following chapters (chs. 7–9), we learn that problems relating to dropping out appear in their most acute form in the ninth grade. The transition into high school is a point of tremendous vulnerability, and a great many students who fail to progress directly from ninth into tenth grade never recover.

The third section of the book presents new models for easing this critical transition (chs. 10, 11) and evaluates their impact. We learn that the most systematic federal study of dropout intervention programs shows some gains for school completion, but little for test-score improvement (ch. 13). In the description of the Talent Development High School model (ch. 14), we are introduced to an important reform being developed at Johns Hopkins for Philadelphia, Baltimore, and elsewhere to try to help students stay—and succeed—in school. Each of these studies and summaries of previous research indicates that there are changes that can make a real difference, but that many obstacles will have to be overcome.

DROPOUT RATES AS A CIVIL RIGHTS ISSUE

High school dropout rates have been a central concern of The Civil Rights Project at Harvard University, which was created in 1996 as a university-based think tank to work on issues of civil rights and racial equity, and to foster understanding of problems and solutions in a society where 40 percent of the nation's young people are nonwhite and where racial and economic stratification are growing. The dropout issue has not traditionally been high on the civil rights agenda, in part because most published data suggested that it was not an urgent problem. However, The Civil Rights Project's research on the statistical trends and local reports convinced us that the dropout problem was very serious and probably worsening in response to educational policies, such as high-stakes, test-driven school reform strategies.

Our preliminary research showed that the basic data were so fundamentally flawed that it was impossible to have a serious conversation about the real dimensions of the issue, and we found that little serious work had been done on dropout policy for decades. Other work that The Civil Rights Project had commissioned, especially the studies on high-stakes testing that led to the book *Raising Standards or Raising Barriers?*, convinced us not only that there were very serious problems, but that the excessive pressure of high-stakes tests could make them worse. Our study of the Houston schools in 2000 foreshadowed the kinds of problems that would become a public scandal in 2002, when a cover-up of very high dropout levels was revealed in a district often featured as a model for test-driven reforms.[9]

Our colleagues at Achieve, Inc., a leading pro-testing organization representing many business and political leaders, agreed that improving graduation rates was critically important. In early 2001, Achieve and The Civil Rights Project cosponsored a national conference, called Dropouts in America, which focused on measuring dropouts and summarizing what was known about positive interventions. The two organizations jointly commissioned leading national experts to prepare papers on the key issues, and we found that there was intense national interest in the subject. The papers ignited policy discussions and local efforts to look seriously into the problems and solutions. Some of them, in much revised form, appear in this book.

Since that conference, The Civil Rights Project has been very active on the dropout issue. When the legislation that eventually became the No Child Left Behind Act was in development, The Civil Rights Project commissioned and presented research to members of Congress and their staffs. We urged that more resources be made available for high school and middle school interventions, and that schools be held accountable not just for test scores, but also for their students' level of high school completion, with a special focus on minority students. By any reasonable definition, a student who does not graduate from high school is "left behind." It is no measure of success for anyone if a school raises its average test scores by flunking out low-scoring students and ruining their futures. Graduation accountability provides an essential balance for schools reacting to pressure to make test-score gains. Our ideas on dropout accountability and on defining dropouts were ultimately included in a portion of the No Child Left Behind Act.

The Civil Rights Project also cosponsored, with a variety of concerned organizations and universities, major regional conferences on dropouts in New York, Phoenix, and Chicago. The Chicago conference, cosponsored by 17 organizations in 2004, drew more than 350 participants, including community groups, educators, political leaders, researchers, and many others concerned that the dropout issue must become a high priority in both civil rights and education. In 2004, state legislatures in Ohio and Illinois, for example, enacted bills designed to help reduce dropouts, signifying a growing interest in the subject. In the 2004 presidential campaign, Democratic candidate John Kerry pledged to lower the number of dropouts in the nation by one million during his first term.

Raising graduation rates is a key item on the opportunity agenda for adolescents from minority communities, who are often simply written off. Though it is seldom said aloud, the basic assumption is that by high school it is too late to do anything to help these young people, and that attention should be focused on saving the next generation. This theory ignores the fact that millions of students must attend high schools that are troubled, low-performing, have poorly qualified faculty, a limited curriculum, and a low level of competitiveness—all of this often in threatening environments. Adolescence is a risky time, even for students with privileged backgrounds, good academic preparation, and families who provide many supports and safety nets for their children. For students in what Balfanz calls "dropout factories," adolescent risks are many times more serious, and there are few if any safety nets. If we wish to change this, we will obviously need new initiatives and leadership that recognize a range of issues, take young people seriously, and address the academic and personal crises they face before their life chances are damaged irretrievably.

LOOKING AHEAD

The fact that so little work has been put into raising graduation rates does not mean that nothing can be done. Although the solutions are as complicated as are the adolescent crises in the ghettos and barrios of our society, there are many things that could make a difference. In some ways raising the graduation rate may be considerably less difficult than raising test scores at this age level.

Our authors have identified a number of possible interventions. For instance, they identify ninth grade as a critical year in determining students' futures. Policies that smooth the transition to high school, create closer contact with teachers, and deliver more individual attention to students can help.

One thing that is both depressing and hopeful about the data is the finding that the dropout problem is concentrated in its most severe form in a relatively small number of high schools around the country. The few hundred high schools that are overwhelmingly minority, low income, and located in central cities are where the dropout crisis reaches catastrophic dimensions. These schools are also located in areas where labor markets are unforgiving for people without high school credentials, so that many young African Americans and Latinos—especially males—face a nearly hopeless situation. If neither the military nor fast-food restaurants want your application, you have few options. The problem is compounded by well-documented, ongoing racial discrimination in the labor market and the lack of access from segregated residential areas to areas where jobs are increasing.

If we are to be serious about improving graduation rates, we must concentrate our efforts on reforming these critical schools, or on getting the students who are in them into schools that are more effective. We might be able to make a fairly dramatic difference in the level of high school completion with a relatively small number of intervention plans in each state, particularly for our black and Latino populations. It is depressing to realize that many of these "dropout factories" that send hundreds of students off a figurative cliff each year don't have as much money to spend on dropout intervention as it will cost to keep even one of their dropouts in prison for a year.

The crisis deserves a comprehensive strategy, one that includes not only high school reform but also support services and collaboration with criminal justice systems, families, health care, and other systems addressing the whole range of problems that are concentrated in these schools. Many of these students need sustained contact with adult mentors who can give them support and help them connect to mainstream society.

When we see a problem as a serious threat, we don't wait until we have scientific proof about the solutions. We start experiments and try to figure out what works and how to refine our efforts. We first adopted Title I and Head Start back in 1964 and 1965 with very little knowledge about their impact because we were concerned about poor children who were way behind in early elementary grades. It has taken a long time to learn how best to structure and target these interventions, but we never turned away from the goal. We need a similar effort, linked to scientific evaluation and ongoing improvements, at the high school level.

Although this book does not present one fully developed program or policy that would solve the dropout problem, there are plenty of reasonable starting points presented in the research here and elsewhere. We need to start major experiments and encourage new and comprehensive approaches. We should deepen research and consolidate our knowledge from existing data. While conducting systematic experiments on relatively well-developed ideas, we also need to pursue the best guesses of local educators and communities, since there are so many different situations and contexts. We should study and disseminate interventions that substantially increase graduation rates. We should encourage research groups and school districts to launch strategies that combine research-based elements and theories of change in multidimensional programs. This is how many of the most important preschool programs and elementary school reforms were launched, and it seems certain that similarly broad, multidimensional approaches will be essential for high schools.

Reforms often try to create for poor students conditions, networks, and support systems that middle-class children find in their families and their neighborhoods and schools. If we start thinking about students who drop out as people who have potential instead of as threats to society, we'll have to recognize the challenges they are actually facing and the incredible losses sustained in communities where most of these young people have no future. If we are to benefit from their talents rather than fear the pathological consequences of their massive exclusion and rejection in the economy, we must help them finish school and give them a chance to succeed as adults in this society.

NOTES

1. The term *Hispanic* is used throughout in tables because the data is collected and reported under that category.
2. U.S. Bureau of the Census, *Educational Attainment in the United States*: March 2002, table 9. Washington, DC: Government Printing Office.
3. Bruce Western, Vincent Schiraldi, and Jason Ziedenberg, *Education and Incarceration* (Washington, DC: Justice Policy Institute, August 2003), pp. 7–9.
4. Center for Labor Market Studies, Northeastern University, *Youth Labor Market and Education Indicators for the State of Illinois* (Chicago: Alternative Schools Network, October 2003).
5. U.S. Bureau of Labor Statistics, "Manufacturing," on-line table, modified October 2, 2003, available at www.bls.gov/ces/.

6. Disconnection and poor attitudes toward school are associated with teen pregnancy (Robert D. Plotnick, "The Effects of Attitudes on Teenage Premarital Pregnancy and Its Resolution," *American Sociological Review, 57* [December 1992]:802), and teen pregnancy, of course, sharply reduces high school completion.
7. U.S. Bureau of the Census, news release, June 29, 2004.
8. Phillip Kaufman, "The National Dropout Data Collection System: Assessing Consistency." Paper presented at the Dropouts in America Conference, Harvard University, Cambridge, MA, January 2001, p. 30. (See ch. 5 for an edited version.)
9. Linda McNeil and Angela Valenzuela, "The Harmful Impact of the TAAS System of Testing in Texas: Beneath the Accountability Rhetoric," in *Raising Standards or Raising Barriers? Inequality and High-Stakes Testing in Public Education,* ed. Gary Orfield and Mindy L. Kornhaber (New York: Century Foundation Press, 2001): 127–150.

CHAPTER 1

Sketching a Portrait of
Public High School Graduation:
Who Graduates? Who Doesn't?[1]

CHRISTOPHER B. SWANSON

Despite nearly universal recognition that completing high school is a key milestone in an individual's schooling and an important indicator of system performance, graduation rates have not been a major focus of educational statistics reporting in the past. Moreover, these important measures have historically generated far less attention and interest than test scores. The No Child Left Behind Act (NCLB) of 2001, however, has sparked a renewed interest in graduation rates. For the first time, this federal law requires that high schools and school systems be held accountable in a meaningful way for graduation rates, as well as performance on academic assessments. This important step in the evolution of federal accountability has generated considerable debate over a variety of issues, including the state of the nation with regard to this key measure of educational fitness; graduation levels among particular student subgroups, such as historically disadvantaged minorities; the ways in which states are implementing graduation rate accountability required under the law; and even the best methods for measuring graduation rates.

This chapter provides the most extensive set of systematic empirical findings on public school graduation rates available to date, for the nation as a whole and for each of the 50 states, using a measure called the Cumulative Promotion Index, or CPI. This indicator offers several significant advantages over other commonly reported graduation rate statistics. It adheres to the definition of the high school graduation rate specified by NCLB, so it could be used for purposes of federal accountability. It relies on enrollment information and diploma counts and avoids the notoriously unreliable dropout data some other methods use. The CPI also requires only two years of data collection, as opposed to four years for most other methods.

Since the CPI indicator makes very modest demands on data systems, it could be calculated today for virtually every public school and district in the country using readily available information. In addition, the CPI employs a focused one-year window of observation, which makes it particularly desirable for application in accountability systems. This is because the CPI places a stronger emphasis on current educational conditions than other approaches have, and thus would detect improvements related to ongoing reform initiatives more quickly.

This study computes graduation rates using data on enrollment and diploma counts from the Common Core of Data (CCD). This U.S. Department of Education database is the most comprehensive national source of information on public schools and local education agencies. The CCD also offers the only means of directly comparing graduation rates for school systems across the country using data defined and reported to the National Center for Education Statistics in a uniform manner. By pairing the CPI indicator with the CCD data, graduation rates for the high school class of 2001 can be computed for virtually every public school district in the nation.

Nationwide, the overall graduation rate for 2001 was 68 percent. As disconcerting as this national statistic may be, focusing on this figure alone would fail to call attention to the truly troubling educational experiences for particular student groups. Results consistently point to certain areas that should be of grave concern to educators and policymakers. When results are broken down by race and ethnicity, we find that more than 75 percent of white and Asian students completed high school with a diploma. By stark contrast, barely half of students from historically disadvantaged minority groups graduated. Graduation rates for black, American Indian, and Hispanic students were 50, 51, and 53 percent, respectively. Male students complete high school at consistently lower levels than females. Graduation rates are also substantially lower for students educated in highly segregated, socioeconomically disadvantaged, and urban school systems. Strong regional disparities consistently emerge from the findings, as does tremendous variation in the performance of individual states.

This chapter provides the most compelling evidence to date that the nation finds itself in the midst of a serious, broad-based, and (until recently) unrecognized crisis in high school completion. This crisis has gone undetected in part due to a lack of in-depth national investigation into the phenomenon based on solid statistics and methods. Understanding the depth and breadth of a problem, however, is a crucial first step in devising a solution. When armed with such knowledge, both policymakers and the public will be better able to identify and implement promising intervention strategies for struggling schools.

This chapter is organized into several main sections. The following section provides a discussion of the data and methods used in this study. Next is an overview of the study's descriptive findings, which include graduation rate statistics for the student population as a whole and results disaggregated for racial/ethnic subgroups and by gender. Graduation rates for different kinds of school districts are also examined. The next section conducts more sophisticated bivariate and multivariate statistical analyses in order to investigate the links between graduation rates and district context, particularly relating to levels of socioeconomic disadvantage and segregation. The final section offers a brief conclusion to the analytic portion of the study.

DATA AND METHODS

The Common Core of Data

The analyses performed for this study are based on data from the Common Core of Data. The U.S. Department of Education annually conducts this census of public sector local educational agencies (districts) and schools for the 50 states, the District of Columbia, and several other nonstate jurisdictions.[2] The CCD data collection is intended to capture all settings in which public education is provided at the elementary and secondary levels. Annual surveys of basic demographic and educational information at the state, district, and school levels are completed by staff of the state education agencies. Detailed methodological descriptions of the CCD can be found in technical documentation published by the National Center for Education Statistics (NCES, 2003a, 2003b).

The CCD represents the most comprehensive source of statistics on basic school and district demographics, high school completion, and dropout currently available. Individual state-operated data systems typically contain information similar to the CCD and in some cases may have far richer collections of variables. But because states often employ different definitions and methods when collecting and reporting their data, there is no guarantee that the information generated by such state systems will be comparable from state to state.

Two principal features of the CCD recommended it for use in this study. The first is its inclusiveness and the systematic nature of the data. The CCD reports data according to common definitions and requires some level of standardization in the data collection procedures used across the states. In fact, it is the only database from which it is possible to calculate graduation rates that can be compared across states with confidence. Secondly, the CCD is a well-known, frequently used database that exists in the public domain. As such, the results from this study can be replicated using information readily available to other researchers, policymakers, educators, and the public at large. State systems do not typically offer this level of accessibility.

All analyses reported in this study were performed at the district level. This effectively bottom-up analytic strategy was devised to provide a more direct examination of local conditions and dynamics than is available in other recently published reports that present only national- or state-level results. In situations where findings in the current study are reported for higher levels of aggregation (e.g., the states or the nation as a whole), district data have been weighted according to size of enrollment in order to produce results representative of the student populations of those broader educational units. Subgroup-specific results are weighted according to subgroup-specific enrollment.

The District Sample

During the focal year for our analysis (the 2000–2001 academic year), there were 14,935 regular school districts in operation throughout the 50 states and the District of Columbia, as reported in the Common Core of Data. In defining our target population for analytic purposes, however, it will be necessary to introduce several additional conditions or restrictions. Our objective is to identify districts that 1) are eligible for the calculation of a graduation rate and 2) should in theory have the necessary reliable information needed to calculate such a rate. It is reasonable to assume, for instance, that we can only calculate a meaningful graduation rate for districts that contain a full complement of secondary-level grades (9–12). Roughly one-quarter of regular school districts in the country do not meet this criterion, the majority of which have only an elementary-level grade span or have ungraded enrollment.

In addition, some level of district stability is required for a reliable graduation rate to be produced. Districts that have been in operation for fewer than four years, for instance, would not have graduated a full cohort of students (i.e., a group of students progressing from ninth grade through graduation). Of the districts serving students during the 2000–2001 school year, a small fraction were not in operation during at least some part of the preceding four-year period. In addition, about one percent of districts had undergone a significant change in boundaries during this period. Such events could effectively alter the identity of a particular district organization and its student body. This is likely to produce large year-to-year fluctuations in enrollments and demographics, resulting in invalid estimates of graduation rates. Taking all of these selection criteria into consideration, we arrived at a target population of 11,110 school districts for which valid graduation rates can be calculated.

A Note on Data Verification

The CCD is a voluntary data collection system operated as a collaborative enterprise between the U.S. Department of Education and state education agencies (SEAs). Once surveys from the states are received, the National Center for Education Statistics engages in a variety of mechanical procedures to clean the raw data. Otherwise, however, the federal agency's operating assumption is that these data are accurate as reported to the states by local agencies through their own established administrative data systems. No provisions exist for routine verification of the data reported to the CCD with local school system personnel. Barring exceptional circumstances, the information provided by the SEAs is assumed to be accurate.

Under most circumstances there is no reason to suspect that significant problems with data quality exist within the CCD, at least if the state administrative systems from which the data originate take steps to assure the accuracy of reported information at the source. In an enormous data system like the CCD, which consists of information from over 95,000 schools and 17,000 local education agencies, the odd undetected reporting error may exist. These isolated irregularities will have a negligible impact on large-scale empirical analyses such as those presented in this chapter. However, to the extent that certain forms of information (e.g., dropout counts) tend to be systematically misreported (e.g., undercounted), the CCD data will also reflect these biases.

This study has taken steps to ensure that its reported findings are based on the most complete and reliable information available. For instance, the CPI method we employ and recommend to measure graduation rates avoids using dropout data, which are often of questionable accuracy. Throughout this report, we also adopt a reporting convention that reflects data quality and completeness. Specifically, we do not present results that are based on low levels of coverage of the student population. In situations where CPI graduation rate estimates represent less than half of the target student population, results are not reported and a notation is provided indicating low coverage. Estimates based on 50 to 75 percent of the student population are reported, but are flagged as reflecting a moderate level of coverage. Estimates covering over 75 percent of students in the target population are reported without notation. Given a richer data source, more sophisticated indicators could be developed to capture other characteristics of the districts examined. While admittedly rudimentary, the reporting criteria linked to student population coverage used here provide a basic but practical indication of data quality.

The Cumulative Promotion Index

This report employs the Cumulative Promotion Index to measure high school graduation rates. The value of the CPI indicator approximates the probability that a student entering the ninth grade will complete high school on time with a regular diploma. It does this by representing high school graduation as a stepwise process composed of three grade-to-grade promotion transitions (9 to 10, 10 to 11, and 11 to 12) in addition to the ultimate high school graduation event (grade 12 to diploma). It should be emphasized that this measure counts only students receiving regular high school diplomas as graduates. This definition of a graduate is consistent with the provisions of the No Child Left Behind Act. The law clearly stipulates that, for purposes of federal accountability, the recipients of a regular standards-based state diploma are counted as graduates, while those who obtain other nondiploma credentials (e.g., certificates of attendance) or equivalencies (e.g., the GED) are not to be considered graduates.[3]

To demonstrate the method for calculating the CPI we use a simplified example. Let us suppose that a particular school district currently has one hundred students enrolled in each grade from ninth through twelfth. Further, we will hypothesize that 5 percent of students currently in grades 9, 10, and 11 will drop out of school this year, and that 5 percent of seniors will fail to earn a diploma at the end of the year. So, for example, we would count 100 ninth graders at our starting point but only 95 tenth graders the following fall. Carrying out the calculation (note 3), we would estimate a graduation rate of 81.5 percent for this district. Given conditions in this hypothetical district (an effective 5 percent annual attrition rate for students at each grade level), only about 82 out of every 100 entering ninth graders would be expected to finish school with a diploma.[4]

The data available in the CCD are cross-sectional and reported at aggregate levels, representing snapshots of schools and district agencies at particular points in time. So, for example, we know how many ninth graders were enrolled in a district in 2000 and how many tenth graders were enrolled in 2001. But we cannot track these students individually over time. The CPI statistics reported in this study are, therefore, based on *estimated* grade-level cohorts from the CCD rather than *true* cohorts of individual students from a longitudinal database. For the purposes of this study, the advantage of the CCD (and a very important one) is that the database provides systematic information that can be used to calculate comparable graduation rates for every school district in the nation. It would be possible to apply the CPI calculation method to longitudinal data following individual students as well, but few states have the established student-tracking systems necessary to generate such data.

The most common strategy for estimating graduation rates when longitudinal data are not available is to follow a single estimated cohort over a four-year period. Typically, this will involve identifying a focal group of ninth graders and comparing data on that group to the students who are twelfth graders (or graduates) four years later. The strategy employed in the CPI method, however, breaks with this common approach by instead following four separate estimated cohorts over a one-year period.

The CPI's shortened window of observation has a number of potential advantages. Over shorter periods of time, large changes in migration rates or grade retention patterns that could potentially undermine the accuracy of a graduation rate indicator are less likely to occur. The CPI indicator can also be estimated very quickly, after two waves of data collection conducted over a one-year interval. From an accountability perspective, the CPI's strategy of heavily weighting contemporary conditions may offer a more appealing (and perhaps even a more legitimate) basis for determining *current* levels of educational system performance, and for implementing sanctions that are experienced in the *present*. Finally, the measure's one-year timeframe may offer an attractive opportunity for a state or other educational agency to move incrementally from a cross-sectional data system toward an ultimate goal of implementing a comprehensive student-tracking system. Existing data systems might be modified, for instance, in order to incorporate limited kinds of longitudinal information collected over short periods of time (e.g., one year). Such a middle-range solution might greatly improve estimates of graduation rates or other outcomes like achievement growth without incurring the financial and political costs of implementing a full-fledged, long-term student-tracking system.

The CPI offers a flexible and intuitive method for measuring graduation rates that is also consistent with the requirements of No Child Left Behind. The CCD database also provides the necessary information about enrollment and high school completers to compute disaggregated graduation rates for student subgroups defined on the basis of race and ethnicity, gender, and race-by-gender categories. In this chapter, the CPI indicator is calculated in the same manner for totals and for subgroups, given the availability of graduation and grade-specific enrollment counts for those groups.

District Characteristics

The analyses presented in this study incorporate information about various district characteristics. These data are used to provide a demographic context for the findings and to explore the relationship between graduation rates and certain aspects of the local educational environment. They include free or reduced-price lunch (FRL) eligibility, racial and ethnic composition, segregation index, limited English proficiency (LEP), special education, per-pupil expenditures, district size, and location. These particular district features have been selected to examine longstanding dimensions of socioeconomic and educational inequality and to draw attention to conditions in the school systems that disproportionately serve the nation's most at-risk youth.

EMPIRICAL FINDINGS

The National Graduation Rate, Using the CPI Method

Table 1 reports the graduation rate for the public high school class of 2001, calculated according to the Cumulative Promotion Index method.[5] We find a national graduation rate of 68 percent, indicating that nearly one-third of ninth graders fail to complete high school with a regular diploma within a four-year period. Nationally, graduation rates have remained relatively stable in recent years. For instance, the graduation rate increased by about only one percent (from 67%) between 2000 and 2001 (see Swanson, 2003a). Before that, graduation rates had hovered between 65 and 66 percent since the mid-1990s. At the national level, at least, there does not appear to have been much change in high school graduation rates in recent years.

The results for the four major geographical regions of the country, as defined by the U.S. Census Bureau, display a moderate degree of variation.[6] Regional graduation rates vary by more than 12 percent, with the highest graduation rates found in the Midwest (75%) and the lowest in the South (62%). The average graduation rate in the West is nearly identical to the nation as a whole, while levels in the Northeast are somewhat higher (71%).

Graduation rates also differ dramatically from state to state (see Table 2). In the highest-performing states, we estimated that about 80 percent of all students complete high school with a diploma. New Jersey, Idaho, North Dakota, South Dakota, and Minnesota all have graduation rates around this level. Other states graduate barely half of their students. Graduation rates in South Carolina, Florida, and Nevada are below 55 percent. This constitutes a gap of nearly 30 points between the highest- and lowest-performing states. It should be stressed that these results pertain to the student population of these states as a whole. As the more detailed results presented below demonstrate, students from historically disadvantaged groups generally graduate high school at rates far below the average.

The lowest-performing states, many of which are in the South, tend to serve predominantly minority and socioeconomically disadvantaged student populations. The opposite pattern is found among states that lead the nation.

TABLE 1

2001 CPI Graduation Rates for All Students: Nation and Region

	Graduation Rate	Gap (Region–Nation)
National Average	68.0	—
Regions		
Northeast	71.0	3.0
South	62.4	–5.6
Midwest	74.5	6.5
West	68.2	0.2

Source: Common Core of Data Local Educational Agency and School Surveys, National Center for Education Statistics.

For example, over half of all students attending public school in Mississippi are black, and the majority are eligible to participate in the national free or reduced-price lunch programs (51 and 64%, respectively), whereas in Idaho 86 percent of students are white and only 35 percent are FRL eligible. As we might expect, Mississippi's graduation rate of 58 percent lags far behind Idaho's 80 percent.

The fact that states with some of the most challenging educational conditions and student populations find themselves so far behind the rest of the nation holds important implications. In an era of performance-based accountability—where failure to make adequate progress toward high educational standards carries serious consequences for struggling schools—these states are not only starting from behind, they may also face a particularly difficult uphill climb in the race to achieve educational excellence.

CPI Graduation Rates for Major Student Subgroups

The analyses above described aggregate graduation rates; that is, results for the overall student population. To the extent possible, given the data available in the CCD, we also calculated disaggregated rates for the main reporting subgroup categories required under the accountability provisions of No Child Left Behind. According to the terms of the federal law, states, districts, and schools are required to report performance measures for their overall student population and to disaggregate results separately for student subgroups defined on the basis of race and ethnicity, gender, English-language proficiency, socioeconomic status, disability classification, and migrant status. These federally mandated performance indicators include achievement test scores and the *graduation rate* at the high school level.[7]

Calculating the CPI rate for a particular student subgroup requires data on graduation counts and grade-specific enrollment for that group. As suggested earlier, the strength of the CCD as a database lies in its breadth of coverage, not in the depth of information it provides. Nevertheless, with the CCD it is possible to disaggregate the CPI graduation rates separately for racial and ethnic subgroups, by gender, and even for race-by-gender categories. Results are reported below for the nation, regions, and states by race/ethnicity, and for the nation and geographic regions by gender and race-by-gender subgroups. The following section of this report considers the other NCLB subgroups indirectly via the composition of a district's student body. That is, we will examine the aggregate graduation rates for districts categorized on the basis of the proportion of students who are limited English proficient, of low socioeconomic status, or receive special education services. The CCD does not collect the separate graduation or enrollment data for these groups that would be needed to compute true disaggregated rates.

Graduation Rates by Race and Ethnicity

The Common Core of Data collects information on graduation and enrollment separately for five major racial/ethnic categories: American Indian/Alaska Native, Asian/Pacific Islander, Hispanic, black (not Hispanic), and white (not Hispanic).[8] National, regional, and state CPI graduation rates disaggregated by race and ethnicity are reported in Table 2.

At the national level we observe dramatic racial disparities in high school completion, with whites and Asians graduating at much higher rates than historically disadvantaged minority groups. Rates for white and Asian students far exceed the national average, completing high school at rates of 75 and 77 percent, respectively. By contrast, graduation rates for American Indian, Hispanic, and black students barely break the 50-50 mark, ranging from just above 50 percent to only 53 percent. This constitutes a racial gap in high school graduation rate of about 25 percent. A graduation gap of this magnitude is large by any standard of comparison.

When graduation rates are viewed across regions, we find considerable variability. For instance, the graduation rate for Asian students nationwide is slightly higher than that for whites (77 versus 75%). However, a closer examination of regional results reveals important differences in the relative performance of these two groups in different areas of the country. Graduation rates for Asian students in the West (where the majority of Asians live) and South reach as high as 79 and 82 percent, respectively. In fact, in these parts of the country, Asians constitute the highest-performing racial/ethnic group and outpace their white peers by margins of 4 and 14 percent, respectively. The situa-

TABLE 2

2001 Graduation Rates by Race/Ethnicity: Nation, Region, State

	All Students	American Indian	Asian	Hispanic	Black	White
National Average	68.0	51.1†	76.8	53.2	50.2	74.9
Regions						
Northeast	71.0	31.8†	65.2†	35.6†	43.8	78.7
South	62.4	58.1†	81.9	55.4	52.3	68.9
Midwest	74.5	40.1†	75.5†	53.1†	46.5	78.7
West	68.2	50.7†	78.8	55.9	54.2	75.0
States						
Alabama	61.4	68.6	66.3†	43.8†	54.0	65.8
Alaska	64.2	46.5†	71.4	58.3	66.3	66.3
Arizona	67.3	—nr	—nr	—nr	—nr	—nr
Arkansas	70.5	69.3†	76.8†	—*	62.7	74.4
California	68.9	49.7†	82.0	57.0	55.3	75.7
Colorado	69.0	40.7†	72.6†	47.6	49.0	75.2
Connecticut	77.0	42.9†	73.7†	50.1	60.7	81.9
Delaware	61.3	*	*	42.2†	53.4	69.7
Dist. of Columbia	65.2	—*	—*	56.1	60.4	—*
Florida	53.0	47.9†	79.9	52.2	41.0	57.9
Georgia	55.5	34.3†	79.8†	43.2	43.7	62.4
Hawaii	66.0	70.9	66.8	59.9	60.7	64.7
Idaho	79.6	—nr	—nr	—nr	—nr	—nr
Illinois	75.0	—*	88.8	57.8	47.8	82.9
Indiana	72.4	33.9†	—*	50.4†	52.9†	74.9
Iowa	78.2	—*	66.2†	40.5†	48.0†	79.3
Kansas	74.1	—*	48.0†	47.6†	52.1	78.9
Kentucky	65.3	—†	63.3†	62.8†	47.5	68.5
Louisiana	64.5	58.1†	74.2	74.2†	57.7†	68.0
Maine	72.1	33.0†	35.2†	—*	—*	72.3
Maryland	75.3	—*	92.9	71.2	64.8	79.9
Massachusetts	71.0	25.4†	60.5	36.1	49.4	73.7
Michigan	74.0	39.5†	—*	36.3†	—*	76.6
Minnesota	78.9	35.7†	66.3†	—*	51.0†	81.4
Mississippi	58.0	—	45.6†	—*	52.6	63.3
Missouri	72.9	22.7†	73.4†	—*	52.3	76.1
Montana	77.1	45.8	—*	56.8†	71.4†	79.3
Nebraska	77.3	32.3†	—*	46.9†	45.2	81.7
Nevada	54.7	47.8	75.1	37.6	40.5	62.0
New Hampshire	73.9	—nr	—nr	—nr	—nr	—nr
New Jersey	86.3†	—*	83.3†	—*	62.3†	86.4
New Mexico	61.2	60.0	64.2†	54.7	55.9†	67.8
New York	61.4	36.2†	61.2	31.9	35.1	75.3

continued on next page

TABLE 2 (continued)

	All Students	American Indian	Asian	Hispanic	Black	White
North Carolina	63.5	33.8†	68.3	58.4†	53.6	69.2
North Dakota	79.5	52.6†	30.6†	—*	72.1†	84.1
Ohio	70.7	22.4†	—*	43.2†	39.6	75.9
Oklahoma	69.8	63.9†	—*	56.2†	52.8	72.1
Oregon	73.6	42.4†	78.4†	56.2†	58.0	71.4
Pennsylvania	75.5	24.9†	63.5†	40.9	45.9	81.3
Rhode Island	73.5	—*	53.8†	67.7	84.1	73.8
South Carolina	50.7	—nr	—nr	—nr	—nr	—nr
South Dakota	79.4	32.1†	61.2†	—*	—*	83.4
Tennessee	57.5	—nr	—nr	—nr	—nr	—nr
Texas	65.0	36.7†	85.3	55.9	55.3	73.5
Utah	78.3	52.8†	69.3†	—*	—*	83.7
Vermont	77.9	—nr	—nr	—nr	—nr	—nr
Virginia	73.8	68.6†	80.4	65.2	62.8	76.1
Washington	62.6	—nr	—nr	—nr	—nr	—nr
West Virginia	70.7	52.8†	—*	—*	58.0	71.3
Wisconsin	78.2	47.0†	73.2†	54.4†	41.1	82.4
Wyoming	72.4	34.4†	—*	57.1†	67.7†	73.3

Source: Common Core of Data Local Educational Agency and School Surveys, National Center for Education Statistics.

nr Value not calculated because necessary data field(s) not reported in CCD.

* Low Coverage: Rate not reported because statistic covers less than 50 percent of student population.

† Moderate Coverage: Rate covers between 50 and 75 percent of student population.

tion in the Midwest and Northeast, on the other hand, proves to be a nearly perfect mirror image. Here white students achieve the highest graduation rates, with Asians lagging behind by about 3 percent in the Midwest and 13 percent in the Northeast. Our regional analysis shows that graduation rates for the other racial and ethnic minority groups—American Indian, Hispanic, and black students—are consistently and substantially lower than those for both Asians and whites. The most dramatic racial gaps are observed in the Northeast, where results indicate that fewer than one-third of American Indian, about 36 percent of Hispanic, and 44 percent of black students can be expected to graduate from high school. Here white students (with a graduation rate of 79%) outperform other groups by extremely large margins: 35, 43, and 47 percent for black, Hispanic, and American Indian students, respectively. In fact, whites in the Northeast graduate from high school at more than *twice* the rate of Hispanic and

American Indian students. To some extent, then, the regional results replicate (and can even amplify) the disparities exhibited in the national findings described earlier.

Not only does the *size* of these racial performance gaps vary greatly across regions, but a systematic patterning of effects in the magnitude of these gaps also becomes evident upon closer examination. In particular, a consistent rank ordering of gaps emerges among the regions. Disparities between whites and minority students are greatest in the Northeast, followed by the Midwest, then the West, with the smallest gaps found in the South. This regional pattern of racial gaps is replicated for each racial/ethnic group, even for Asians, who outperform whites in two regions of the country. It is interesting to note that the largest racial gaps exist in the parts of the country with the highest overall graduation rates—the Northeast and Midwest. Not only do members of racial/ethnic minorities in these regions fare more poorly than their white peers, but their graduation rates are lower than members of the same groups in the West and South. Overall graduation rates in the West and South are lower than in other regions of the country, although racial gaps are generally less pronounced.

Graduation Rates by Gender and Race-Gender Subgroups

Findings in Table 3 show a substantial and systematic gender disparity in graduation. Nationally, female students graduate from high school at a rate of 72 percent, compared to 64 percent for males, constituting an 8 percent gender gap. Large gender gaps by race exist among Hispanic and black students, with females graduating at rates 11 and 13 percent higher than males in these groups, respectively. This pattern of gender gaps by race generally pertains across regions, although the Northeast proves to be an exception. In that part of the country, the largest gender gap is found among Asians, with graduation rates for female students exceeding those of males by 13 percent. The average size of the gender gap across racial/ethnic groups is of approximately equal size for each region (about 8%).[9]

These race-by-gender findings also further confirm the most prominent patterns of results described for the separate regional, gender, and race analyses above. Females, for instance, consistently outperform males from the same racial/ethnic group across the nation and for each of the four regions. The same regional stratification of the racial gap in graduation rates described earlier can also be found with remarkable consistency, separately for females and for males within each racial/ethnic group. Without exception, for both females and males, the ranking in the size of the racial gap runs from highest in the Northeast, followed by the Midwest, the West, with the lowest in the South.

TABLE 3

2001 National and Regional CPI Graduation Rates,
by Gender and Race-by-Gender Subgroups

| Race by Gender Group | Nation | Census Region | | | |
		Northeast	South	Midwest	West
Female (all)	*72.0*	*71.0*	*62.4*	*74.5*	*68.2*
American Indian/AK Nat	51.4†	34.2†	58.1†	40.2†	—*
Asian/Pacific Islander	80.0†	72.1†	82.9†	75.7†	81.6
Hispanic	58.5	42.9	60.4	57.8†	61.0
Black	56.2	44.9	59.4	52.0	57.5
White	77.0	79.9	72.1	80.2	78.5
Male (all)	*64.1*	*64.9*	*58.8*	*70.9*	*64.7*
American Indian/AK Nat	47.0†	27.7†	53.3†	33.0†	47.2
Asian/Pacific Islander	72.6†	58.7†	78.2†	70.9†	74.5
Hispanic	48.0	34.6†	49.5	44.6†	50.3
Black	42.8	35.7	44.4	39.2	47.5
White	70.8	74.5	64.9	75.3	71.5

Source: Common Core of Data Local Educational Agency and School Surveys, National Center for Education Statistics.

* Low Coverage: Rate not reported because statistic covers less than 50 percent of student population.

† Moderate Coverage: Rate covers between 50 and 75 percent of student population.

Placing Subgroup Results in Perspective

Graduation rates can differ sharply across subgroups. As one way to place the implications of these disparities into context, let us suppose that one were to set a goal of graduating two-thirds of students, a modest target, but one close to the overall national graduation rate. This exercise proves quite illuminating. Students from historically disadvantaged racial groups (American Indian, Hispanic, black) fail to reach a 66 percent graduation rate for the nation and for each geographic region. In every state for which graduation rates disaggregated by race can be calculated, at least one minority group falls short of the 66 percent mark. With respect to gender, at least two-thirds of female students graduate for the nation as a whole and in every region. Males, however, meet this goal only in the Midwest. In fact, only female and white students consistently achieve a 66 percent graduation rate nationally and for each region.

Prior to NCLB, graduation rates were not part of formal educational accountability systems in most states. In some cases graduation rates were not even systematically measured. Findings from this study suggest that in the coming years we can expect states to report widespread failure to meet accountability goals if performance on graduation rates is held to even a modest subgroup goal (e.g., 66%). Given the widespread disparities, raising the graduation rates of males, and particularly of students from historically disadvantaged minority groups, may prove to be a tremendous challenge for school systems nationwide.

INVESTIGATING THE ROLE OF DISTRICT CONTEXT

Descriptive Analysis of Graduation Rates by District Type

The ability to calculate truly disaggregated graduation rates using the CCD is limited to the race, gender, and race-by-gender subgroups examined above. Information on other student characteristics of educational and social interest, however, is collected by the CCD at aggregate levels. It is possible, therefore, to compare graduation rates for districts that (as a whole) vary according to characteristics such as the percentage of students who come from socioeconomically disadvantaged backgrounds or who are English-language learners. The district compositional findings reported below provide estimates of district-level graduation dynamics. Even at an aggregate level, our results point to strong and consistent patterns in graduation rates between higher-performing educational settings and the school systems that serve the nation's more disadvantaged students. Were actual disaggregated data available, we would expect these disparities to be even more strongly pronounced.

Much as in the case of the subgroup results, findings for the aggregate district analysis reported in Table 4 display consistent and often dramatic differences between graduation rates in more and less advantaged districts. As we would expect, for instance, nationwide graduation rates in districts where most students are members of racial/ethnic minorities lag almost 18 percentage points behind majority-white school systems (56% versus 74%, respectively). A similar gap exists between districts classified as more or less socioeconomically advantaged. Graduation rates for high- and low-FRL districts are 58 and 76 percent, respectively. Districts with a higher than average proportion of LEP students have graduation rates about ten points lower than districts with fewer English-language learners. A margin of about half this size separates districts serving high versus low numbers of special education students. Nationally, we find the highest graduation rates in suburban districts and the lowest in central cities (73% versus 58%).

Without exception, the general patterns that emerge in the national findings are also evident when the analysis is taken to the regional level. However, differences are most pronounced in the Northeast, where graduation rates are at least 33 percentage points lower in predominantly minority, high-LEP, high-FRL, and central-city districts than they are in relatively more advantaged educational environments.

Characteristics of Districts Serving Racial and Ethnic Minorities

This study's basic descriptive results, presented above, reflect some important and well-known relationships among student characteristics, district context, and graduation rates. Of course, factors such as those examined above are closely related. For instance, minority students tend to be disproportionately poor, live in highly segregated communities, and attend schools in large, chronically low-performing urban school systems. Such contextual factors may help to explain, at least in part, the low graduation rates found for historically disadvantaged racial and ethnic groups.

A recent study by the Urban Institute found that the average black or Hispanic student attends high school in a district where just over half of all students qualify for the free or reduced-price lunch programs.[10] By comparison, white students typically attend school in districts where less than a third of their classmates are FRL-eligible. For blacks and Hispanics, most of their fellow students are also members of racial and ethnic minority groups. The average white student is enrolled in a district where more than three-quarters of students are also white.

Asian, Hispanic, and black students attend school in districts that are much larger than those of whites. In fact, the district of the average black student is more than five times the size of the average white student's school system. Many of the nation's largest school districts are located in urban areas.[11] Accordingly, we find that nearly half of all Hispanic and black students attend center-city school districts. American Indians, on the other hand, are more likely than all other groups to attend schools in towns and rural communities. Although distinctive in many respects, impoverished rural school systems share many of the same challenges faced by the large urban districts that often occupy center stage in debates over a variety of educational issues.

In certain respects, however, the districts attended by the various racial/ethnic groups do not differ very much. Average levels of per-pupil educational expenditures do not vary considerably across racial and ethnic groups, nor does the percentage of special education students in the district. This is not to say, of course, that school funding and special education are unrelated to graduation rates, either for individual students or in the aggregate for districts. These findings do suggest, however, that these contextual factors are not likely to be major explanations of observed differences in graduation rates across racial/ethnic groups.

TABLE 4

2001 National and Regional CPI Graduation Rates, by District Type

District Characteristic	Nation	Census Region			
		Northeast	South	Midwest	West
Racial Composition					
Majority White	74.1	80.0	66.5	78.6	73.7
Majority Minority	56.4	46.4†	56.6	48.2†	62.4
Free/Reduced-Price Lunch					
Low (<38%)	76.0	81.5	69.7	79.4	74.6†
High (>38%)	57.6†	48.4†	57.6	57.4†	62.4†
LEP Participation					
Low (<9%)	70.3†	76.4†	64.3	75.6†	74.4†
High (>9%)	60.1†	42.8†	57.3	61.2†	65.8†
Special Education					
Low (<13%)	69.7	78.0	62.7	78.0	68.6
High (>13%)	65.0	63.5	62.1	71.0	64.6†
Location					
Central City	57.5	47.7	57.2	58.5	62.5
Suburb	72.7	81.6	64.7	79.9	72.2
Town	69.1	74.9	61.7	76.6	69.8
Rural	71.9	79.0	63.9	79.6	69.5†

Source: Common Core of Data Local Educational Agency and School Surveys, National Center for Education Statistics.

† Moderate Coverage: Rate covers between 50 and 75 percent of student population.

MODELING GRADUATION RATES:
LINKS TO POVERTY AND SEGREGATION

The connections between graduation rates and other district characteristics discussed above all point in the direction one would expect, given the large body of existing research on educational performance. Additional district context analyses not reported here show that graduation rates are significantly lower in school systems with higher levels of poverty (percentage FRL eligible) and segregation, more students from racial and ethnic minorities, and more students enrolled in special education programs. Students who attend school in central cities and in larger districts also complete high school at levels lower than in non-urban and smaller school systems. Although levels of funding appear modestly related to graduation rates, this relationship is small and not statistically significant.

These analyses show that poverty and segregation are both strongly associated with lower graduation rates. We also know, however, that poverty and segregation are strongly associated with each other. Highly segregated communities also tend to be disproportionately poor. So, we might well ask whether segregation has an independent effect on graduation rates over and above that of poverty. To gain more detailed insight to such complex relationships, we must rely on multivariate statistics that are able to account (or statistically control) for the independent contributions of more than one predictor.

Even after simultaneously modeling the full set of district characteristics described earlier (FRL elegibility, segregation, special education, expenditures, size, and location), we still find that a district's level of socioeconomic disadvantage continues to show a very strong relationship to graduation rates. Even holding all other factors in the model constant, for every 10 percent increase in FRL eligibility, we would expect the graduation rate to drop by 3.8 percent. All else being equal, statistically significant negative effects are found for segregation, district size, and special education enrollments. Graduation rates are also significantly lower in central-city and rural districts (controlling for other factors) than they are in suburban areas, the point of comparison for this particular analysis.

Our supplementary analyses indicate that district poverty level has by far the strongest independent effect on graduation rates among the district characteristics examined. The effect of poverty is nearly twice the size of the next stroangest predictor. However, segregation levels and district size continue to display sizeable relationships with a district's overall graduation rate, even after controlling for other factors.

The Impact of District Poverty for Racial/Ethnic Subgroups

Our final analysis models the relationship between district context and graduation rates for students from specific racial and ethnic groups. To do this, we estimate a set of five separate regression analyses, with the outcomes being the disaggregated graduation rates for five major racial/ethnic groups. These final regression models include the same set of predictors as our earlier analysis: FRL eligibility, segregation level, district size, district locale, special education enrollments, and per-pupil expenditures. To predict the graduation rate for the average member of each racial/ethnic group, we combine the results from these new regression models with information about the kinds of districts attended by the typical student from each group.

The relationship between a district's poverty level and graduation rates for each racial/ethnic group are displayed in Figure 1. As before, we use the per-

FIGURE 1

Estimated Graduation Rate Trajectory by District Poverty for the
Average Student of Each Major Racial/Ethnic Group

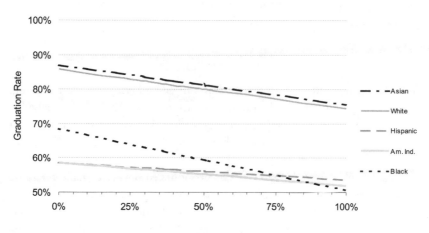

Percent Free or Reduced-Price Lunch

centage of students who are FRL eligible as a proxy for poverty. This graph illustrates the strength of the association between graduation rates (on the vertical axis) and socioeconomic disadvantage (on the horizontal axis), once we have accounted for the effects of the other district characteristics included in the regression analyses.

We find that graduation rates for average Asian and white students are much higher than for students from historically disadvantaged minority groups. Average graduation rates for whites and Asians are always expected to be higher than for black, Hispanic, and American Indian students, regardless of district poverty levels. In fact, to take one example, the predicted graduation rate for whites in districts with extremely high poverty levels (i.e., where all students would qualify for free or reduced-price lunch) would be more than 15 percent higher than the rate for the average Hispanic student in a district with the lowest poverty level.

The steepness of the slopes observed in the graph reflects the strength of the association between district poverty and graduation rates for the respective racial/ethnic groups. The strongest relationship here is for black students. This indicates that socioeconomic disadvantage and graduating from high school are much more closely linked within this student population. In effect, graduation rates for black students suffer much more in high-poverty environments and are helped much more in low-poverty settings than is the case for other racial/ethnic groups. Black graduation rates approach 70 percent in very low-poverty districts, a rate about 10 percentage points higher than similarly situated Hispanic or American Indian students. In stark contrast, graduation rates for blacks in very high-poverty districts would plummet to about 50 percent, the lowest levels observed among the five racial/ethnic groups.

CONCLUSION

The findings presented in this study paint a highly sobering, indeed troubling, portrait of high school completion in this nation. Members of historically disadvantaged racial/ethnic groups (American Indian, Hispanic, black) finish high school at rates far lower than their white peers. Nationally this racial gap approaches 25 percent. Males also graduate at consistently lower levels than females, although the gender gap is not as pronounced. Districts that serve more socioeconomically or educationally disadvantaged populations also graduate substantially fewer students. Graduation rates in districts with higher than average levels of poverty and minority enrollment lag behind more advantaged systems by about 18 percent. Similarly, a 15 percent graduation gap can be found between suburban and urban districts.

These findings offer researchers and educational decisionmakers a valuable resource for better understanding the depth and breadth of the graduation crisis that exists in many places around the country. Given the nature of the data, however, one should be cautious about drawing causal inferences from the analyses presented above. For instance, we observed strong and significant relationships between graduation rates and a variety of district characteristics. Some part of this association may be truly causal. Poverty or segregation may have a direct or indirect impact on the educational experiences of students in ways that affect their odds of graduating from high school. Some part of these observed associations, however, probably also captures the influence of other district characteristics not included in our analyses and/or multiple causal factors. For instance, high-poverty districts attract less qualified teachers, which results in less effective and less engaging instruction, producing lower levels of academic achievement, which in turn may lead students to drop out of high school at higher rates.

The goal of future research should be to continue to explore these important relationships more thoroughly using more comprehensive data. This research knowledge will provide us with better tools for diagnosing the seriousness of the high school completion crisis and for more conclusively identifying leading culprits behind low graduation rates. More importantly, armed with better knowledge, we will be able to develop more successful interventions to combat high school graduation crises wherever they exist.

APPENDIX:
COMPARISON OF ALTERNATIVE GRADUATION RATE INDICATORS

A national graduation rate of 68 percent may strike many readers as surprisingly low, particularly given the much higher rates that often appear in government reports and other frequently cited sources.[12] Those sources, of course, rely on various methods for determining the graduation rate. These methodological variations in turn may result in systematically divergent estimates of the percentage of students graduating from high school.

To provide a point of comparison for the estimation method used in this study, Table A2.1 reports results generated using the CPI and three other approaches for calculating the high school graduation rate. These alternative estimates were calculated using the Common Core of Data, the same data source on which the CPI analyses are based. Along with the graduation rate, we also provide a basic quality indicator for each method—the inclusiveness of its estimate. This *estimate coverage* is captured by the percentage of districts and the student population nationwide for which a value can be calculated using the CCD. As noted earlier, the CCD is the most comprehensive and systematic source of basic information about schools and school districts currently available.

The first row of results in Table A2.1 indicates that the CPI estimate displays a very high level of coverage. The CPI can be calculated for 85 percent of school districts, which serve over 93 percent of the national high school population. In addition, estimates can be calculated for each of the 50 states and the District of Columbia. The relatively higher level of student coverage (compared to district coverage) found here suggests that the CPI is somewhat more likely to be available for larger school districts.

Perhaps one of the simplest and most intuitive approaches for approximating a graduation rate is the Basic Completion Ratio (BCR). The BCR estimate is calculated by dividing the number of graduates in a given year by the number of ninth graders three school years before.[13] Although rudimentary in some respects, this method can be valuable for producing a rough estimate of the graduation rate in the aggregate where very limited data are available.[14]

Using data from the CCD, we find a BCR rate of 68.3 percent for 2001. This value is very close to the CPI estimate of 68.0 percent reported above. Estimated coverage for the BCR method is also somewhat higher than CPI, due largely to its minimal data demands. While the CPI and BCR methods produce similar results on a broad national level, this similarity will not necessarily carry downward to more local units of analysis. The BCR approach will tend to be less stable at more localized levels, in part because changes in the student population (e.g., due to population growth and migration) over the indicator's four-year window of observation will affect the accuracy of the BCR estimate. The CPI method, by contrast, minimizes the potential bias introduced by population change by using two data points separated by a one-year period of observation. Over such a short period of time, large shifts in student demographics are highly unlikely.

One of the most commonly cited high school completion measures in circulation today was developed by the National Center for Education Statistics (NCES). This statistic, often described as a "leaver rate," approximates the high school graduation rate by calculating the percentage of students who leave high school as completers versus dropping out (Young & Hoffman, 2002). Most states are currently incorporating a modified version of this statistic into their NCLB-mandated accountability plans, in which only regular diploma recipients are counted as graduates (Swanson, 2003b, 2003c). This modified indicator will be identified as "NCES-G" in this report to distinguish it from the agency's official statistic.[15]

It should first be noted that the NCES-G statistic displays very low levels of national coverage and can be computed for only 54 percent of districts and 45 percent of the national student population. This coverage pattern indicates that the NCES-G estimate is disproportionately unavailable for larger school districts (the opposite of the pattern found for CPI). For the class of 2001, the NCES-G measure can only be estimated for 34 states. The poor coverage for the NCES-G indicator can be traced to a large amount of missing data on high school dropouts. As the indicator's formula shows, dropout data are essential for calculating the statistic. In past years, many states either have not reported dropout data to CCD or have done so in a manner that does not conform with standards established by the NCES. However, even when the NCES-G rate can be computed, it produces results that are systematically higher than the CPI indicator. For instance, Table A2.1 reports an NCES-G graduation rate of about 80 percent for the districts for which estimates are available, a level about 12 percent higher than either the CPI or BCR estimates.[16] Due to the low level of indicator coverage, however, this NCES-G rate should not be considered representative of the nation as a whole.

A final alternative approach examined in this study—the Serial Persistence Rate (SPR) method—approximates the graduation rate by estimating the percentage of students in an estimated cohort who are expected to remain enrolled in

TABLE A2.1

2001 National Graduation Rates, Using the CPI and Alternative Methods

Method for Calculating Graduation Rate	District Coverage (%)	Student Coverage (%)	States Covered (out of 51)*	Graduation Rate Estimate
Cumulative Promotion Index (CPI)	84.9	93.5	51	68.0
Basic Completion Ratio (BCR)	96.3	99.2	51	68.3
National Center for Education Statistics (NCES-G)	53.7	44.8	34	80.4†
Serial Persistence Rate (SPR)	53.9	45.1	34	82.1†

Source: Common Core of Data Local Educational Agency and School Surveys, National Center for Education Statistics.

* Count of states included the District of Columbia.

† Estimate should not be considered representative of the nation as a whole due to low levels of indicator coverage.

school from grade 9 through grade 12. The SPR value is calculated by multiplying together a set of grade-specific persistence rates over a four-year period. These persistence rates are computed as one minus the grade-specific dropout rate.[17]

This estimation strategy has some serious limitations. Unlike the other measures compared above, SPR does *not* directly measure high school graduates and effectively assumes that students who do not drop out should be counted as high school graduates. No distinction, for instance, is made between diploma recipients and those receiving other credentials (e.g., certificates of attendance or possibly GEDs). Despite the obvious shortcomings of this method, several states have been authorized to employ similar indicators as part of their NCLB accountability plans (see Swanson, 2003b). Nonetheless, such allowances might be reasonable, at least if the objective is to produce a very rough estimate of the true graduation rate.

Again using data from the CCD, we find that levels of SPR indicator coverage here are quite low (54% of districts and 45% of students). As was the case for the NCES-G indicator, the low coverage is due to the SPR measure's reliance on dropout data. The Serial Persistence Rate method projects a graduation rate of 82 percent. This value exceeds the results for the CPI by a considerable margin, although it is quite similar to the NCES-G estimate.

Findings for the NCES-G and SPR measures have both produced estimates of the graduation rate that: 1) offer poor coverage of the national student population and 2) point toward a graduation rate considerably higher than the CPI and BCR. As discussed above, the low levels of coverage are a product of states failing to collect and report dropout data consistent with the CCD's technical standards. Increasing numbers of states are now providing such data. However, because the NCES-G and SPR measures require four consecutive years of dropout counts, it will be several years before coverage for these indicators improves substantially.

The apparent overestimation of the graduation rate produced by both of these indicators (compared to the CPI), however, is the result of a separate set of complicating factors for which a resolution is unlikely in the near future. The NCES and SPR methods rely primarily on information about the prevalence of high school dropout data in order to indirectly estimate the graduation rate. Researchers have long argued that dropout data are notoriously unreliable. In particular, counts of dropouts tend to be systematically underreported. As a result, when dropout data are used to indirectly estimate the graduation rate, graduation rates tend to be inflated.

The reasons underlying the underreporting of dropout counts are certainly multiple and complicated. On the one hand, it is possible that certain schools or school systems could intentionally manipulate dropout data. Blatant attempts to distort the true dropout and graduation rates, however, are more likely to be the exception than the rule. After all, it is important to recognize that information on dropouts is inherently challenging to collect, certainly posing more difficulty than obtaining enrollment data or even counts of graduates. For instance, ascertaining the status of a ninth grader who attended a particular school during the spring one academic year but who is no longer in attendance the following fall requires that this student's status be tracked in some fashion over time. This student may have dropped out, moved to a different school in the same district, transferred out of state, switched to a private school, or may have even died over the summer. Determining which of these actually occurred may be difficult, particularly in situations where a systematic student-tracking system is not in place or has a limited scope, student populations are highly mobile, or the administrative offices responsible for tracking such students are overworked, understaffed, underresourced, and have other pressing responsibilities. Such conditions certainly exist to a greater or lesser extent in districts around the country. The more serious these problems are, the more likely it will be that school systems are unable to determine the status of students no longer enrolled, perhaps even after a good-faith attempt has been made to locate those individuals.

At some point, school systems must make decisions regarding how to classify students with an effectively "Unknown" status. Formal (or informal) procedures typically exist to govern the disposition of such individuals in administrative records, and sometimes rules are also in place to specify how such students will be counted (or not) when computing official dropout or graduation rates. School systems may recategorize these Unknown students as Dropouts, classify them as Transfers, or retain them in Unknown status. Little systematic information is available about key features of these processes around the country. As a result, we have little way of knowing which reclassification strategies are more prominent, whether these reassignments are the product of formal administrative rules or informal shop-floor practices, whether these decisions are made at the school or district level, or how much these practices might affect the accuracy of reported data on dropouts. Given the obvious incentives for underreporting and disincentives for overreporting dropouts, however, it seems very likely that the kinds of ambiguity described above will continue to contribute to the systematic undercounting of dropouts.

If these suppositions are accurate, we would expect to find deflated dropout rates and inflated graduation rates, at least when the latter rely on dropout data to produce an estimate. The findings reported in Table A2.1 are consistent with these expectations. The dropout-dependent NCES and SPR rates are considerably higher than those produced by both the CPI and BCR approaches, neither of which employs dropout data. As a result, we believe that methods for indirectly estimating graduation rates using dropout data should be avoided or at the very least viewed with considerable caution, unless the reliability of the dropout data can be certified with confidence. Unfortunately, extensive databases like the CCD or many statewide data systems may provide few rigorous mechanisms to positively verify and safeguard the quality of data reported by the local systems. By utilizing information that is less susceptible to biased reporting (e.g., graduation and enrollment counts), we believe that the CPI approach is able to provide a more accurate estimate of the true graduation rate than other methods in wide use today.

NOTES

1. This chapter is adapted from the author's recent study, *Who Graduates? Who Doesn't? A Statistical Portrait of Public High School Graduation, Class of 2001*, which was released by the Urban Institute in 2004. The graduation rate indicator used in this study—the Cumulative Promotion Index, or CPI—has been developed by the author as an alternative method for estimating graduation rates that is appropriate for use in contemporary accountability systems and is also based on widely available and reliable data on enrollment and diploma counts. The views expressed in this chapter are those of the author and are not necessarily those of the Urban Institute or its board of trustees.

2. Since the CCD includes information only about public schools and school districts, it cannot be used to examine graduation rates or other conditions in the nation's private schools.

3. The equation below illustrates the formula for calculating the CPI using graduates from 2001 as an example. The most recent high school completion data available in the CCD are from the 2000–2001 academic year.

$$CPI = \left[\frac{E_{2002}^{10}}{E_{2001}^{9}}\right] * \left[\frac{E_{2002}^{11}}{E_{2001}^{10}}\right] * \left[\frac{E_{2002}^{12}}{E_{2001}^{11}}\right] * \left[\frac{G_{2001}}{E_{2001}^{12}}\right]$$

where

G_{2001} is the count of students who graduated with a regular high school diploma during the 2000–2001 school year

E_{2001}^{9} is the count of students enrolled in grade nine at the beginning of the 2000–2001 school year

E_{2002}^{10} is the count of students enrolled in grade ten at the beginning of the 2001–2002 school year

4. Example: $$CPI = \left[\frac{95}{100}\right] * \left[\frac{95}{100}\right] * \left[\frac{95}{100}\right] * \left[\frac{95}{100}\right] = .815$$

5. The Appendix presents a comparison between the CPI and three other approaches commonly used to calculate high school graduation rates.

6. The Census Bureau divides the nation into four regions as follows: Northeast (Connecticut, Maine, Massachusetts, New Hampshire, New Jersey, New York, Pennsylvania, Rhode Island, Vermont); Midwest (Indiana, Illinois, Iowa, Kansas, Michigan, Minnesota, Missouri, Nebraska, North Dakota, Ohio, South Dakota, Wisconsin); South (Alabama, Arkansas, Delaware, District of Columbia, Florida, Georgia, Kentucky, Louisiana, Maryland, Mississippi, North Carolina, Oklahoma, South Carolina, Tennessee, Texas, Virginia, West Virginia); and West (Alaska, Arizona, California, Colorado, Hawaii, Idaho, Montana, Nevada, New Mexico, Oregon, Utah, Washington, Wyoming).

7. Under NCLB, gender and migrant status are mandated categories for purposes of public reporting but not for accountability determination. Subgroup accountability for academic assessments is a *required* part of determining adequate yearly progress (AYP) for test-score performance. With respect to graduation rates, however, the use of subgroup accountability for determining AYP is left up to the states.

8. In keeping with the conventions of social science research, this report will refer to these racial/ethnic subgroups using the terminology employed in the original data collection instruments (i.e., the CCD surveys).

9. For detailed results that report state graduation separately according to race-by-gender categories, see *Who Graduates? Who Doesn't?* (Swanson, 2004).

10. See Swanson (2004) for detailed results of the district context analyses referenced in this chapter.

11. There are, of course, exceptions to the generally observed relationship between district size, location, and socioeconomic level. A number of states, for instance, organize school districts around county boundaries. As a result, there are situations where such county-wide districts may be among the largest in the nation and yet also some of the highest-performing, serving relatively affluent suburban populations (e.g., Montgomery County, Maryland; Fairfax County, Virginia).

12. See Kaufman, Alt, and Chapman (2001).

13. For example, spring 2001 graduates divided by ninth graders in the fall of 1997.
14.

$$BCR = \frac{G_y}{E_{y-3}^9}$$

where:

G_y is the count of students who graduated with a regular high school diploma during the *y* school year, and

E_{y-3}^9 is the count of students enrolled in grade 9 in year *y*–3.

15.

$$NCESG_y = \frac{G_y}{G_y + D_y^{12} + D_{y-1}^{11} + D_{y-2}^{10} + D_{y-3}^9}$$

where:

G_y is the count of students who graduated with a regular high school diploma during the *y* school year, and

D_y^{12} is the count of students who dropped out of grade 12 during the *y* school year.

16. Results remain essentially unchanged when the analysis is limited to only those districts with valid rates for all four calculation methods compared here. Using this restricted analytic sample, estimated graduation rates are as follows: CPI (68.5), BCR (68.8), NCES-G (79.4), and SPR (81.2). See also Swanson (2003a) for a more detailed analysis of CPI and NCES-G graduation rates for the 2000 school year.

17.

$$SPR_y = \left[1 - DR_{y-3}^9\right] * \left[1 - DR_{y-2}^{10}\right] * \left[1 - DR_{y-1}^{11}\right] * \left[1 - DR_y^{12}\right]$$

where:

DR_{y-3}^9 is the annual dropout rate for grade 9 in year *y*–3.

REFERENCES

Kaufman, P., Alt, M. N., & Chapman, C. D. (2001). *Dropout rates in the United States: 2000* (NCES 2002-114). Washington, DC: U.S. Department of Education, National Center for Education Statistics.

Massey, D. S., & Denton, N. A. (1988). The dimensions of racial segregation. *Social Forces, 67,* 281–315.

National Center for Education Statistics. (2003a). *Documentation to the NCES Common Core of Data Local Education Agency Universe Survey: School year 2001–02.* Washington, DC: U.S. Department of Education.

National Center for Education Statistics. (2003b). *Documentation to the NCES Common Core of Data Public Elementary/Secondary School Universe Survey: School year 2001–02.* Washington, DC: U.S. Department of Education.

Swanson, C. B. (2003a). *Keeping count and losing count: Calculating graduation rates for all students under NCLB accountability.* Washington, DC: Urban Institute. Available at http://www.urban.org/url.cfm?ID=410843.

Swanson, C. B. (2003b). *NCLB implementation report: State approaches for calculating high school graduation rates.* Washington, DC: Urban Institute. Available at http://www.urban.org/url.cfm?ID=410848.

Swanson, C. B. (2003c). *Ten questions (and answers) about graduates, dropouts, and NCLB accountability.* Washington, DC: Urban Institute. Available at http://www.urban.org/url.cfm?ID=310873.

Swanson, C. B. (2004). *Who graduates? Who doesn't? A statistical portrait of public high school graduation, class of 2001.* Washington, DC: Urban Institute. Available at http://www.urban.org/url.cfm?ID=410934.

Young, B. A., & Hoffman L. (2002). *Public high school dropouts and completers from the Common Core of Data: School years 1991–92 through 1997–98.* Washington, DC: U.S. Department of Education, National Center for Education Statistics.

CHAPTER 2

Graduation Rate Accountability under the No Child Left Behind Act and the Disparate Impact on Students of Color

DANIEL J. LOSEN

Nationally, high school graduation rates are low for all students, with only an estimated 68 percent of those who enter ninth grade graduating with a regular diploma in twelfth grade (see ch. 1). But, as Table 1 makes clear, rates are substantially lower for most minority groups, and particularly for males. According to the calculations used in a report[1] issued jointly by the Urban Institute, The Civil Rights Project at Harvard University, Advocates for Children of New York, and the Civil Society Institute, in 2004, only 50 percent of all black students, 51 percent of Native American students, and 53 percent of all Hispanic students graduated from high school.[2] Black, Native American, and Hispanic males fare even worse: 43, 47, and 48 percent, respectively, and less than 33 percent in some states, including New York and Ohio.[3]

As our economy continues to grow into the service and information age, the economic implications of failing to earn a high school diploma are greater than ever.[4] At an absolute minimum, adults need a high school diploma if they are to have any reasonable opportunity to earn a living wage. Students who earn a GED have a much higher rate of unemployment than diploma recipients and are much more likely to need welfare or other forms of government assistance.[5] Most businesses need workers with technical skills that require at least a high school diploma. Yet the United States is allowing a dangerously high percentage of students to disappear from the educational pipeline before graduating from high school, a situation that is receiving little notice.

In 2001, Congress made an important move to remedy this situation by including graduation rate reporting and accountability provisions in the No Child Left Behind Act (NCLB). This law passed with bipartisan support and was signed into law on January 8, 2002. Unfortunately, neither the reporting

TABLE 1
National Graduation Rates by Race and Gender

By Race/Ethnicity	Nation	Female	Male
American Indian/AK Nat	51.1	51.4	47.0
Asian/Pacific Islander	76.8	80.0†	72.6†
Hispanic	53.2	58.5	48.0
Black	50.2	56.2	42.8
White	74.9	77.0	70.8
All Students	68.0	72.0	64.1

Source: Orfield, Losen, Swanson, and Wald, *Losing Our Future* (see note 2).
† Moderate Coverage: Rate covers between 50 and 75 percent of student population.

nor the graduation rate accountability provisions of the law were seriously monitored or enforced. At the same time, the test-score accountability provisions were being rigidly implemented. Anecdotal evidence shows how high test-score accountability inadvertently creates incentives for encouraging low-scoring students to drop out, in subtle and not so subtle ways, which is referred to as a "push-out" phenomenon.[6] If low-scoring students drop out, their school's average test score rises. To some extent the incentives to push students out are exacerbated by the failure to enforce graduation rate accountability, which was added to the law purposefully to mitigate this problem.[7]

This chapter begins with a description of law, policy, and practice with regard to graduation rate reporting and accountability. It then examines specific ways in which NCLB's implementation of reporting and accountability has likely failed to mitigate this crisis, despite the act's tremendous potential to do so. This chapter concludes with recommendations to policymakers on how to revitalize the potential of graduation rate reporting and accountability and with a call for broader reforms to NCLB's entire accountability system. The evidence suggests that there have already been unintended negative consequences.

HOW GRADUATION RATE ACCOUNTABILITY FITS INTO THE LARGER SCHEME OF NCLB

The incentives in test-driven accountability systems can lead to unscrupulous practices that are harmful to low-achieving students. It is important to note that although nothing in NCLB requires exit exams like those used in Florida or New York, the law's primary emphasis on test scores for school-level accountability may create the same push-out incentives, because failure to meet test-score goals can lead to drastic sanctions against the school. One reason lawmakers added graduation rate accountability to NCLB was to diminish the incentive for schools to pressure low-achieving students to leave. To provide a clearer picture of how graduation rate accountability has the potential to mitigate the push-out phenomenon, it is necessary to understand the general purpose and accountability system of NCLB.

One central principle is that schools, districts, and states be evaluated on the basis of academic performance and progress toward uniform standards for achievement. Standards-based reform theorizes that if the standards are aligned appropriately to enriching curriculum, then tests and other academic measures aligned to this curriculum can be used routinely to assess educational achievement, diagnose educational strengths and weaknesses, and help improve instruction based on the assessments. An accountability scheme based on this theory called adequate yearly progress (AYP) was written into the law in 1994 but substantially revised in 2001.

The central element of this AYP evaluation changed dramatically with the passage of NCLB. Before 2001, each state set its own academic goals for reading and math and created benchmarks to encourage every school to reach them. With NCLB's passage, all schools and districts were required to demonstrate that their students have achieved 100 percent proficiency in reading and math in 12 years (by 2014). To ensure that this goal will be met, each state is required to establish annual benchmarks for academic outcomes for its schools and districts. The state monitors the progress of the districts, which in turn are required to monitor their schools in order to ensure that each school is making adequate yearly progress toward the 100 percent goal.

If a school or district fails to make adequate yearly progress for two years in a row, it is flagged for technical assistance and "identified for improvement."[8] Parents are notified that they can transfer their children out or use school funds to purchase private educational services. If the failing institution cannot improve through the technical assistance provided by the overseeing agency, that agency *must* intervene.[9] NCLB provides choices that range from harsh—whereby schools can be closed, federal funds restricted, and staff fired—to the least aggressive approach, whereby the agency may require a school or district to hire a consultant and submit a school improvement plan.[10] Decisions about interventions are made by the agency responsible for oversight.[11]

The overwhelming desire of many states and school districts aiming to avoid the test-driven accountability sanctions of NCLB has likely contributed to the push-out phenomenon referred to above. The following scenario illustrates this incentive: Imagine that a school has 1,000 ninth-grade students.

Three hundred are very low achievers and fail a proficiency test. The remaining 700 are predominantly moderate achievers who pass. The school does not make the AYP testing goals. The next year the pressure is higher because coming in under the goal for two years will result in state intervention. NCLB requires that an even higher percentage of the students who are enrolled will have to pass the test for the school to make AYP; 95 percent of the enrolled tenth graders must take the test. However, if 200 of the 300 low achievers leave for a GED program or simply drop out before the year gets underway, the "leavers" will not be tested or counted for test-based accountability. As a result, the smaller test pool will have far fewer low achievers, and the test scores of this group should rise considerably over those of the original. Without one additional dollar spent on instruction or academic support for the low achievers, the school's test profile will have improved dramatically in just one year.

NCLB also requires that racial and ethnic minorities, English-language learners, students with disabilities, and students from low-income families make adequate yearly progress as defined in the statute. If *any* of these groups of students does not meet the state's standards, the educational institution in question has not made adequate yearly progress. It is well established that students in these groups are disproportionately low achieving. Despite the great benefits that could accrue from a sound system of subgroup accountability for academic achievement, students in these groups may be pressured to leave when test scores alone determine whether schools and districts are sanctioned.

With the passage of NCLB, graduation rates were added to the requirements as academic indicators. Graduation rate accountability provisions were inserted into the act's definition of adequate yearly progress, in part to create a counterincentive for school officials to hold on to, rather than push out, struggling and disadvantaged students.[12] The original intent of the legislation was that a district's or school's failure to achieve adequate graduation rates would also result in failing to make adequate yearly progress.[13] If a school failed to meet adequate rates for two consecutive years, it would be sent into "school improvement status."[14] However, a review of federal and state graduation rate accountability implementation suggests that the U.S. Department of Education has allowed confusion and inconsistency to reign.[15] In fact, in some instances, the Department of Education has taken steps that demonstrably weaken the graduation rate accountability provision in the law.

DEEPENING THE CRISIS

The intersection of weak graduation accountability with strong test-score accountability could deepen the crisis. Rather than act as an obstacle to push-out practices, the law's uneven implementation might be deepening the dropout crisis. The federal and state governments have basically undermined NCLB's graduation reporting and accountability in three ways:

- With federal approval, states have promoted standards for calculating graduation rates that violate the definition in the statute and yield inflated rates.
- The U.S. Department of Education issued regulations that all but eliminated graduation rate accountability for major racial and ethnic groups and others.
- Most states have extremely weak graduation rate accountability schemes, yet all have won the approval of the Department of Education.

The Perpetuation of Misleading Graduation Rates

The No Child Left Behind Act says that graduation rates are to be *"defined as the percentage of students who graduate from secondary school with a regular diploma in the standard number of years."*[16] This seems straightforward.

The Department of Education's draft guidance, however, began by suggesting that states could create their own definition of graduation rates. They corrected this error with another, telling states to use the National Center for Education Statistics' definition of "graduation rate" when no such definition existed (see ch. 5). The administration erred a third time when they sent draft regulations that conflicted with the statute to the states. They told states that for defining graduation rates they could use the statutory definition "or another definition." They acknowledged the problem but only partially corrected it when the final regulations were issued in December 2002. The corrected regulations told states that the other definition could only be one that was more accurate and that measured graduation rates based on the number of students who entered high school.[17]

The final regulations also watered down the requirement that annual progress be made in improving graduation rates. The law adds graduation rates to the test-based measures of adequate yearly progress required of each school and district. But the administration's regulations made it so that yearly progress is required only on test scores. According to the administration, schools and districts need only set a fixed goal for graduation rates, and that goal, it turns out, can be whatever a state wants it to be—50 percent, 40 percent, 90 percent—it doesn't matter.

Following their attempts to clear up the confusion, administration officials made matters worse with confusing public statements about what states had to do to calculate graduation rates. For example, in reference to a question about how to count graduates, Christine Wolfe, director of policy for the Undersecretary of Education, told one reporter, "There are many folks who would have liked a national definition in the statute." However, congressional lawmakers didn't believe such a definition was appropriate.[18]

Moreover, this description by an administration official was not only inaccurate, it also telegraphed the low priority the DOE placed on graduation rate accountability. Also, the low water mark came many months later, when the department announced that, in its interpretation, the law did not require subgroup accountability for graduation rates, though accountability for racial and ethnic subgroups was a fundamental idea of the law.

No Subgroup Accountability

In a controversial decision, U.S. Secretary of Education Ronald Paige issued regulations stating that graduation rates did not have to be disaggregated by minority subgroups for accountability purposes, except for the "safe harbor" provision.[19] The secretary's interpretation of the law hinged on the lack of unequivocal language mandating such accountability for graduation rates. Instead, he rested his argument on his personal belief that mere reporting of disaggregated data would ensure the intended subgroup accountability. The secretary, in defending this reading, cited other regulations that he had authorized, and not the statute, to insist that:

> Section 200.19(d)(2) makes clear that the State must disaggregate its other academic indicators, including graduation rate, by each subgroup in order to report that information under section 1111(h) of the ESEA and to calculate whether schools that do not meet the State's annual measurable objectives but have decreased for each subgroup the percentage of students below proficient by at least 10 percent can be considered to have made AYP. As indicated in Sec. 200.19(d)(2)(ii), however, the State need not disaggregate its other academic indicators for determining AYP. The Secretary is confident that publicly reporting disaggregated data on the other academic indicators will ensure that schools, LEAs, and the State are held accountable for subgroup performance.[20]

In other words, schools need to be responsible for minority groups only on test scores, not for whether most black or Latino students in a school actually drop out. This decision represented a substantive departure from the law's disaggregation requirement for accountability purposes in testing. It is controversial because it appears to have incorrectly interpreted the text of the statute and the will of Congress. It means that each state is now required only to set a graduation rate for students *in the aggregate.*

Further, as the statistics on graduation rates presented in Chapter 1 bear out, in every state, using even a modest graduation rate target of 66 percent, many districts that would pass in the aggregate would fail based on the rates of many of the subgroups.[21] That said, as the following survey results point out, even in the aggregate, there is little graduation rate accountability.

Weak State Accountability Systems

A survey of state graduation rate accountability reveals that the Department of Education guidance, regulation, and monitoring contributed to the creation of weak state graduation rate accountability systems.

Method

The following accountability survey was performed by The Civil Rights Project from the fall of 2003 through January 2004. According to a report by The Education Trust, all states submitted various accountability plans to the federal government in September 2003. Some left out graduation rate accountability entirely, but all were approved. A review of each state's website was conducted for available information on graduation rate accountability and officially reported graduation rates. In many cases there was no posted graduation rate goal or minimum requirement for NCLB accountability. For every state, researchers followed their website review with an interview of the appropriate state official. Frequently more than one official was interviewed. In many cases, these interviews were the primary source of the information on each state listed below.

The terms *floor* and *disaggregated accountability for initial adequate yearly progress (AYP) determinations* were selected to categorize how graduation rate accountability worked, especially with regard to minority subgroups. States with "floors" require schools or districts to achieve an absolute minimum graduation rate in order to make AYP. States without floors usually allow some degree of improvement over the prior year to suffice if the graduation rate standard was not met. To determine whether there was a floor or a "soft" accountability system, each interviewee was asked whether a school or district that fell below the stated goal could still make adequate yearly progress by showing some improvement in the rate from the prior year. If the interviewee answered *yes*, then the system was put into the soft category and excluded from the category of states that were listed as having a floor.[22] In this report, we describe states that allow something less than compliance with an absolute floor to satisfy AYP as "soft states."[23]

The phrase "disaggregated accountability for initial AYP determinations" indicates that a state's accountability system separately considered the graduation rates of the major racial and ethnic subgroups when the initial AYP deter-

TABLE 2

State Graduation Rate Accountability Summary*

Absolute Floor for AYP?	State's Goal for Graduation Rate	Required Degree of Graduation Rate Improvement	Does State Disaggregate Graduation Rates by Race for Initial AYP Determinations?
No = 39 Yes = 10 N/A = 1	Range 50–100%	Between 1/10 of 1% and 10% annually	No = 40 Yes = 9 N/A = 1

Source: Orfield, Losen, Swanson, and Wald, *Losing Our Future* (see note 2).

*Due to limited information on the state website and no response to inquires, these measures are unavailable for Delaware.

mination was made. This category excluded states that only disaggregated graduation rates for accountability when a school or district's subgroup failed to meet a testing standard and was seeking to implement the "safe harbor" provision, which provides a second chance to make AYP. Specifically, to make AYP under the safe harbor provision, the school or district in question must show that an otherwise underperforming subgroup both decreased by 10 percent its failure to meet or exceed proficiency and improved its graduation rate.[24]

Findings

As of February 2004, two years after the president signed NCLB, no meaningful graduation rate accountability was in place (see Table 2).[25] In fact, 39 states set a "soft" AYP goal for graduation rates. Only ten states set a true floor for adequacy in graduation rates, whereby schools and districts that do not meet the stated goals for two consecutive years are designated as having failed to make AYP.[26]

The ten states that were identified as having a floor are Illinois, Colorado, Maryland, Nebraska, North Dakota, Oregon, Rhode Island, Tennessee, West Virginia, and Alaska. The nine states that disaggregated for AYP graduation rates are Hawaii, Colorado, Illinois, Kansas, North Dakota, Oklahoma, Oregon, South Dakota, and Wisconsin.

State Examples

The Texas system is representative of the 39 soft systems. The Texas plan requires schools to either meet the 70 percent benchmark *or show improvement*. The required "improvement" in Texas is tiny, just 1/10th of one percent per year for any school or district that falls below the 70 percent goal. The New York plan is slightly more rigorous. New York sets a lower graduation rate goal

TABLE 3
Ohio Graduation Rates by Race and Gender

	All Students	Female	Male
Ohio Students as Reported			
Ohio Students CPI	70.7	73.8	67.0
By Race/Ethnicity			
American Indian/AK Native	22.4	—	—
Asian/Pacific Islander	—	—	—
Hispanic	43.2	45.5	32.7
Black	39.6	45.6	32.4
White	75.9	78.2	72.3

Source: Orfield, Losen, Swanson, and Wald, *Losing Our Future* (see note 2).

of 55 percent and requires a full one percent improvement for schools and districts as part of the goal to achieve AYP.

California sets a lofty goal of 100 percent, yet gives passes on AYP for "any improvement." Given that Native Americans, blacks, and Hispanics are currently graduating at rates of between 49 and 57 percent, we estimate that meeting California's 100 percent goal could take over 500 years if they disaggregated for graduation rate accountability. However, the state of California, like Texas, New York, and most others, disaggregates for test score accountability but not for graduation rate accountability,[27] except where improvement in graduation rates could help an otherwise struggling school make AYP by using the safe harbor provision. In other words, if a school's or district's aggregate graduation rate is high enough, and if the racial and ethnic subgroups meet the test-proficiency goal, the state does not look at the graduation rates of racial and ethnic subgroups when determining AYP.

In fact, not only were systems similar to those in New York, California, and Texas approved in many states, but "off the record" some state education officials suggested that the Department of Education's approval of weaker systems had encouraged them to employ "softer" graduation rate requirements than they had originally proposed.[28] Despite the trend toward very weak systems, four states—Colorado, Illinois, North Dakota, and Oregon—have implemented graduation rate accountability plans that both include a floor and require that data be disaggregated by race. Unfortunately, three of the four—Illinois, North Dakota, and Oregon—are among the majority of states that use accounting methods that tend to inflate graduation rates.

Thus far, the resistance to rigorous graduation rate accountability at both the state and federal levels casts serious doubt on whether there is the political will to educate *all* children to high standards. Despite the oft-stated goal of leaving no child behind, under current accountability systems, schools can be deemed "highly performing" even if half of their minority freshmen never graduate.

OHIO: A CASE STUDY

NCLB's test-driven accountability could exacerbate resource inequality and make the dropout crisis even worse. A case study in Ohio revealed that the state has an officially reported graduation rate and a graduation rate goal, but neither is readily accessible. Whatever the rate and goal are, elements of the state's accountability system put Ohio squarely within the group of soft accountability states. This means that Ohio schools are among those that can meet the AYP requirements if they make any improvement whatsoever from one year to the next. Furthermore, if a minority subgroup is very low, that low rate alone will never trigger an accountability intervention, even if the rate goes lower.

Based on the CPI (see ch. 1), Ohio's graduation rate of 70.7 percent is slightly better than the national average. For Native Americans and blacks, however, the rates are the lowest and second lowest in the nation, 22.4 percent and 39.6 percent, respectively (see Table 3). Not surprisingly, the racial gaps in graduation rates compared to whites are among the highest in the nation. For Native Americans the gap is 53.5 points, for blacks 36.3 points, and for Latinos 32.7 points.

Ohio's Crisis Is Pronounced at the District Level

One thing that stands out in Ohio's largest districts is that graduation rates are extremely low—consistently between 20 and 40 percent—in high-minority districts (see Table 4). With rates this low, it is hard to imagine that Ohio is doing all it can to foster academic success in these districts. In fact, the state's highest court has declared the school finance system unconstitutional for its inadequate support to lower-income areas.[29] The state legislature has reportedly rebuffed the court and has yet to comply with the mandated requirements.

Persistent Racial Gaps and Racial Isolation

The district data showing low graduation rates in high-minority districts are consistent with the findings in Chapter 1 that both segregation and having a primarily minority population in a district have a strong relationship with low graduation rates, independent of poverty (see Table 5). In Ohio, the district composition difference is pronounced, with a graduation rate gap of more than

TABLE 4
Ohio's Ten Largest Districts

District	Enrollment	Largest R/E Group	% Minority	% FRL	Total	Nat. Am.	Asian	Hisp.	Black	White
									CPI Graduation Rates	
Cleveland	75,684	Black	80.7	75.7	30.0	34.3	70.8	31.3	29.0	30.9
Columbus City	64,511	Black	62.9	55.5	34.4	12.0	40.3	36.2	37.5	29.4
Cincinnati City	46,562	Black	74.3	57.2	32.4	—	31.7	21.4	25.7	56.4
Toledo City	37,738	Black	53.9	53.2	38.8	—	93.3	32.6	32.5	45.2
Akron City	31,464	White	50.9	50.2	54.3	—	—	29.5	46.1	61.7
Dayton City	23,522	Black	72.3	69.8	36.3	—	—	—	39.8	26.3
South-Western City	19,216	White	14.6	29.4	60.2	—	—	28.7	—	60.2
Lakota Local	14,659	White	10.3	3.8	—	—	—	—	—	85.0
Westerville City	13,571	White	15.6	7.0	81.0	—	—	34.4	—	82.5
Parma City	13,197	White	4.4	17.6	65.6	—	—	—	44.4	66.0

Source: Orfield, Losen, Swanson, and Wald, *Losing Our Future* (see note 2).

FRL = Free or Reduced-Price Lunch

TABLE 5

Ohio Graduation Rates by District

Racial Composition	% of Dists	CPI (%)
Majority White	96.8	77.3
Majority Minority	3.2	40.6

Source: Orfield, Losen, Swanson, and Wald, *Losing Our Future* (see note 2).

50 points between the majority white district of Westerville (81.0%) and major-ity minority district of Cleveland (30.0%). Moreover, the large gender differ-ences within each racial group are significant and are not explained by poverty.[30]

While only 3.2 percent of Ohio's districts have a majority of minority stu-dents, these more segregated districts include the largest cities. In fact, districts with low graduation rates and in "academic emergency" according to the state are those that most of Ohio's minority students attend. Specifically, Ohio's 2002 performance report identified 12 school districts as being in a state of aca-demic emergency. Ten of the 12 districts were well above Ohio's average black enrollment (approximately 16%), and most were high-poverty urban school districts. The data below indicated that a disproportionate percentage of black children in Ohio were attending districts in a state of academic emergency.[31]

Approximately 50 percent of all enrolled black students attend the failing districts, compared to only about 7 percent of white students in these districts. What this means for the high-poverty, predominantly high-minority districts is that despite the state's clear failure to meet its resource obligations to these dis-tricts under state law, NCLB entrusts the state with sanctioning these same dis-tricts for underperforming.

Ohio fails to hold schools and districts accountable for minority students' low graduation rates. Because there are a small number of very large and highly segregated districts, this accountability loophole would not mask the issue en-tirely, but in places like Akron and Westerville and in large suburbs, it very well could. Under this soft accountability system, increasing dropout rates for low-achieving minority students could be reported as improved achievement at no extra cost.

Many Ohio Districts Would Fail AYP under the CPI Method

Ohio typifies what would happen if a true floor were established for graduation rates applied to minority subgroups, and if no pass were given for mere "im-provement." In this example, failing to make a rate of 66 percent would trigger identification as "failing AYP." With rates so low in Ohio, just one of the state's largest districts (Westerville) would "make AYP." If held accountable for the minority students as well, none of these large districts would pass muster. There is, however, some evidence that Ohio is enforcing graduation rate accountability to some degree. Specifically, on August 15, 2003, a presentation to the state legislature said six districts and 27 schools failed to make AYP based on graduation rates in 2003–2004.

Implications for the Nation

All the states for which disaggregated graduation rates could be calculated would fail if a real standard for graduation rates and meaningful accountability were imposed. Assuming a minimum district graduation rate requirement of 66 percent and graduation rates estimated in a consistent and accurate manner across the nation, 46 states[32] and the District of Columbia would fail to meet this benchmark either for their student population as a whole or for at least one minority subgroup. In Pennsylvania, for example, graduation rates for whites are among the highest in the nation (81%), while fewer than half of Latino and African American students earn a diploma (41% and 46%, respectively) (see ch. 1).

RECOMMENDATIONS[33]

1. *Action must be taken to ensure that accurate graduation rates are reported to the public, and that these rates are disaggregated for all major student subgroups.* Under an accurate system, the number of graduates, the number of dropouts, the number of confirmed transfers, and legitimate removals from school rosters should be equivalent to 100 percent of the entering high school class. The National Center for Education Statistics should begin collecting the number of graduates at each school by race for inclusion in the Common Core of Data (CCD). Districts currently collect the data from individual schools and report it to the CCD. Since schools must collect the school data, this requirement would also help detect reporting errors and identify schools that are failing to report any data.

2. *States should be strongly encouraged to institute longitudinal tracking of all students through a unique common identifier system that would follow students throughout their schooling.* When this system in a given state achieves a sufficiently high level of coverage, it should produce the publicly reported statistics on graduation and dropouts. An estimated system like Swanson's CPI (see ch. 1), should be used to check even individualized tracking systems. Such cross-checking would help detect errors or the inappropriate exclusion of certain groups of students (i.e., those who enroll in a GED program should be included in the cohort) from the longitudinal individualized system.

3. *Pending the development of ideal systems, states should implement the congressional mandate for accurate graduation rate reporting and accountability.* While such systems are being developed, the legal obligation for graduation rate accountability under NCLB should still be fulfilled.

4. *Graduation rate accountability must include a reasonable graduation rate floor.* A pass for accountability purposes should be available to some schools and districts falling under the floor, but be tied to significant and steady improvement over a period of years. To be approved, accountability systems must be more rigorous, eliminate all incentives to raise test scores by excluding students, and focus school leadership on graduation as a central goal.

5. *The regulations that specifically removed the requirement of disaggregation of graduation rates for determining adequate yearly progress and sanctions should be rescinded.* Nothing in the NCLB statute suggests that graduation rates should be excepted from disaggregated accountability. The exception for graduation rate heightens the incentive of school officials to push out low-achieving minority students.

6. *Incentives to push students out of school should be replaced with rewards for keeping students in school.* Improved accountability for low graduation rates alone will not solve the dropout crisis. The research in this book suggests that multiple factors may contribute to a student's eventual dropping out of school. Further research is needed to identify and evaluate effective intervention and dropout-prevention programs, as well as those policies and practices under a school's control that may exacerbate the crisis. Certainly policymakers should increase the use of Title I funds in high schools, particularly for transition and dropout-intervention programs.

7. *The extremely low graduation rates of black, Native American, and Latino males cry out for immediate action informed by research.* While the plight of minority male children is no secret in America, there is little research, intervention, or accountability directed specifically at subgroups of minority males.

NOTES

1. The reported rate estimates used in this table are based on enrollment data. No estimates are flawless, but as discussed later in this chapter, the rates reported here are among the most accurate available.

2. Gary Orfield, Daniel Losen, Chris Swanson, and Johanna Wald, *Losing Our Future: How Minority Youth Are Being Left Behind by the Graduation Rate Crisis.* Cambridge, MA: The Civil Rights Project at Harvard University, 2004. www.civilrightsproject.harvard.edu.

3. *Id.*

4. *Id.*

5. Russell W. Rumberger, *Why Students Drop Out of School and What Can Be Done,* Chapters 1 and 3 in this volume.
6. See *Losing Our Future,* supra note 2.
7. 20 U.S.C. Sec. 6311 (b)(2)(C)(vi). Stat 1447.
8. *See* 20 U.S.C. § 6311(b)(1), 115 STAT 1444.
9. *See* 20 U.S.C. § 6311, 115 STAT 1444; 20 U.S.C. § 6317, 115 Stat 1479.
10. 20 U.SC 6317(b) 115 Stat 1479–1498.
11. The local education agency (LEA) does not set AYP or the indicators for "needs improvement," but LEAs are responsible for intervening when benchmarks are not met.
12. The concern that AYP is not made by increasing dropouts is shared by the secretary. "Discussion: The Secretary agrees that the graduation rate should not include students who have dropped out of school as students who have transferred to another school. With the passage of the NCLB Act, the expectations for schools to make AYP have increased; it is critically important that schools do not make AYP simply because students have dropped out of school. The Secretary also agrees that graduation rate should be measured from the beginning of high school in order to capture students who drop out before reaching 12th grade." Title I—Improving the Academic Achievement of the Disadvantaged, 67 Fed. Reg. 71, 710-43 (Dec. 2, 2002), available at www.ed.gov/legislation/ FedRegister/firule/2002-4/120202a.html.
13. One provision of the law makes clear that having high graduation rates should not suffice to make AYP if an educational entity failed to achieve adequate test performance. However, another provision does allow an entity to avoid accountability consequences if the percentage of nonproficient scores is reduced by 10 percent over the prior year, *and* the school meets or exceeds its graduation rate goal, or other academic indicator. The provision is commonly referred to as the "safe harbor" (emphasis added), 20 U.S.C. § 6311(b)(2)(I)(i), (West 2000 & Supp. 2003).
14. 20 U.S.C 6311 (b)(2)(vi), 115 STAT 1447.
15. Jeff Archer, "Graduation-Rate Plans Called All Over the Map,*" Education Week*, October 1, 2003, p. 5.
16. 20 U.S.C. § 6311((b)(2)(C)(vi); 115 STAT.1447. (Emphasis Added)
17. *See* 34 C.F.R. § 200.19.
18. Lynn Olsen, "Study: Formulas Yield Widely Varied Graduation Rates," *Education Week*, May 21, 2003, available at www.educationweek.org/ew/ewstory.cfin?slug=37grad.h22 last visited September 13, 2004.
19. *See* 34 C.F.R. § 200.19 (d)(2); Title I—Improving the Academic Achievement of the Disadvantaged; Final Rule; Federal Register: December 2, 2002 (Volume 67, Number 231) [Rules and Regulations]. Further, the fact that graduation rates were added to the definition of "adequate yearly progress" in the statute did not seem to convince the secretary that any method of measuring "yearly progress" on graduation rates was required for "making adequate yearly progress." "The regulations do not require states to proffer graduation rate goals or hinge accountability success on making yearly progress." 34 C.F.R. § 200.19(b)(2) (2002). For the secretary's comments, see also Final Rule; Federal Register: December 2, 2002 (Volume 67, Number 231) at 71743.
20. *Id.* at 71741. *available at* http://www.ed.gov/legislation/FedRegister/finrule/2002-4/ 120202a.html.
21. In the appendix to *Losing Our Future,* for each of 12 states I found that many of the ten largest districts in each state would not meet a 66 percent graduation rate. For each of the

12 states, I provided some state/district analysis describing how many districts in the given state would not meet that cutoff. Chris Swanson of the Urban Institute suggested this cutoff because it is slightly below the national average and represents that approximately one-third of the entering class fails to earn a regular diploma on time.

22. The description sent for confirmation did not include the words "floor" or "soft" because researchers found that in their interviews, some officials objected to these terms. For example, as least one official insisted on using the word "floor" even though there was complete agreement that it did not constitute a "floor" as defined for the survey.

23. In June 2003, the administration approved the plans of all 50 states, even though most had not met NCLB's requirements and few had any information on graduation rate accountability. The information in this report is based on a combination of reviewing state websites and interviewing a designated employee for each state. The interviews and website reviews were conducted between October 1, 2003, and January 25, 2004. Each state was given an opportunity to confirm the information reported about them.

24. 20 U.S.C. Sec. 6311 (b)(2)(I).

25. In some cases state officials insisted they had set a clear floor for AYP determinations. Further questions, however, often revealed the loophole that any increase in rates would permit the school or district to avoid AYP any time the rate improved over the prior year's rate. When asked hypothetically whether AYP would be granted if a district slipped 20 points one year and improved 1/10th of one percent the next, many said yes.

26. For a thumbnail description of each state, see *Losing Our Futures,* at Appendix 2, pages 74–80.

27. The one exception, "safe harbor," is discussed supra in the text at p. 46.

28. For example, an education official in a southern state told us that although they currently have a genuine "floor" in their plan now, they are likely going to move toward a softer requirement of "any improvement" for graduation rate accountability.

29. *DeRolph v. State*, 97 Ohio St.3d 434, 2002-Ohio-6750. This case, now referred to as DeRolph IV, is based on a complaint filed in 1991 against the state of Ohio. The Ohio Supreme Court eventually ruled in 1997 that Ohio's school system violated the state constitution. *See* De Rolph v. State, 677 N.E.2d 733 (Ohio 1997) [De Rolph I].

30. Christopher B. Swanson, *Who Graduates? Who Doesn't? A Statistical Profile of Public High School Graduation, Class of 2001.* Washington, DC: Urban Institute, 2004. http://www.urban.org/url.cfm?ID=410934.

31. Daniel J. Losen, Challenging Racial Disparities: The Promise and Pitfalls of the "No Child Left Behind" Act's Race Conscious Accountability, *Howard Law Review* (Winter 2004).

32. The four left off, Arizona, Idaho, New Hampshire, and Vermont, did not disaggregate their data by race, and their overall rate was above 66 percent.

33. The recommendations do not constitute a comprehensive list of the actions, remedies, and programs needed to improve on-time high school graduation rates in this country. Rather, they offer a narrower set of recommendations that directly address some of the reporting and accountability issues discussed in this book.

CHAPTER 3

Locating the Dropout Crisis: Which High Schools Produce the Nation's Dropouts?

ROBERT BALFANZ

NETTIE E. LEGTERS

It is hard to find a critical social or economic issue that does not ultimately intersect with the American high school: It is central to the long-term health of the U.S. economy. It is vital to Justice Sandra Day O'Connor's hope that the need for affirmative action will recede within 25 years. Yet from Benton Harbor to Los Angeles, from Akron to San Antonio, from Chicago's south side to rural South Carolina, close to half of the students in those communities do not graduate from high school, let alone leave high school prepared to fully participate in civic life. It is no coincidence that these locales are gripped by high rates of unemployment, crime, ill health, and chronic despair. For many people in these and other areas, the only real and lasting pipeline out of poverty in modern America, a solid high school education followed by postsecondary schooling or training, is cracked and leaking.

Recognition of the importance of the American high school to the economic and social well-being of the nation has been building over the past decade. High schools have been the orphans of school improvement efforts, as states and districts have chosen to invest the too few dollars available for low-performing schools in schools serving younger children. High schools still receive only 5 percent of federal funds available for low-performing schools (Alliance for Excellent Education, 2004). Policymakers and education decision-makers are now realizing that support for preschoolers and elementary school students must be sustained through the secondary grades in order to keep achievement and attainment gains from fading as students face the academic and social challenges of their middle and high school years.

The emerging high school reform movement is at risk, however, of having only a superficial impact if reform experiments are not successfully brought to scale. Worse, current reform investments could result in wider achievement gaps if they do not tackle head on, with systematic focus and adequate resources, the high schools that are producing the greatest number of the nation's dropouts.

Recent reports reveal, however, that there is much confusion among policymakers and the lay public about the scale and scope of the dropout problem. Researchers from major research institutes that span the political spectrum have shown that federal dropout statistics underestimate the number of students who drop out of high school (Greene, 2002; Swanson, 2004). Others have shown that state- and school-level reporting of graduation rates under No Child Left Behind (NCLB) is subject to significant error (Education Trust, 2004; Orfield, Losen, Wald, & Swanson, 2004). One reason for this is that the most widely used method to calculate graduation rates for NCLB, the graduation rate formula developed by the National Center for Education Statistics (NCES), is ultimately dependent on high schools accurately self-reporting how many students drop out (Swanson, 2003). Recent investigations into dropout reporting in New York City and Houston indicate how difficult this is to do.

As a result, there is no ready understanding of how many high schools have high dropout and low graduation rates, where they are concentrated, or the extent to which they dominate the educational opportunities provided to different groups of students. It is not known, for example, the extent to which all states and large cities have significant numbers of high schools that have large numbers of dropouts, or if the problem is concentrated in a subset of states and cities.

PROMOTING POWER AS AN INDICATOR OF HIGH SCHOOLS WITH HIGH DROPOUT AND LOW GRADUATION RATES

There is currently no available direct and common measure of high school dropout or graduation rates at the school level. Available federal measures can provide estimates at the state and district levels only (Kaufman, 2001). Under NCLB, states are allowed to use different graduation measures, so it is not even possible to use common state-level measures to identify which high schools have high dropout rates nationwide.

Fortunately, available federal data can be used to develop an indirect measure. The Common Core of Data (CCD) compiled by the National Center for Education Statistics provides enrollment rates by grade for every public high school in the United States. We have used this to develop a measure we call promoting power, which compares the number of freshmen at a high school to the number of seniors four years later (or the number of tenth graders to seniors three years later in schools with a 10–12 grade span). Ideally, we would compare freshmen to the number of graduates four years later—but the CCD does not currently provide data on the number of graduates at individual high schools.[1]

We argue that using the ratio of freshmen to seniors four years later provides a reliable indicator of the extent to which a high school is succeeding in its core mission of graduating its students. The underlying assumption of the promoting power measure is that high schools in which the number of seniors closely approximates the number of freshmen four years earlier will have high graduation rates and low dropout rates because most students will have remained in school, been promoted in a timely fashion, and be on course to graduate. Conversely, a high school where there are half as many seniors as freshmen is likely to be a school where on-time graduation is not the norm. We make no claim that promoting power equals the graduation or dropout rate in the schools we identify. We do believe, however, that the cumulative evidence on indirect measures of the graduation rate that use student enrollments, most notably the work of Christopher Swanson and John Warren, supports the efficacy and accuracy of using promoting power to identify high schools with high dropout and low graduation rates.

In our analysis of high schools across the country, we use two cut points to identify those that have high dropout and low graduation rates. The first cut point is high schools in which there are 50 percent or fewer seniors than there were freshmen four years earlier. We classify these high schools as those with the worst promoting power in the United States because students in these schools have less than a 50/50 chance of graduating on time, if at all. The second cut point we use is high schools in which there are 60 percent or fewer seniors than there were freshmen. We added this second point because analysis of the data revealed a large number of high schools with promoting power between 50 and 60 percent. We believe it is analytically useful to isolate the high schools with the worst promoting power and to identify all high schools in which graduation is likely not the norm. Identifying high schools with promoting power of 60 percent or less provides a good estimate of the number of high schools with severe dropout rates, and thus can be used to locate the high schools that produce the majority of the nation's dropouts.

Data

Analyses in this study are based on data drawn from the Common Core of Data. The CCD includes information for the universe of all public elementary and secondary schools, school districts, and other educational administrative and operating units across the United States. We included all high schools (defined as schools with a tenth grade) located in the 50 states or the District of Columbia that enrolled 300 or more students, were typed as "regular" or "vocational" high schools in the CCD, and had a grade span of at least grades 10–12 (to enable calculation of the promoting power measure). The application of our filters resulted in a sample size of 10,296 schools for the class of 1993; 10,709 schools for the class of 1996; 10,915 schools for the class of 1999; and 11,129 schools for the class of 2002. Altogether, between 50 and 60 percent of all public schools in the 50 states or the District of Columbia with a tenth grade were included in each cohort.

We constructed the promoting power variables by calculating the ratio of twelfth-grade enrollment in 1992–1993 to ninth-grade enrollment in 1989–1990; twelfth-grade enrollment in 1995–1996 to ninth-grade enrollment in 1992–1993; twelfth-grade enrollment in 1998–1999 to ninth-grade enrollment in 1995–1996; and twelfth-grade enrollment in 2001–2002 to ninth-grade enrollment in 1998–1999. For grade 10–12 schools, we calculated the ratio of twelfth-grade enrollment in 1992–1993 to tenth-grade enrollment in 1990–1991; twelfth-grade enrollment in 1995–1996 to tenth-grade enrollment in 1993–1994; twelfth-grade enrollment in 1998–1999 to tenth-grade enrollment in 1996–1997; and twelfth-grade enrollment in 2001–2002 to tenth-grade enrollment in 1999–2000. Variables for school size, location, and student enrollment by race/ethnicity and by gender were drawn directly from the CCD data files. Proportions of students of various races/ethnicities in the total enrollment were calculated by dividing the enrollment of a given ethnic group (Native American, Asian, Hispanic, black, or white) into the total school enrollment. An additional variable for total school minority concentration was also calculated from the data using the proportion of Native American, Asian, Hispanic, or black students in the total enrollment. The data used in calculating additional variables and in analysis were taken from the final (twelfth-grade) year of each cohort. While this information is available for most included schools, the education agencies in Tennessee did not report enrollment figures by race/ethnicity to NCES. Therefore, the schools in this state are not included in analyses of student race/ethnicity or of school minority concentration.

HOW MANY HIGH SCHOOLS HAVE WEAK PROMOTING POWER?

One in five high schools in the United States has weak promoting power, indicating unacceptably low graduation rates and high dropout rates. In the United States there are currently between 900 and 1,000 high schools in which surviving to

TABLE 1

Number of Schools with Weak Promoting Power in the United States

Class	Total # of High Schools*	< 50% Promoting Power		< 60% Promoting Power	
		# of High Schools	% of High Schools	# of High Schools	% of High Schools
2002	11,129	930	8%	2,007	18%
1999	10,915	903	8%	1,968	18%
1996	10,709	783	7%	1,717	16%
1993	10,296	530	5%	1,254	12%

*Regular and vocational high schools with more than 300 students

the senior year is at best a 50/50 proposition. In these high schools, which represent about 8 percent of all regular and vocational high schools with enrollments of 300 or more students, the senior class has half or less than half the number of students the freshman class had four years earlier. If the standard used to classify a school as having weak promoting power is relaxed slightly to include high schools with 60 percent or fewer seniors than freshmen, the number of chronically low-performing schools doubles to 2,000. This represents nearly one in five (18%) of regular and vocational schools that enroll 300 or more students. These high schools collectively educate over 2,600,000 students.

The number of high schools with weak promoting power grew substantially during the 1990s. Comparing the class of 2002 to the classes of 1993, 1996, and 1999 indicates that the number of high schools with weak promoting power grew substantially during the 1990s, as seen in Table 1. Between 1993 and 2002, the number of high schools with the lowest rates of promoting power increased by 75 percent and overall the number of high schools with weak promoting power increased by 60 percent. This stands in contrast to only an 8 percent increase in the total number of schools.[2]

The gap between promoting power for high schools with the weakest promoting power and the national norm is a striking 40 to 60 percentage points. Promoting power of 80 percent or higher is the norm for regular and vocational high schools in the United States. This can be seen in Figure 1. Promoting power is 40 to 60 percentage points lower in the 930 high schools with the worst promoting power (50 percent or less).

FIGURE 1

Number of High Schools by Different Levels of Promoting Power,
Class of 2002

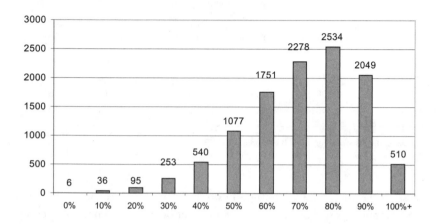

WHO ATTENDS HIGH SCHOOLS THAT PRODUCE
THE NATION'S DROPOUTS?

In high schools with weak promoting power, the overwhelming majority of students represent racial or ethnic minorities. A school in which more than half of the students come from minority backgrounds is five times as likely to have weak promoting power as a school in which the majority of students are white. It is rare for a high school that is predominately attended by white students to have weak promoting power. The nation's dropout factories are overwhelmingly the province of minority students. This can be seen in Figure 2. In 2002, there were 4,417 high schools with enrollments of 300 or more that had 90 percent or more white students. Only 27, or one percent, of these schools had 50 percent or fewer seniors than freshmen. In contrast, 29 percent of the nation's majority minority high schools (712 out of 2,468) have senior classes with 50 percent fewer seniors than freshmen. When the comparison is made at the 60 percent level of promoting power, the contrast is even starker. Only 3 percent of high schools in the United States that enroll 90 percent or more white students have weak promoting power, compared to 49 percent of schools in which more than half the students are minorities, and a stunning 66 percent of high schools that enroll 90 percent or more minority students.

Fifty years after the Brown vs. Board of Education decision, nearly half of the nation's African American students, nearly 40 percent of its Latino students, and only

FIGURE 2
Percentage of High Schools by Minority Concentration That Have Weak Promoting Power, Class of 2002

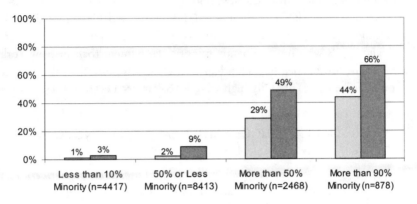

□ < 50% promoting power ■ < 60% promoting power

11 percent of white students attend high schools in which graduation is not the norm. The prevalence of weak promoting power among majority minority schools when combined with the continuing segregation or resegregation of schools in many locales (Orfield & Chungmei, 2004) means that 50 years after *Brown vs. Board of Education* approximately 46 percent of the nation's African American and 39 percent of its Latino students attend high schools in which graduation is not the norm. This compares to only 11 percent of white students. Separate and unequal high schools are unfortunately alive and well in our nation. (See Appendix, Table 1A, for ste-level data.)

Two Exceptions to the Rule:
Selective High Schools and High Schools in Affluent Suburbs

Not all majority minority high schools have weak promoting power. Selective high schools in the nation's major cities rank among the nation's best. These high schools often educate predominantly minority students and have strong promoting power. This is illustrated in Table 2, which shows minority concentrations and promoting power in selective high schools located in New York City, Newark, and Philadelphia.

Another exception, at least in the New York metropolitan area, are high schools located in affluent suburbs. Table 3 compares promoting power in the 14 majority minority high schools found in four affluent counties near New York City to promoting power in the majority white schools in these areas.

Overall in these counties majority minority schools have the same high level of promoting power as majority white schools.

One striking difference between these largely minority high schools in New York's affluent suburbs and majority minority high schools with weak promoting power in New York City is the amount of funding available to provide quality education. Average per-pupil spending is $4,500 per pupil higher in suburban high schools with predominantly minority enrollment than in New York City, and the lowest-spending suburban district spends more than the average per-pupil in the New York City high schools (Balfanz & Legters, 2003).

WHERE ARE HIGH SCHOOLS WITH WEAK PROMOTING POWER LOCATED?

The majority of weak promoting-power high schools are located in northern and western cities and throughout the southern states. There are two key points regarding the location of the high schools that produce the majority of the nation's dropouts. First, the high schools with the worst promoting power are concentrated within a relatively small subset of cities and states. Second, when the standard for low promoting power is raised from 50 to 60 percent fewer seniors than freshmen, the location of schools with weak promoting power becomes more diffuse. At this level, a high school with weak promoting power can be found in every state except North Dakota. However, the majority of schools with weak promoting power remain located in northern and western cities and throughout the southern states.

High schools with the worst promoting power are concentrated in a subset of the nation's cities. The high schools with the worst promoting power (50% or less) are primarily found in the nation's cities. Only 20 percent of high schools that enroll more than 300 students are located in large- and medium-sized cities, yet among them are 60 percent of the nation's high schools with the lowest levels of promoting power.

All cities, however, are not the same. Fifteen of the nation's 100 largest cities have no high schools with weak promoting power (see Appendix, Table A2). These are primarily western cities, and in ten of the 15 cities minority students do not make up the majority of students in the school system. Long Beach and Anaheim, California, stand out as exceptions. They are the only two urban school districts in which minority students equal two-thirds or more of the student population that have no weak promoting-power high schools.

At the other end of the spectrum are ten cities that educate primarily minority students and have ten or more high schools with very weak promoting

TABLE 2

Promoting Power in Selective-Admissions High Schools in New York City,
Philadelphia, and Newark, Class of 2001

District	School	Percent Minority	Promoting Power for Class of 2001
New York City	Bronx HS of Science	63%	82%
	Stuyvesant HS	57%	98%
Newark	University HS	100%	101%
	Arts HS	95%	75%
	Technology HS	92%	74%
	Science HS	81%	76%
Philadelphia	Central HS	60%	85%
	Girls HS	77%	87%
	Creative Arts HS	52%	93%

TABLE 3

Promoting Power by High School Minority Concentration
in Bucks County, PA; Somerset County, NJ; Fairfield County, CT[a];
and Westchester County, NY,[b] High Schools, Class of 2001

Concentration of Minority Students	Number of Schools	Total # of 9th-Grade Students in 1997–98[c]	Total # of 12th-Grade Students in 2000–01	Ratio of 2000–01 12th Graders to 1997–98 9th Graders
50% or more minorities	14	4,526	4,151	92%
Less than 50%	70	18,729	16,944	90%
Total	84	23,255	21,095	91%

[a] Excludes Bridgeport School District

[b] Excludes Yonkers City School District

[c] For grade 10–12 schools in the sample, this number corresponds to the number of 1998–1999 10th graders.

power. They include the nation's three largest cities (New York, Los Angeles, and Chicago), and these ten cities collectively contain nearly one-third (29%) of the nation's high schools with the lowest levels of promoting power. These cities are listed in Table 4.

Thirty-four cities have four or more high schools with promoting power of 50 percent or less. This accounts for 86 percent of the high schools in the 100 largest cities and 43 percent of high schools in the nation in which the senior class has half as many or fewer students than the freshman class four years earlier.

In some cities, students have virtually no other choice but to attend a high school with weak promoting power. What is most significant about promoting power in many of the nation's largest cities, however, is not the number of high schools with weak promoting power but their concentration. In half of the nation's largest 100 cities, 50 percent or more of high school students who attend regular or vocational high schools with more than 300 students attend high schools with weak promoting power (see Appendix, Table A2). In 21 cities, this climbs to 75 percent of high school students and, for the class of 2002, it reaches an incredible 100 percent in St. Louis and Indianapolis. In these cities, attending high schools where graduation is not the norm is inescapable.

Spotlight on New York City

New York City dwarfs all other city school districts in size. With more than a million students, its student population is four times greater than Philadelphia's and more than ten times greater than most major cities. Given this, the fact that New York City has the greatest number of low-performing high schools is no surprise. But since more than 100 high schools have weak promoting power, the scale of the city's reform challenge is particularly daunting. What stands out in New York City is not only the sheer concentration of poorly performing high schools, but how low promoting power is in many of its schools. For the class of 2002, there were more than 30 high schools in which the senior class was less than one-third the size of the freshman class four years earlier. The challenge of the reform task in New York City can be seen in Table 5. It shows that, on average, in the high schools with the worst promoting power in New York City, more than a third of entering ninth graders are over age, and less than 20 percent have met eighth-grade standards in English and math. Average attendance rates are in the 70s. This great educational challenge is clearly not being met with enhanced resources. In addition to the relatively low per-pupil expenditures cited earlier, on average, one in five teachers in these schools is not certified and two in five teachers have fewer than five years' experience. Moreover, the typical low-performing high school in New York City with very weak promoting power is over capacity.

High schools with the worst promoting power are also concentrated in a subset of states. More than two-thirds of the high schools with the lowest promoting power (50% or less) are located in just 11 states (Georgia, Florida, Texas, South Carolina, North Carolina, New York, Ohio, Illinois, Michigan, Pennsylvania, and California), which have 55 percent of the total U.S. population. If four

TABLE 4

Ten Cities with the Greatest Number of Weak Promoting-Power
High Schools, Class of 2002

City	Popu-lation Rank	< 50% Promoting Power		< 60% Promoting Power	
		# of High Schools in City	% of High Schools in City	# of High Schools in City	% of High Schools in City
New York	1	92	68%	110	81%
Chicago	3	31	50%	42	68%
Los Angeles	2	26	46%	39	68%
Philadelphia	4	20	61%	20	61%
Houston	8	18	72%	20	80%
Dallas	9	18	69%	21	81%
Detroit	10	18	69%	19	73%
Jacksonville (Duval)	13	12	63%	15	79%
Cleveland	36	12	86%	12	86%
Milwaukee	22	10	67%	13	87%
Total		257		311	

more southern and southwestern states are included (Mississippi, Louisiana, New Mexico, and Arizona), nearly 80 percent of the nation's high schools that produce the highest number of dropouts are included.

In the northern industrial (Rust Belt) states, weak promoting power schools are overwhelmingly attended by minority students and located in large and medium-sized cities. More than one-quarter of the high schools with the worst promoting power are located in five northern industrial states (Ohio, Michigan, Illinois, Pennsylvania, and New York). These high schools are located almost entirely in the large- and medium-sized cities of these states, and are overwhelmingly attended by minority students. Ninety percent of the high schools with the worst promoting power in these states are majority minority.

While these states are at about the national average for the percentage of all high schools with weak promoting power, they are well above the national average for percentage of minority students attending schools with weak promoting power. When the standard for weak promoting power is set at the 60 percent level, in four of the states (Ohio, Michigan, Pennsylvania, and New York) more than 70 percent of all majority minority schools have weak promoting power.

More than half the African American students in Illinois, Ohio, Michigan, New York, and Pennsylvania attend high schools in which the majority of stu-

TABLE 5

Characteristics of High-Minority (90% or More), Low Promoting-Power
(30% or Less) New York City High Schools

		Range	
	Average	Min.	Max.
Percentage of Entering 9th Graders			
Over-Age for Grade	35.0%	11.0%	78.0%
Meeting Standards in English	17.9%	0.0%	41.9%
Meeting Standards in Math	8.9%	0.0%	29.1%
Attendance Rate for 2001	78.0%	67.0%	90.0%
Percentage Fully Licensed/Permanently Assigned Teachers in 2001	80.0%	49.0%	97.0%
Percentage Teachers with Less Than 5 Years Teaching Experience in 2001	39.0%	15.0%	71.0%
School Capacity 2001	107.0%	76.0%	174.0%

dents do not graduate on time, if at all. By contrast, the percentage of white students attending high schools with weak promoting power in these states is below the national average. As a result, African American students in these states are up to ten times more likely to attend a high school with very low graduation rates than white students. Even more striking gaps can be found by looking at the high schools with the worst promoting power in Illinois, Ohio, Michigan, New York, and Pennsylvania. As Figure 3 shows, very few white students in these states attend these high schools, but between one-third and one-half of African American students do.

In the South, high schools with weak promoting power can be found in high numbers throughout the states. High schools with weak promoting power are not found only in the northern industrial states. In fact, in terms of both total number and level of concentration, five southern states—Georgia, South Carolina, North Carolina, Florida, and Texas—lead the nation. More than one-third of high schools with weak promoting power can be found in these five states. Across these five states, as seen in Figure 4, the percentage of regular and vocational high schools with weak promoting power (at the 60% level) ranges from 34 percent in North Carolina and Texas to a stunning 53 percent in Georgia and 58 percent in South Carolina.

One result of the pervasiveness of weak promoting power high schools in these states is that, across all minority groups (Native Americans, Asians, Hispanics, and blacks), as well as among white students, the percentage of students

FIGURE 3

Percentage of African American and White Students Attending a
High School with Very Weak Promoting Power (50% or less) in Five
Northern Industrial States, Class of 2002

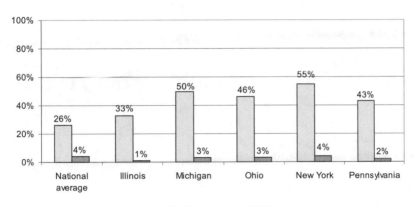

who attend a high school with weak promoting power is above the national average (see Appendix, Table A1).

Only in the South do large numbers of white students attend high schools in which on-time graduation is not the norm. In some states, this appears to be partly a function of rural poverty. In North and South Carolina, most of the high schools with weak promoting power are located in small towns or rural areas. In these areas, which are typically one–high school counties, there are about equal numbers of majority white and primarily minority high schools with weak promoting power. In Georgia and Florida, however, high schools with weak promoting power are pervasive in both rural and urban areas.

Spotlight on Texas

Texas is different. In many respects, Texas' distribution of weak promoting-power high schools more closely resembles a northern industrial state than a southern state. As seen in Table 6, the majority of weak promoting-power high schools in Texas are found in urban areas, and they are almost exclusively majority minority high schools. More than half of the state's 240 high schools with weak promoting power are located in cities; 91 percent of these high schools are majority minority, and 56 percent are more than 90 percent minority.

Table 7 shows that in most of Texas' central-city school districts, which educate predominantly minority students, three-fourths or more of the high

FIGURE 4

Percentage of High Schools* with Weak Promoting Power
in Five Southern States, Class of 2002

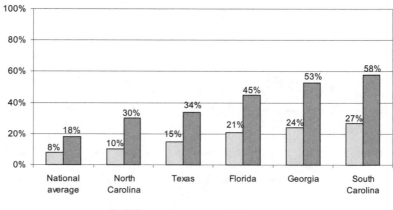

☐ < 50% promoting power   ■ < 60% promoting power

*Regular and vocational high schools enrolling more than 300 students.

schools have weak promoting power. In these districts, students have few opportunities to attend a high school in which graduating is the norm.

The Rest of the Nation

There are only five states, all with small minority populations (Maine, New Hampshire, North Dakota, Idaho, and Wyoming), in which high schools with weak promoting power are rare. In these states, 90 percent or more of all students, regardless of majority or minority status, attend high schools with good promoting power. Montana, Utah, and West Virginia stand out as states in which all groups, except for Native Americans, attend high schools with decent promoting power at high rates. In each of these states, roughly one in five Native Americans attends a high school in which graduation is not the norm. This is still considerably better, however, than in Arizona, New Mexico, South Dakota, and North Carolina, states with large Native American populations, where nearly half or more of all Native American high school students attend a high school with weak promoting power.

Delaware and Rhode Island stand out as two small states in which students across all groups attend high schools with weak promoting power at relatively high rates. New Mexico and Colorado share that distinction among larger states. (See Appendix, Table A3, for state-level data.)

TABLE 6

Number of Weak Promoting-Power (60% or Less) High Schools by Locale
in Five Southern States

State	Total	Locale			
		Cities	Urban Fringe	Towns	Rural
North Carolina	106	16	24	18	48
South Carolina	101	10	28	15	48
Georgia	156	34	44	41	37
Florida	162	51	61	15	35
Texas	240	134	46	36	24
Total	765	245	203	125	192

TABLE 7

Minority Concentration of High Schools with Weak Promoting Power (PP)
(Less Than 60%) in Major Texas Cities, Class of 2002

City	# of High Schools with Weak PP	% of High Schools with Weak PP	% of School District Students That Are Minority
Dallas	21	81%	88%
Houston	20	80%	86%
Austin	8	80%	58%
San Antonio	7	88%	95%
Fort Worth	7	75%	71%
El Paso	5	50%	81%
Corpus Christi	3	60%	73%

POLICY IMPLICATIONS

This study locates the nation's dropout crisis in approximately 2,000 high schools. These high schools are found in nearly every state, but are concentrated in northern and some western cities, southern and southwestern states, and three mega-districts—New York City, Chicago, and Los Angeles. Currently, close to one in five students attends a high school with weak promoting power. Among minorities, the rate approaches one in two. There are cities and rural counties where students have virtually no choice but to attend a public high school in which graduation is not the norm.

Until the nation's dropout factories are reformed or replaced, the promise of the American high school as an engine of economic growth and social transformation will not be met. Indeed, given their fierce concentration in areas populated by large numbers of poor and minority youth, these high schools not only deny many the promise of equal educational opportunity, they also act as a wedge that is driving the country further apart.

Transforming the high schools that produce the majority of the nation's dropouts is a daunting challenge that current reform efforts have not even begun to confront. Traditional approaches to school reform have applied a "pipeline" approach to improving education achievement and attainment, favoring investment in the early grades, with minimal direct intervention in high schools themselves. Recent findings from Chicago, however, show that this approach in itself is not enough. In Chicago, targeting reform resources to the elementary grades, ending social promotion with an eighth-grade gateway exam, expanding summer school and other extra help structures, implementing high-stakes accountability and assessments for students, teachers, and administrators, and providing only general technical assistance to high schools did not lead to substantial improvements in the graduation rate (Allensworth, 2004). The message from Chicago is clear—low-performing high schools cannot be fundamentally improved by attempts to "inoculate" children early and encouraging high school teachers and students to work harder at existing practices within the traditional organizational structure of large, nonselective neighborhood high schools (Lee, 2002). High schools with high dropout rates need to be directly targeted and radically reinvented if they are going to see substantial improvement.

Similarly, current federal policy and programs provide necessary but insufficient guidance and resources for the systemic overhaul needed to improve national graduation rates. Recent reports by The Education Trust (2004) and The Civil Rights Project at Harvard University (2004) demonstrate that No Child Left Behind has no real teeth at the high school level. States have been allowed to adopt minimal improvement targets for graduation rates and most have done just that. Throw in the lack of a uniform measurement standard for graduation rates and it becomes clear that NCLB, in its current form, will neither accurately identify the nation's dropout factories nor prod many of them to improve.

The U.S. Department of Education currently funds two initiatives that provide some direct funding for high school reform—the Comprehensive School Reform (CSR) and the Small Learning Communities (SLC) grants program. Both fight annually for their survival and provide neither enough funding nor guidance to reform the nation's most troubled high schools. Each, for example, only provides funds for three years, not long enough to see even one class through to graduation. The Department of Education is also seeking additional funds to provide instructional supports to students who enter high school unprepared for high-standard high school work. This too is welcome, but its initial goal is very modest—to support demonstration programs in a small number of districts. As a result it does not come close to providing sufficient support to assist all high schools with severe dropout rates.

Other advocates of increased attention to high school reform are also aiming too low to effectively solve the problem of high schools with weak promoting power. There are bills before Congress, for example, that call for a literacy coach to be placed in every low-performing high school. This would clearly be beneficial, especially if coaching was connected to curriculum specifically designed to support the skill development of adolescent learners. The strategy entirely ignores mathematics, however. Failing ninth-grade algebra is the reason many students are left back in ninth grade, which in turn is the greatest risk factor for dropping out.

Three high school reform approaches promise to promote fundamental change to the traditional organizational structure of large, nonselective neighborhood high schools—the creation of new small schools, the creation of new medium to large theme-based schools, and converting large high schools into multiple small learning communities that operate with varying amounts of autonomy within the larger school building. Evidence from this and other studies strongly suggests, however, that an exclusive emphasis on any one of these strategies will fall far short of resolving the nation's dropout crisis. To point:

New Small School Creation: A substantial amount of local and private foundation resources currently support a movement to replace large comprehensive high schools with small high schools of typically 300 or fewer students. The hope here is that the creation of new, small high schools will provide students with an energized faculty and a higher degree of personalized attention and instruction, which in turn will lead to substantially greater graduation rates. While based on a compelling and largely research-based theory, this movement's singular focus on new school creation is its Achilles heel in the face of the number, concentration, and location of high schools with weak promoting power revealed in this report. Among the 50 cities in which half or more of the student population attends high schools with weak promoting power, 39 have five or more weak promoting power high schools. To replace these high schools with small schools would require starting, staffing, and sustaining between 25 and 50 high schools in most of these cities, with many more than 100 new high schools needed in the largest cities. The question that remains to be addressed is the extent to which the financial, human, and social capital exists to accomplish this overwhelming task. In cities and rural counties hard pressed by shrinking middle-class populations and tax bases, as well as shortages of skilled principals and a near continual churn of superintendents and CEOs, will it be possible to find and sustain the civic capacity and investment in personnel development needed to equitably create, successfully run, and manage 25, 50, or 100-plus new high schools?

New Medium to Large School Creation: In some cities, efforts are underway to create somewhat larger new high schools serving from 600 to 800 students. While the economies of scale afforded by these schools make them a potentially more feasible option for school systems with limited resources, early anecdotal evidence recommends caution. The dual pressures of a high-standards environment and expectations of private and local funders (typically present when schools require new buildings or major renovations to existing buildings) can result in the shunting of equity concerns as new school leaders scramble to implement rigorous curriculum and achieve dramatic results in a short time period. In one such school that replaced a declining neighborhood high school, the new school remained nonselective but adopted an open-enrollment system to attract students from across the city who were interested in its technology focus. The school's brand-new curriculum and energized teachers were not prepared, however, to meet the needs of the substantial number of students coming in two or more grade levels behind in basic literacy and mathematics skills. As a consequence, the school has a significantly higher transfer rate than other high schools in the city. Just as telling, the enrollment slots reserved for students from the surrounding neighborhood now go unfilled; neighborhood families have concluded that the school is for "other people's children" (read "white and privileged").

Existing High School Conversions: Different approaches to break free from bureaucratic inertia and create smaller, more personalized and flexible learning environments, such as converting large schools into multiple small learning communities, face different challenges. First, not all low-performing high schools are good candidates for conversion. Some (we estimate perhaps 1% to 5% of the 2,000) are such demoralized environments, so lacking in leadership, teaching capacity, and community support, that any effort to turn them around would be quixotic at best. Second, attention to the process of conversion is very important to its outcome. Evidence is emerging that high schools that pursue a phased-in or voluntary approach to converting into multiple small learning communities or schools-within-a-school can produce marked inequities. The first smaller units to be developed typically attract the strongest teachers, entrepreneurial leaders, the most motivated students, and community resources, leaving subsequent efforts to struggle with fewer resources. Striking images are emerging of large low-performing high schools in which a section has been turned into a new, better-resourced small high school, where the fortunate few are provided with access to a better education under the daily gaze of the unfortunate majority still stuck attending a marginally smaller dropout factory. The alternative, converting an entire school at the same time, is an extremely intensive experience requiring substantial technical expertise and commitment to working through difficult staffing, curriculum, facilities, and scheduling challenges.

Transforming the Nation's Dropout Factories: What Would It Take?

Despite growing interest in high school reform and an increasing number of reform experiments, nothing close to a systematic plan to transform the nearly 2,000 high schools with low graduation rates and high dropout rates currently exists. Such a plan must be forged, however, if we are going to overcome the feasibility, equity, and quality challenges that current reform efforts are facing. Failure to do so runs the risk that current attempts to reform high schools will fall so short of the mark in transforming the high schools that produce the majority of the nation's dropouts that the energy behind the reform movement may dissipate before substantial progress can be made.

Enough is known about reforming low-performing, high-poverty neighborhood high schools to transform them. Working models and success stories exist.[3] The challenge is to develop the capacity, know-how, and will to implement what is known to work in all the high schools in need. First and foremost, it needs to be recognized that truly comprehensive reform is required. A dominant focus on one or even several levers of improvement will not be enough. Increased personalization and student outreach; high standards; intensive instructional programs to close achievement gaps; improved teacher quality, professional development, and teacher supports; engaging school programs; and strengthened connections among high schools, colleges, and employers are all needed in large, sustained, and coordinated measures. To date, however, this has rarely occurred because schools and districts have lacked the energy, know-how, and resources to do all that is needed. Instead, districts and schools focus on one or two areas of needed reform and then become disappointed and frustrated when the results are not sufficient.

The findings in this report, however, are hopeful in this regard. They show it is possible to identify the number and location of high schools that produce the majority of the nation's dropouts. This means that reforms and resources can be targeted. Transforming 2,000 high schools, moreover, is not beyond the bounds of human agency, especially when the payoff is potentially so large economically, educationally, and socially. In order to get the energy needed to sustain this effort, it will be important to bring into the high school reform movement all who stand to benefit from the demise of the nation's dropout factories —groups interested in economic growth, social justice, youth development, crime reduction, rural prosperity, and urban renaissance, at the local, state, and national levels. In order to get the necessary know-how to the high schools in need, it will be necessary to invest in the development of technical assistance groups who can shepherd school systems and schools through an effective reform process and join them into networks of reformed and reforming high schools. In order to gather and distribute the financial resources necessary to fundamentally change high schools with weak promoting power, a federal commitment to raise the budgets of 2,000 high schools by 10 percent or more will be needed. Because of the tight correlation between weak promoting power and poverty, this could be accomplished by funding Title I to its authorized levels, using the increase to provide high schools with their fair and proportional share of Title I funding. In return for the additional funding, high schools could be required to implement proven reforms. In order to develop, support, and sustain the human resources needed to bring about major improvements in teaching and learning, states and school districts will need to commit to putting a high-quality teacher in every classroom in every high school with weak promoting power and sustaining these teachers with ongoing professional development.

In addition to human and financial resources, a pragmatic approach will be required. No single reform strategy or set of comprehensive reforms will work for all high schools and all locations. In large cities with multiple high schools in need of reform, a mix of strategies will likely be the most productive and efficient approach. In other words, a combination of new small high schools, middle schools transformed into high schools, and existing high schools both broken up into several small high schools and converted into wall-to-wall small learning communities with a common principal but clearly defined separate spaces, teaching staffs, and student bodies. It will also need to be recognized that the same strategy that works in Detroit might not be the most effective in rural South Carolina. In fact, the data in the report on the location of high schools with weak promoting power makes clear that three very different strategies might be needed: a district strategy for cities in which half or more of the students attend a high school with weak promoting power; a state strategy for southern and southwestern states where schools with weak promoting power can be found throughout the state; and a school-level strategy for states and school districts in which schools with weak promoting power exist but are not the norm.

Finally, the middle-grades connection cannot be overlooked. Every high school with weak promoting power is fed by one or more low-performing middle-grades schools. The major reason students repeat the ninth grade and enter the dropout track is that they fail too many ninth-grade courses. Ninth-grade course failure is, in turn, driven in good part by students' lack of intermediate academic skills, weak reading comprehension and fluency abilities, and underdeveloped mathematical knowledge: in short, the academic outcomes of a good middle-grades education. The connection between poor middle schools and high schools with weak promoting power can be seen vividly in the fact that the very areas that have the highest concentration of high schools with weak promoting power—the urban North and the South—are also the areas with the lowest eighth-grade NAEP scores, particularly among minorities (Flanagan & Grissmer, 2002). Hence, high school reform must ultimately be seen as part of a broader secondary-school reform movement.

CONCLUSION

There are about 2,000 high schools in the United States where graduation is not the norm. These are high schools in which the senior class routinely shrinks to 60 percent or less, often much less, of the freshman class that entered four years earlier. These high schools are located throughout the nation, but are concentrated in about 50 large cities and 15 primarily southern and southwestern states. High schools with weak promoting power are overwhelmingly attended by minority students. Outside of the rural South, it is rare to find white students in appreciable numbers attending high schools with the high dropout and low graduation rates signaled by weak promoting power. Consequently, high schools with weak promoting power are the engines driving the low national graduation rate for minority students and the growing number of dispossessed young adults who are neither employed nor in school. These high schools must be specifically targeted for reform if the American high school is to fulfill its pivotal role as the means by which children who grow up in poverty can become adults who lead the nation. Transforming the nation's dropout factories into high schools that prepare all their students for postsecondary schooling or training and successful adulthood should thus be an urgent national priority. The promoting power indicator allows us to identify the number and location of the high schools that produce the bulk of the nation's dropouts. We now know where these schools are. It is time to go about the hard work of fixing them.

NOTES

1. It does provide it at the district level, and these data have been used by a number of scholars (Greene, 2002; Haney et al., 2004; Swanson, 2004; Warren, 2003) to develop indirect common measures of graduation rates at the state and district levels.
2. Both Haney et al. (2004) and Warren (2003) find that the graduation rate declined at the state level during the 1990s as well.
3. See, for example, Legters, Balfanz, Jordan, & McPartland (2002), Toch (2003), NASSP (2004).

REFERENCES

Allensworth, E. (2004). *Ending social promotion: Dropout rates in Chicago after implementation of the eighth-grade promotion gate.* Chicago: Consortium on Chicago School Research.

Allensworth, E., & Easton, J. (2001). *Calculating a cohort dropout rate for the Chicago Public Schools: A technical research report.* Chicago: Consortium on Chicago School Research.

Balfanz, R. (2000). Why do so many urban public school students demonstrate so little academic achievement? In M. Sanders (Ed.), *Schooling students placed at risk.* Mahwah, NJ: Erlbaum.

Balfanz, R., & Legters, N. (2001). *How many central city high schools have a severe dropout rate, where are they located, and who attends them? Estimates from the Common Core of Data.* Paper presented at the Dropouts in America Conference, The Civil Rights Project at Harvard University and Achieve, Inc., Cambridge, MA.

Balfanz, R., & Legters, N. (2003). *Weak promoting power, minority concentration, and high schools with severe dropout rates in urban America: A multiple cohort analysis of the 1990s.* Paper presented at the Making Dropouts Visible Conference, The Civil Rights Project at Harvard University and Achieve, Inc., Cambridge, MA.

Baltimore City Public School System (BCPSS). (1995). *Maryland School Performance Program Report, 1995.* Baltimore, MD: Author.

Baltimore City Public School System (BCPSS) (1997). *Maryland School Performance Program Report, 1997.* Baltimore, MD: Author.

Carnevale, A., & Desrochers D. (2004). *Standards for what? The economic roots of K–16 reform.* Princeton, NJ: Educational Testing Service.

Corvers, S., & Franklin, B. (2003). *A second look at Louisiana dropout, completion, and graduation rates.* Paper presented at the annual meeting of the American Educational Research Association, Chicago.

Flanagan, A., & Grissmer, D. (2002). The role of federal resources in closing the achievement gap. In J. Chubb & T. Loveless (Eds.), *Bridging the achievement gap.* Washington DC: Brooking Press.

Greene, J. P. (2002). *Public school graduation rates in the United States* (Civic Report No. 31). New York: Manhattan Institute for Policy Research.

Haney, W., Madaus, G., Abrams, L., Wheelock, A., Miao, J., & Gruia, I. (2004). *The education pipeline in the United States 1970–2000.* Boston: Boston College, National Board on Educational Testing and Public Policy.

Harvey, J., & Houseman, N. (2004). *Crisis or possibility? Conversations about the American high school.* Washington, DC: National High School Alliance.

Johnston, R. C. (2000, Sept. 20). Chicago study questions results of retention. *Education Week,* p. 3.

Kaufman, P. (2001). *The national dropout data collection system: Assessing consistency.* Paper presented at Dropouts in America Conference, Civil Rights Project at Harvard University and Achieve, Inc.

Kominski, R. (1990). Estimating the national high school dropout rate. *Demography, 27,* 303–311.

Legters, N., Balfanz, R., Jordan, W., & McPartland, J. (2002). *Comprehensive reform for urban high schools: A talent development approach.* New York: Teachers College Press.

Lee, V. (Ed.). (2002). *Reforming Chicago's high schools: Research perspectives on school and systems level change.* Chicago: Consortium on Chicago School Research.

Maryland State Department of Education (MSDE). (1997). *1996–1997: The fact book.* Baltimore, MD: Author.

National Association of Secondary School Principals. (2004). *Breaking ranks II: Strategies for leading high school reform.* Washington, DC: Author.

Neild, R., & Balfanz, R. (2001) *An extreme degree of difficulty: The educational challenge of the ninth grade in Philadelphia's neighborhood high schools.* Baltimore, MD: Johns Hopkins University, Center for Social Organization of Schools.

Orfield, G., Losen, D., Wald, J., & Swanson, C. (2004). *Losing our future: How minority youth are being left behind by the graduation rate crisis.* Cambridge, MA: Civil Rights Project at Harvard University.

Orfield, G., & Lee, C. (2004). *Brown at 50: King's dream or Plessy's nightmare?* Cambridge, MA: Civil Rights Project at Harvard University.

Roderick, M., Choing, J., & DaCosta, K. (1998). *The Student Life in High School Project: First follow-up student outcomes.* Chicago: University of Chicago, School of Social Service Administration.

Roderick, M., & Camburn, E. (1999). Risk and recovery from course failure in the early years of high school. *American Educational Research Journal, 36,* 303–343.

Steinberg, J. (2000, October 10). Frustrated parents hope their votes will change schools' ways. *New York Times,* p. A23.

Swanson, C., & Chaplin, D. (2003). *Counting high school graduates when graduates count: Measuring graduation rates under the high stakes of NCLB.* Paper prepared for the annual meeting of the National Economic Association. Washington, DC: Urban Institute, Education Policy Center.

Swanson, C. (2004). *Who graduates? Who doesn't? A statistical portrait of public high school graduation, class of 2001.* Washington, DC: Urban Institute, Education Policy Center.

Toch, T. (2003). *High schools on a human scale: How small schools can transform American education.* Boston: Beacon Press.

Wald, J., & Losen, D. (Eds.). (2003). Deconstructing the school to prison pipeline. *New Directions for Youth Development, 99.* San Francisco: Jossey-Bass.

Warren, J. R. (2003). *State-level high school graduation rates in the 1990s: Concepts, measures, and trends.* Paper presented at the annual meeting of the American Sociological Association, Atlanta.

APPENDIX: ADDITIONAL TABLES

TABLE A1
Percentage of Minority Students in Weak Promoting-Power Schools:
60 Percent Promoting-Power Cutoff

State	Nat. Amer.	Asian	Hispanic	Black	White
Alabama	20%	22%	20%	33%	17%
Alaska	37%	15%	17%	22%	21%
Arizona	55%	16%	37%	8%	12%
Arkansas	1%	0%	1%	15%	1%
California	14%	13%	31%	35%	8%
Colorado	27%	25%	47%	41%	14%
Connecticut	6%	7%	37%	34%	3%
Delaware	33%	41%	53%	41%	29%
Florida	39%	40%	39%	52%	41%
Georgia	41%	38%	57%	68%	37%
Hawaii	14%	21%	15%	12%	11%
Idaho	1%	1%	2%	0%	2%
Illinois	15%	8%	35%	52%	5%
Indiana	12%	11%	57%	39%	7%
Iowa	4%	11%	11%	25%	4%
Kansas	13%	11%	25%	22%	6%
Kentucky	14%	18%	28%	42%	17%
Louisiana	34%	26%	47%	38%	23%
Maine	2%	1%	3%	2%	3%
Maryland	11%	2%	21%	20%	4%
Massachusetts	7%	22%	34%	21%	7%
Michigan	18%	17%	39%	64%	9%
Minnesota	20%	11%	4%	24%	1%
Mississippi	16%	16%	21%	36%	21%
Missouri	4%	12%	16%	40%	3%
Montana	22%	0%	0%	0%	0%
Nebraska	20%	9%	17%	48%	7%
Nevada	11%	11%	24%	35%	12%
New Hampshire	9%	1%	1%	2%	4%
New Jersey	20%	6%	22%	39%	1%
New Mexico	45%	38%	51%	46%	32%
New York	24%	49%	68%	68%	8%
North Carolina	65%	27%	36%	47%	24%
North Dakota	0%	0%	0%	0%	0%
Ohio	22%	13%	24%	60%	7%
Oklahoma	9%	17%	38%	40%	9%
Oregon	8%	6%	9%	23%	4%
Pennsylvania	14%	24%	48%	63%	4%
Rhode Island	34%	35%	55%	45%	13%
South Carolina	55%	39%	58%	65%	46%
South Dakota	52%	15%	22%	15%	11%
Texas	27%	25%	52%	52%	20%
Utah	21%	0%	0%	0%	0%
Vermont	1%	15%	15%	20%	7%
Virginia	7%	4%	7%	23%	5%
Washington	22%	19%	29%	30%	13%
West Virginia	21%	8%	8%	5%	7%
Wisconsin	17%	11%	32%	59%	2%
Wyoming	3%	6%	4%	2%	6%
Total	26%	19%	39%	46%	11%

TABLE A2

1993–2002 Promoting Power in 100 Largest Cities: 60 Percent Cutoff

City	2002 No. of HSs	2002 % of HSs	1999 No. of HSs	1999 % of HSs	1996 No. of HSs	1996 % of HSs	1993 No. of HSs	1993 % of HSs	% Minority
New York City	110	81%	91	76%	83	80%	57	51%	83%
Chicago	42	68%	43	77%	46	81%	41	69%	89%
Los Angeles	39	68%	29	57%	40	78%	40	80%	88%
Philadelphia	26	79%	27	82%	25	76%	16	48%	79%
Dallas	21	81%	20	80%	21	88%	21	88%	88%
Houston	20	80%	21	81%	20	80%	19	73%	86%
Detroit	19	73%	19	73%	18	72%	19	86%	96%
Jacksonville	15	79%	13	68%	10	63%	3	19%	49%
Louisville	14	70%	7	33%	9	41%	5	25%	31%
Milwaukee	13	87%	15	94%	14	93%	9	60%	73%
Tampa	13	68%	5	33%	4	29%	1	8%	42%
Cleveland	12	86%	13	87%	10	59%	14	78%	82%
Memphis	11	41%	13	46%	10	37%	8	30%	93%
Baltimore	11	65%	12	75%	10	67%	11	73%	88%
St. Petersburg	11	69%	12	75%	12	86%	1	7%	23%
Atlanta	10	91%	9	90%	7	64%	5	42%	95%
Fort Worth	9	75%	5	45%	9	82%	8	67%	71%
Columbus	9	53%	12	71%	12	71%	12	67%	61%
St. Louis	8	100%	8	100%	7	88%	7	100%	80%
Denver	8	73%	9	90%	8	80%	5	50%	69%
Shreveport	8	80%	9	82%	10	100%	10	91%	60%
Austin	8	80%	8	80%	8	80%	7	70%	58%
Nashville	8	53%	9	69%	7	54%	7	54%	49%
San Antonio	7	88%	6	75%	8	100%	8	100%	95%
Augusta	7	70%	6	67%	6	67%	3	33%	69%
Oklahoma City	7	78%	7	78%	7	88%	4	50%	66%
Albuquerque	7	64%	8	73%	7	58%	4	33%	55%
Pittsburgh	7	64%	6	60%	7	64%	5	45%	51%
New Orleans	6	32%	6	32%	7	37%	7	37%	95%
Honolulu	6	16%	9	26%	1	3%	2	6%	94%
Kansas City	6	86%	2	29%	7	70%	3	33%	82%
Cincinnati	6	67%	6	75%	4	67%	5	56%	67%
Buffalo	6	43%	8	57%	5	36%	3	20%	63%
Akron	6	75%	6	75%	2	25%	2	50%	46%
Las Vegas	6	25%	2	10%	0	0%	3	23%	40%
Oakland	5	83%	4	67%	4	67%	4	67%	95%
Newark	5	50%	4	40%	6	67%	3	33%	90%
El Paso	5	50%	6	60%	7	88%	6	75%	81%
Boston	5	33%	4	27%	4	27%	0	0%	80%
Rochester	5	83%	7	100%	5	71%	6	86%	80%
San Diego	5	26%	3	17%	4	22%	3	18%	74%
Fresno	5	63%	5	71%	6	86%	4	57%	73%
Indianapolis	5	100%	5	100%	5	100%	7	100%	64%
Tucson	5	50%	5	50%	5	50%	4	40%	50%
Toledo	5	71%	5	71%	6	86%	4	57%	49%
Mobile	5	36%	8	62%	13	87%	8	53%	48%
Tulsa	5	56%	6	67%	7	78%	6	67%	48%

continued on next page

Table A2   (continued)

City	2002 No. of HSs	2002 % of HSs	1999 No. of HSs	1999 % of HSs	1996 No. of HSs	1996 % of HSs	1993 No. of HSs	1993 % of HSs	% Minority
Charlotte	5	36%	4	33%	2	18%	2	18%	47%
Richmond	4	67%	1	17%	3	50%	3	60%	95%
San Francisco	4	29%	7	54%	3	23%	4	33%	88%
Phoenix	4	50%	1	13%	0	0%	0	0%	76%
Norfolk	4	80%	5	100%	4	80%	5	100%	67%
Baton Rouge	4	31%	8	62%	4	31%	2	15%	60%
Minneapolis	4	57%	5	71%	4	57%	3	43%	60%
Grand Rapids	4	100%	3	60%	3	60%	3	50%	56%
Tacoma	4	80%	2	40%	1	20%	2	40%	40%
Santa Ana	3	75%	2	50%	3	75%	4	100%	97%
Birmingham	3	33%	7	78%	8	73%	8	80%	94%
Jersey City	3	60%	3	60%	4	80%	3	60%	92%
Stockton	3	100%	0	0%	3	100%	3	100%	85%
Corpus Christi	3	60%	4	80%	4	80%	0	0%	73%
Greensboro	3	38%	8	57%	2	14%	1	8%	41%
Arlington	3	60%	0	0%	0	0%	1	25%	39%
Omaha	3	43%	0	0%	1	14%	0	0%	36%
Raleigh	3	21%	1	8%	2	17%	0	0%	31%
Yonkers	2	50%	1	33%	1	33%	0	0%	73%
Sacramento	2	40%	2	40%	3	60%	4	80%	72%
Riverside	2	40%	1	25%	2	50%	3	75%	50%
Portland	2	20%	2	20%	3	30%	3	30%	34%
Virginia Beach	2	20%	2	20%	2	22%	0	0%	32%
Fort Wayne	2	33%	3	50%	1	17%	1	17%	29%
Des Moines	2	40%	2	40%	0	0%	0	0%	24%
Montgomery	1	20%	0	0%	1	20%	0	0%	69%
Bakersfield	1	7%	4	31%	6	50%	1	10%	53%
Irving	1	33%	2	67%	2	67%	1	33%	52%
Fremont	1	20%	3	60%	2	40%	0	0%	49%
Aurora	1	25%	0	0%	0	0%	0	0%	44%
Colorado Springs	1	20%	2	40%	0	0%	0	0%	25%
Lexington	1	20%	1	17%	2	33%	0	0%	25%
Scottsdale	1	20%	1	20%	1	25%	1	25%	13%
Long Beach	0	0%	0	0%	0	0%	0	0%	77%
Anaheim	0	0%	0	0%	1	13%	0	0%	66%
San Jose	0	0%	1	17%	1	17%	0	0%	63%
Seattle	0	0%	0	0%	0	0%	5	50%	60%
St. Paul	0	0%	0	0%	0	0%	0	0%	55%
Lubbock	0	0%	0	0%	0	0%	0	0%	49%
Garland	0	0%	1	17%	1	20%	0	0%	41%
Glendale	0	0%	0	0%	0	0%	0	0%	39%
Wichita	0	0%	2	25%	3	38%	0	0%	39%
Chesapeake	0	0%	0	0%	0	0%	0	0%	37%
Anchorage	0	0%	0	0%	0	0%	0	0%	30%
Madison	0	0%	1	25%	0	0%	0	0%	26%
Mesa	0	0%	1	20%	0	0%	0	0%	22%
Spokane	0	0%	0	0%	1	17%	0	0%	13%
Lincoln	0	0%	0	0%	0	0%	0	0%	12%

TABLE A3

Low-Promoting Schools by State, Locale, and Minority Concentration: 60 Percent Cutoff

State	Total No. of HSs	% of HSs in State	Type of Location				Minority Concentration			
			City	Urban Fringe	Town	Rural	<10% Minority	<50% Minority	Majority Minority	>90% Minority
Alabama	71	21%	10	16	14	31	12	43	28	13
Alaska	9	28%	0	0	5	4	0	6	3	2
Arizona	37	26%	18	6	4	9	0	6	31	13
Arkansas	5	3%	2	0	2	1	0	0	5	3
California	129	16%	74	49	1	5	1	12	117	64
Colorado	32	20%	16	13	3	0	0	14	18	4
Connecticut	13	9%	11	2	0	0	0	0	13	6
Delaware	8	28%	1	6	0	1	0	3	5	0
Florida	162	45%	51	61	15	35	6	116	46	15
Georgia	156	53%	34	44	41	37	8	67	89	37
Hawaii	6	16%	1	5	0	0	0	0	6	2
Idaho	2	3%	0	0	0	2	1	2	0	0
Illinois	63	15%	54	7	2	0	2	10	53	40
Indiana	30	9%	16	8	3	3	6	18	12	6
Iowa	4	2%	4	0	0	0	0	4	0	0
Kansas	9	7%	4	1	3	1	2	5	4	1
Kentucky	39	19%	6	13	6	14	20	34	5	0
Louisiana	64	31%	18	19	9	18	3	28	36	16
Maine	4	5%	0	1	0	3	4	4	0	0
Maryland	17	10%	11	4	1	1	1	2	15	9
Massachusetts	24	9%	16	6	1	1	4	12	12	4
Michigan	79	16%	37	30	1	11	13	32	47	26
Minnesota	6	2%	4	0	0	2	0	0	6	2
Mississippi	52	31%	9	5	17	21	3	16	36	19
Missouri	25	10%	13	6	3	3	5	8	17	8
Montana	1	3%	0	0	0	1	0	0	1	1
Nebraska	4	5%	3	0	1	0	0	3	1	0
Nevada	8	17%	1	4	1	2	0	3	5	0
New Hampshire	5	8%	0	1	2	2	5	5	0	0
New Jersey	24	8%	12	12	0	0	0	1	23	20
New Mexico	27	42%	7	4	9	7	0	5	22	8
New York	145	20%	128	9	2	6	8	16	129	81
North Carolina	106	34%	16	24	18	48	3	51	55	10
Ohio	75	12%	52	10	6	7	13	35	40	19
Oklahoma	15	11%	12	2	1	0	0	4	11	3
Oregon	7	5%	2	2	2	1	0	5	2	0
Pennsylvania	48	9%	40	5	2	1	0	10	38	19
Rhode Island	7	18%	4	3	0	0	2	4	3	1
South Carolina	101	58%	10	28	15	48	3	51	50	13
South Dakota	3	10%	1	1	0	1	0	2	1	1
Tennessee	58	23%	28	9	11	10	–	–	–	–
Texas	240	34%	134	46	36	24	1	59	181	96
Utah	1	1%	0	0	0	1	0	0	1	1
Vermont	3	7%	1	0	2	0	2	3	0	0
Virginia	26	10%	18	2	0	6	2	4	22	6
Washington	32	14%	9	12	5	6	4	22	10	0
West Virginia	6	6%	1	1	1	3	4	6	0	0
Wisconsin	16	5%	14	0	1	1	0	3	13	8
Wyoming	1	5%	0	0	1	0	1	1	0	0
Total	2007	—	905	477	247	378	139	735	1214	579

– Insufficient data are available to calculate minority concentration for Tennessee.

The work of Carolyn Henry Barber, our chief research assistant on the project, has been invaluable. Her mastery of the dataset and the speed with which she was able to process our many requests was phenomenal. We would also like to thank Chris West, Barbara Colton, and Gregg Howell for their assistance in putting this report together. We would like to thank The Civil Rights Project at Harvard University for helping to shepherd this research through its many phases and helping it make a difference. Finally, we would like to acknowledge the teachers and students whose daily struggle to provide and receive a good high school education inspired us to conduct this research in the first place.

CHAPTER 4

High School Dropout,
Race/Ethnicity, and Social Background
from the 1970s to the 1990s

ROBERT M. HAUSER

SOLON J. SIMMONS

DEVAH I. PAGER

The earning power of high school dropouts—like the earning power of high school graduates—has declined relative to that of college graduates (Hauser, 1993; Murphy & Welch, 1989). Indeed, most high school dropouts are unable to compete for jobs that pay enough to keep them out of poverty. By 1990, the economic consequences of failing to complete high school had reached unprecedented levels. In this context, President George H. W. Bush and the nation's governors (U.S. Department of Education, 1990) proclaimed as one of six national education goals that the high school completion rate would reach 90 percent by 2000.[1] Since the middle 1980s, there has been a steady stream of new reports about the familial and economic correlates of dropping out of high school (Astone & McLanahan, 1991; Ekstrom, Goertz, Pollack, & Rock, 1986; Haveman, Wolfe, & Spaulding, 1991; Krein & Beller, 1988; McLanahan, 1985; Sandefur, McLanahan, & Wojtkiewicz, 1992). In 1988, the National Center for Education Statistics (NCES) began producing a regular series of annual reports on trends in high school dropout rates among different groups of young people (Kaufman, Alt, & Chapman, 2001).[2] Thus, the association of high school dropouts with educational and economic deprivation, minority status, and family disruption is well documented, as is the global trend in high school dropout rates, which have generally—but not always—declined since the 1970s.

The possible impact of higher educational standards on high school dropout rates, especially test-based promotion and graduation, has stimulated new interest in the issue. Some believe that higher standards or the expectation of eventual failure has accelerated or will accelerate marginal students' decisions to leave school, and that high standards pressure school administrators to encourage leaving school before graduating (Haney, 1993, 2000). Others declare that lower rates of high school completion are acceptable if that is the price of demonstrated higher competence among those who graduate. However, there is as yet little evidence about the effects of higher standards on students' decisions to drop out of school, eventual high school completion, or, in fact, on the academic achievements of high school graduates. That is, we are as yet poorly equipped to assess the costs and benefits of tradeoffs between the quality and quantity of high school graduates that may be entailed in standards-based educational reforms.

This chapter will not greatly reduce our ignorance about these important matters. Indeed, it is not clear how long we may have to wait for convincing evidence about the effects of new educational policies on dropout rates, or whether the effects of visible policy changes may be swamped by other changes, such as changes in the overall economy. Rather, this chapter attempts to outline the social and historic context of the dropout problem since 1970: Who drops out of high school? What are the major social and economic characteristics affecting high school dropout? To what degree can social and economic background differences among racial and ethnic groups account for their different chances of dropping out? How have changes in social and economic background interacted with and contributed to trends in high school dropout rates? The unique contribution of this analysis lies in its temporal scope, in the comparability of measurements across that period, and in its use of multivariate methods to estimate the independent effects of social and economic background factors.

NATIONAL DROPOUT DATA OVER THREE DECADES

In light of changes in the social and economic circumstances of their families of orientation, we use a large set of repeated national cross-sectional surveys to assess trends and differentials in dropping out among whites, African Americans, and Hispanics over the past three decades. We review overall trends and trends among different groups of students, the changing social background of high school students, and the effects of social background on high school dropout rates. Most importantly, we report new findings about the racial and ethnic trends and group differences in high school dropout rates that remain after family background has been controlled statistically.

The analysis is based on data from some 167,400 youths aged 14 to 24, covered in October Current Population Surveys (CPS) from 1972 to 1998, who could have dropped out of high school before completing the tenth, eleventh, or twelfth grade. We use a definition of "dropout" developed by Kominski (1990; Kominski & Adams, 1993) at the U.S. Census Bureau and featured in the NCES annual reports on trends in high school dropout rates. Briefly, a tenth- or eleventh-grade dropout is someone who has completed at most the ninth or tenth grade, who is not enrolled in school in October of the survey year, and who was enrolled in school during the previous October. Thus, a tenth-grade dropout is a non-enrolled youth who completed the ninth grade in the survey year or who had completed the ninth grade in an earlier year, was enrolled in school during the previous October, but did not complete the tenth grade. A similar definition applies to an eleventh-grade dropout. At the twelfth-grade level the definition is the same, except that students who completed high school during the survey year are identified separately and counted as non-dropouts.

The CPS data and this definition of dropout have strengths and weaknesses. The CPS data are from a well-designed national survey and—with known exceptions—they are highly comparable across time. This is a great advantage over most local and state data (Kaufman, 2000). The definition of dropout is truly a measure of leaving school, not failure to complete high school; a student may in fact enter and leave school several times during the high school years. It probably assesses high school dropout more accurately in the Hispanic population than measures based on high school completion or current school enrollment, because it excludes youth who have never been enrolled in regular high schools in this country. Moreover, because the definition of dropout focuses on enrollment and grade completion in the year preceding the survey, it is possible to link survey data on enrollment and dropout for the vast majority of high school students to social and economic characteristics of the parental household.

On the negative side, there are problems of population coverage in the Current Population Survey, especially for black males (see ch. 5). The coverage problem is corrected to some degree by the weighting procedures used by the Census Bureau. All the same, one should be cautious in using these data because the remaining bias is likely to lead to underestimation of dropout rates.

The definition of school dropout combines individuals who did not continue from one grade to the next in the survey year with those who dropped out from the next higher grade level during the previous academic year as if they were in the same cohort. For example, dropouts in the tenth grade include students who left school after completing ninth grade, as well as those who left school after starting tenth grade in the previous academic year. The definition also fails to identify return enrollees among the current students at each grade level. Finally, the base of students at risk for dropping out in tenth grade does

FIGURE 1

Cumulative High School Dropout Rate by Race/Ethnicity:
Persons 14 to 24 Years Old, 1973 to 1997

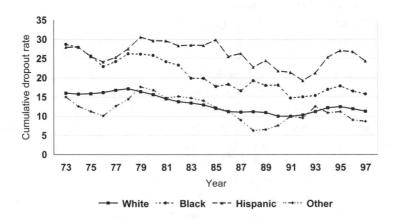

not include students who failed the tenth grade in the previous academic year, unless they dropped out before the October survey.[3] Despite these problems the definition is useful, perhaps more so than definitions based on grade completion and enrollment by a specific age, which fail to take account of variation in age-grade progression (Hauser, 1997, 2001).[4]

TRENDS IN HIGH SCHOOL DROPOUT

The dropout rate among African Americans and Hispanics was high throughout the 1970s, 25 to 30 percent for each group (Figure 1). It rose toward the end of that decade, but was still lower among blacks at the end of the 1970s than at the beginning. In the late 1970s, the black and Hispanic rates diverged. Dropout rates gradually declined among African Americans to between 15 and 20 percent, while it peaked at close to 30 percent among Hispanics in 1985, and then declined to about 20 percent in 1993 when the black rate was 15 percent. Thus, dropping out has been consistently higher among Hispanics than African Americans since the late 1970s.

Dropout rates for all groups rose sharply in the early to mid-1990s (Figure 1). This rise is probably an artifact of changing survey methods in the early 1990s. Almost all of the change reflects an anomalous jump in dropout rates at the twelfth-grade level, which was in no way paralleled in the tenth or eleventh grades.[5] The overall decline in dropout resumed after 1995. Dropout rates have been much lower among non-Hispanic whites (hereafter, whites) and other

FIGURE 2

Trends in Cumulative High School Dropout by Metropolitan Location:
High School Students at Risk of Dropout, 1972 to 1998

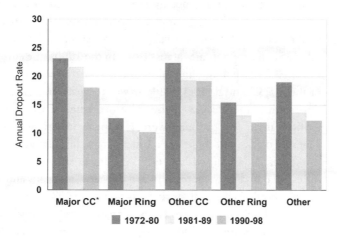

* CC = Central City

races/ethnicities than among African Americans or Hispanics. Except for brief periods in the mid-1970s and late 1980s, the level and trend among "others" has closely tracked that of whites. Among whites, the dropout rate was 15 to 17 percent through the mid- to late-1970s and then began a slow, consistent decline to about 11 percent by the early 1990s. Despite the more rapid decline of dropout rates among African Americans than among whites, racial-ethnic differentials remain large. Based on the NCES dropout report for October 1999 (Kaufman, 2001), we estimate the three-year high school dropout rates to be 11.5 percent among whites and others, 18.3 percent among African Americans, and 21.6 percent among Hispanics.

Some believe that school location—in cities or suburbs—accounts for a large share of racial/ethnic differentials in dropout rates. To test this, we have examined trends and differentials in dropout rates by school location (Figure 2). The clearest contrast is between central cities and their suburban rings; dropping out is consistently greater in central cities. For example, during the 1990s, the cumulative dropout rate was 18.0 percent in major central cities and 19.2 percent in other central cities, while it was 10.2 percent and 11.9 percent in their respective suburban rings. In addition, the overall decline in dropout rates appears in all but one area: There was essentially no change in dropout rates in other central cities during the 1980s and 1990s.[6] The decline is most consistent in the large central cities, from 23.1 percent in the 1970s to 21.6 percent in the 1980s and 18.0 percent in the 1990s. The largest decrease in drop-outs occurred in the other (small metropolitan and non-metropolitan) areas in the 1970s and 1980s, from 19.0 to 13.7 percent.

These same differentials and trends by metropolitan status occur for each major racial and ethnic group. For example, clear differences in dropout rates between central cities and their rings occur for whites and African Americans, along with a decrease in dropout rates across time. In the 1990s, the cumulative dropout rate was 12.8 percent among whites and 15.0 percent among African Americans in the major central cities, while it was 8.3 percent among whites and only 7.3 percent among blacks in the suburban rings of those cities. In other metropolitan areas, dropout rates were 17.0 percent among whites and 19.9 percent among blacks, but there was a much larger differential in the sub-urban ring—10.3 percent among whites and 17.3 percent among blacks. Thus, neither the differential in dropout rates between African Americans and whites, nor that between central cities and their rings, is merely a consequence of racial separation between schools in those two types of areas. However, it should also be kept in mind that minorities are more likely than whites to be located in the central cities, where dropout rates are higher.

Data for the largest metropolitan areas bear out our analysis. In New York City, for example, the estimated dropout rates were 15.0 percent for whites, 18.4 percent for blacks, and 23.1 percent for Hispanics. In the Los Angeles sub-urbs, dropout rates were 11.5 percent for whites and 26.4 percent for Hispan-ics. In the city of Los Angeles, dropout rates were 15.1 percent for whites, 20.0 percent for African Americans, and 28.0 percent for Hispanics. In Chicago, dropout rates were 14.7 percent among whites, 26.2 percent among African Americans, and 30.2 percent among Hispanics. Thus, these data for specific ar-eas support our overall finding that racial/ethnic differentials in dropout rates are large within residential sectors of major metropolitan areas.

TRENDS IN SOCIAL BACKGROUND

Trends in high school dropout rates should be viewed in the context of popula-tion change. Thus, we begin by reviewing key characteristics of high school stu-dents, combining the data across grades 10 to 12 in each survey year. In passing, we also comment on the measurement of some of the social and economic background characteristics that later enter our multivariate analysis of dropout. While there are no great surprises, we believe this review of the evidence is nec-essary because it describes the characteristics of high school students at risk of dropping out, rather than the characteristics of families or those of all children of high school age.

Basic Demographic Characteristics

From the 1970s to the 1990s, the proportion of African American high school students rose from 13.1 to 15.8 percent, while the share of Hispanics rose from 5.3 to 11.6 percent, and the share of others rose from 1.5 to 4.3 percent. Consequently, the proportion of whites fell from 80.0 to 68.3 percent of high school students. This is partly a result of differential fertility and immigration, but is also a result of decreasing high school dropout rates among minorities, relative to the white majority.[7]

The largest share of high school students—between 34 and 38 percent— lives in small metropolitan areas or in non-metropolitan areas. There has been a slight decline in the share of students in the 17 largest metropolitan areas—in both their central cities and suburban rings—from just over 10 percent to just under 10 percent in the central cities and from 17 to 15 percent in their suburbs. The share of students in other metropolitan centers has also declined, from 15.5 to 13.2 percent. However, the share in suburban rings of other metropolitan centers rose from 23 percent in the 1970s and 1980s to almost 26 percent in the 1990s.

Figure 3 shows trends in the distribution of high school students in each racial ethnic group by metropolitan residence. Each group has a distinctive residential distribution, which has persisted in spite of major population redistribution. Few white students live in central cities, and more than 80 percent are almost equally divided between suburban rings and small cities or nonmetropolitan areas. Half or more of African Americans and almost as large a share of Hispanics live in the central cities of metropolitan areas. However, about 30 percent of African American high school students and 20 percent of Hispanics live outside the large metropolitan areas. Other racial and ethnic minorities are roughly similar in residential distribution to Hispanics, but they are increasingly less likely to live in major central cities.

White students are becoming less likely to live in one of the major metropolitan areas, while their representation in smaller cities and non-metropolitan areas has been stable. A constant share of whites resides in the other large metropolitan areas that were not among the top 17 in 1970. Within both types of areas there has been a relative shift of whites from central cities to suburbs. Among blacks there has been a declining share of students in central cities— from 54 percent in the 1970s to 47 percent in the 1990s, roughly balanced by their increasing share in the suburbs of other metropolitan areas from 10 to 16 percent, but not by growth in the suburbs of the major metropolitan areas.

Among Hispanics, there was little change in metropolitan distribution from the 1970s to the 1990s. The main trend was a shift away from central cities, other than in the 17 major areas. However, among other racial-ethnic groups there was a pronounced shift away from central cities and into suburban rings. The percentage of students in central cities dropped from 42 to 34 percent, while the share of students in suburban rings rose from 58 to 66 percent.

There has been a modest regional redistribution of high school students over the past three decades, away from the East and Midwest into both the South and West. The share of students in the East declined from 23 to 19 percent, in the Midwest from 29 to 25 percent. In the South, the share of high school students grew from 30 to 34 percent, while it rose in the West from 18 to 22 percent.

There are distinctive distributions of racial and ethnic groups by region. Whites are almost equally distributed over the four Census regions, and there have been small interregional shifts corresponding to those in the total population. African American students remain concentrated in the South—where more than half reside—and only about 10 percent of black high school students live in the West. The largest share of Hispanic high school students—about 45 percent—lives in the West, and there was a decline in the share of Hispanic students who live in the East from about 21 to 16 percent. Students of other racial and ethnic groups are even more concentrated in the West than Hispanics, but their share in other regions has gradually increased from 33 to 46 percent.

The vast majority of high school students are age 16 to 18 at the time of the October surveys, but a modestly increasing share is 19 or older or 15 or younger. There are also characteristic differences in age distributions between white students and African American, Hispanic, or other high school students. These reflect strong differentials in age-grade progression, as well as dropout rates (Hauser, 2001; Hauser, Pager, & Simmons, 2004). Blacks and Hispanics are more likely than whites to be age 19 or older when they are still in high school. Among whites, even in the 1990s, no more than 8 percent of high school students were age 19 or older, but 13 percent or more of blacks and Hispanics were 19 or older in each period, and the percentage was only slightly lower among students of other racial/ethnic groups. Since the likelihood of dropping out increases with age, the difference in age distributions could partly account for observable differences in dropout rates between whites and minorities.

Family and Socioeconomic Background Factors

Some family background factors changed over time in ways that should tend to increase the risk of high school dropout, but others changed in a favorable direction or did not change at all. Female head of household among African American high school students grew from 38 percent in 1973 to about 54 per-

FIGURE 3   Trends in Metropolitan Distribution by Race/Ethnicity: High School Students at Risk of Dropout, 1972 to 1998

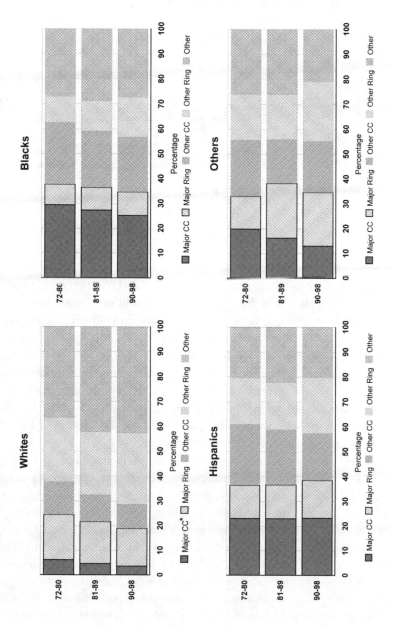

* CC = Central City

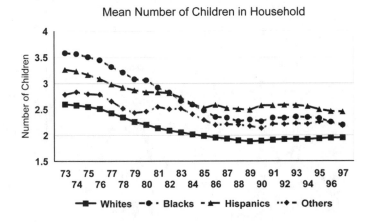

FIGURE 4

Trends in Household Structure by Race/Ethnicity:
High School Students at Risk of Dropout, 1973 to 1997

Mean Number of Children in Household

cent in 1994. Among Hispanics, female head of household increased from 20 to 39 percent. Among whites, female head of household increased from 11 to 16 percent, and the level and trend were similar among students of other racial/ethnic groups. There have been no consistent trends in the share of household heads without occupations—possibly excepting a slight downward shift among African Americans after the early 1980s. There are, however, persistent ethnic differences in the share of student households with working heads. Only about 11 percent of white high school students live in a household without a working head, compared to 31 percent of African Americans, 25 percent of Hispanics, and 21 percent of students of other race/ethnicity.

Figure 4 shows the mean number of children in the household younger than 19—one indicator of family structure associated with low educational outcomes. The declining number of children per household is a dramatic change in family structure. Since large numbers of siblings (of which the number of resident children is a somewhat defective proxy) have long been associated with low levels of education, we would expect this trend to contribute to a decline in high school dropout.[8] In the early 1970s, there was an average of 3.6 children younger than 19 in the households of African American high school students, but this had fallen to 2.2 children by 1997. Among Hispanics, the mean number of children per household fell from 3.3 to 2.5, and among whites it decreased from 2.6 to 2.0. Among students of other race/ethnicity, the number of children per household declined as much as among whites, from 2.8 to 2.2.

In terms of parental education, whites are consistently more advantaged than African Americans, who are consistently more advantaged than Hispanics (Figure 5). Parental education increased from the 1970s to the 1990s among whites and blacks, but mainly undulated among Hispanics. The mean years of school completed by white household heads was 12.2 years in 1973, and it grew to 13.6 years by 1997. The educational attainment of white mothers rose similarly from 11.8 to 13.2 years. Among blacks, the mean schooling of household heads grew from 9.2 years in 1973 to 12.3 years in 1997, and the mean schooling of African American mothers grew from 10.0 to 12.4 years.[9] Among Hispanics, the mean years of schooling of parents was about nine years for the decade after 1973, and there may have been some growth in the schooling of household heads after 1983.[10] We suspect that the meager growth in schooling among the parents of Hispanic high school students partly reflects the continuing immigration of Hispanics. The mean educational attainment for parents of students of other race/ethnicity was just short of 11 years in 1973, and by 1997 it had increased to 13.3 years among household heads and 12.7 years among mothers. We would expect these trends in parental schooling to lead to lower dropout rates among all groups except Hispanics.

Occupational status is much higher among the heads of white households than of black or Hispanic households.[11] Occupational status of household heads has increased regularly among whites, blacks, and others, but not among Hispanics. Other things being equal, these trends will tend to reduce high school dropout rates in the first three groups. Farm occupations are rare among the heads of households of high school students, and they are declining among whites and blacks. At one time, farm background was associated with lower life chances, but here we find that the net effect of farm background on dropout rates is negative in all racial and ethnic groups. Thus, other things being equal, the decline in farm background will tend to increase high school dropout rates.[12]

The CPS household income item is not of high quality (Hauser, 1991), but it is a useful, if rough, indicator of economic standing. There were great differences in household incomes among whites, blacks, and Hispanics; in constant 1988 dollars, white families earned about $27,000, Hispanic families about $14,500, black families about $12,000, and other families about $20,600. The economic cycles of the past 30 years are evident within each racial and ethnic category, but they are more clearly defined among African Americans and others than among whites or Hispanics. In the case of Hispanics, cyclical effects are overlaid on a gradual decline of real income from the 1970s to the 1990s, from about $17,000 to about $13,300.[13] There appears to be no overall trend toward growth or decline in the real family incomes of the other three categories of student households over the past three decades.

FIGURE 5

Trends in Parental Schooling by Race/Ethnicity:
High School Students at Risk of Dropout, 1973 to 1997

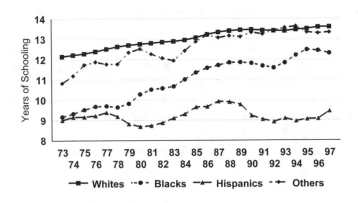

Mean Years of Schooling of Mothers

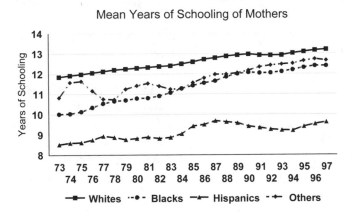

Home ownership is a crude measure of wealth. It may also reflect stability in the economic and social situation of a household, or in the quality of neighborhoods where students live. In any of these cases, we would expect home ownership to be associated with lower chances of dropping out of high school. The white advantage of home ownership is even sharper than that of household income. About 85 percent of white high school students came from families in owner-occupied housing, compared to about 65 percent of Hispanics and 55 percent of blacks and others. After 1981 there was a slight decline in home ownership among the families of white graduates, a sharp fall among Hispanics, and a slight and irregular decline among blacks. Home ownership has been relatively stable only among students from other racial-ethnic groups. Owner occupancy is associated with reduced dropout rates, so we would expect the declining prevalence of home ownership among blacks and Hispanics to increase high school dropout rates.

RACE/ETHNICITY AND HIGH SCHOOL DROPOUT

The observed association between race/ethnicity and high school dropout rates may be explained in part by differences in residential location and in family and socioeconomic background. Moreover, we have seen that the distributions of those factors have changed over time. Thus, we have looked to see how well the potential explanatory factors account for trends and differentials in high school dropout rates among racial/ethnic groups.

Our models demonstrate that regional and metropolitan location explains only a small fraction of the observed racial/ethnic differentials (Figure 6). As shown earlier, racial/ethnic differentials in dropout rates appear within local areas; they are not merely a matter of residential location. However, when family and socioeconomic background factors are controlled, the effects of minority status are reversed. That is, among people of equivalent social origins, minorities are less likely to drop out than whites. For example, at the tenth-grade level in all three minority groups, the odds of dropping out are about 0.6 less than among whites. This reversal is largest in the tenth grade, and it is much smaller at the twelfth-grade level. However, the finding strongly suggests that differentials in high school dropout rates between minority and majority students are primarily a function of family and socioeconomic background and only secondarily depend on residential location.

We have tested this finding by looking at the October CPS data in other ways. For example, we have run the same models independently in each of three successive nine-year periods. The findings are similar in each period. Overall differentials in dropout are largest between Hispanics and whites, but the differentials between blacks and whites are also quite large. These effects are reduced modestly when metropolitan and regional location are controlled, and they are reversed when family and socioeconomic background is controlled. We have also carried out a parallel analysis where the sample has been split into four age groups—16 and under, 17, 18, and 19 and older. The findings are similar in each age group.

Our finding that family and socioeconomic background account for or even reverse minority disadvantage in dropout rates is not unique. It is also not widely known, and the reasons for the reversal are not well understood. While the CPS data cannot tell us why this happens, one plausible explanation is that opportunities outside of school are greater for whites than for minorities. That is, other things being equal, minorities stay in school longer than whites because they lack attractive opportunities outside of school. However, that explanation cannot be tested with the data presented here.

DEMOGRAPHIC AND SOCIOECONOMIC FACTORS IN DROPOUT RATES

In general, dropout rates increase with grade level, but regardless of race/ethnicity, the odds of dropping out are much higher in the twelfth grade. They are highest among Hispanics, where the odds increase by 3.5 relative to the tenth grade and by 3 relative to the eleventh grade. Among whites the increase between tenth and twelfth grade is more than 2.5, and among blacks and others it is about 1.5.

The risk of dropping out increases with age. At age 19 and higher the chance of dropping out increases sharply and rapidly. There are also consistent racial/ethnic differentials in the effects of being older. The effects are much larger among Hispanics and others than among whites or blacks. However, we would not place too much emphasis on the large effects of ages well above 19; recall that these effects pertain to a small fraction of students enrolled in regular schools. The effect of age is very important because grade retention is the major influence on low grade placement of older students. That is, students who have been retained are over age for grade and thus more likely to drop out.

Even after controlling other variables, metropolitan residence remains a significant and consistent source of differences in the chances of dropping out. Simply put, the main finding is that dropout rates are higher in the central cities of the 17 major metropolitan areas than in any other metropolitan or non-metropolitan areas. The effects of location on blacks' likelihood of dropping out of school are particularly large. Blacks in suburbs are a third less likely to drop out than those in major cities, and those in smaller and non-metropolitan areas are 46 percent less likely than those in major cities to leave school.

In every racial and ethnic group, dropout rates are consistently greater in the Midwest, South, and West than in the East. The odds of dropping out are at least 8 percent higher in every ethnic group and in each of three non-Eastern regions; in most cases the odds of dropping out are at least 20 percent higher. Whites do better in the South and West than in the East or Midwest. Among blacks, except for the lower dropout rates in the East, there is relatively little regional variation. In particular, African Americans are not at a much greater disadvantage in the South, relative to the Midwest or West, despite the history of discriminatory practices in that region. Similarly, there is relatively little varia-

FIGURE 6

Effects of Race/Ethnicity on the Odds of High School Dropout by Grade Level

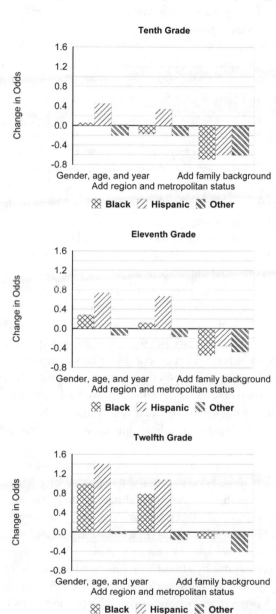

Note: Effects are differences in odds relative to whites.

tion in dropout rates for Hispanics across the Midwest, South, and West. The largest regional differentials occur among youth of other race-ethnicity. Their chances of dropping out are much higher in the Midwest and South than they are in the East or West. Those effects may reflect the differing ethnic composition of the "other" category in different regions of the nation, but the CPS data do not permit a more thorough investigation of that issue. It is worth noting, however, that because of the heavy concentration of "others" in the West, the large effects in the Midwest and South do not pertain to a great number of students.

There are substantial variations among racial and ethnic groups in the effects of family structure. For example, among whites, having a female head of household (vs. male) increases the odds of dropping out by 47 percent, and having a non-employed head of household increases the odds by 28 percent. In most cases, the effects of female head of household and non-employment of the household head are much larger among whites than minority populations. The most striking comparison is the effect of female head of household. Whites with a female head of household are 47 percent more likely to drop out than those with a male head of household; by contrast, blacks with a female head of household are only 6 percent more likely to drop out than those with a male head of household. However, an additional child in the household increases the odds of dropping out equally—about 8 percent—among whites, blacks, and Hispanics.

The effects of the elementary and secondary schooling of parents are quite small, but there are substantial effects of their postsecondary schooling. These effects are similar across racial and ethnic groups. For example, each year of a mother's postsecondary schooling is associated with a 10 percent decline in the odds of dropping out. This implies a difference of 40 percent between youths whose mothers completed high school and those whose mothers completed college.

Other socioeconomic background variables also affect the chances of dropping out, but those effects are usually largest among whites. A 10-point shift in the household head's occupational status reduces the odds by 10 to 14 percent among whites and others, but by only 3 to 5 percent among African Americans and Hispanics. The effects of a head of household with a farm occupation are enormously variable by race and ethnicity. Farm occupation reduces the odds of dropping out by almost half among white youth, but by only 14 percent among African Americans. However, among Hispanics it increases the odds by about 5 percent, and among other racial/ethnic groups it increases the chances of dropping out by 273 percent. The effect of income is larger among whites than among minorities, and the effects are successively smaller among blacks, Hispanics, and others. Home ownership has a consistently large and salutary effect on dropout rates in every racial and ethnic group. It is associated with at least a 30 percent decline in the odds of dropping out in every group, and among whites the effect is a 46 percent decline. Again, these large effects are difficult to interpret, as they may indicate the influence of neighborhood quality or stability, or of family wealth.

SOCIAL BACKGROUND AND TRENDS IN DROPOUT

The significant effects of residential location and social background on dropout rates, together with changes in location and background, imply that the observed trends in overall dropout rates may be explained in part by changes in student population characteristics. We tested this hypothesis by comparing the observed rates with those that are adjusted by regional and metropolitan location and family and socioeconomic background (Figure 7).

There are great differences in findings among the four racial/ethnic groups. Within each group—as we should expect from the glacial speed of population change—the overall shapes of the observed and adjusted trend lines are similar. Among whites, and to a lesser degree African Americans, the adjusted trend lines always lie above the observed trend lines. This implies that changes in location and background have tended to reduce the chances of dropping out. That is, dropout rates would be higher if it were not for favorable changes in location and background. Thus, among whites in the late 1990s, the odds of dropping out would have declined by only about 10 percent after 1972 if not for favorable changes in location and background. Because of those changes, along with the secular trend, the odds of dropping out are about 30 percent lower than they were in 1972. The effect of changing population composition is less among African Americans than among whites. Were it not for changes in location and background, the odds of dropping out among blacks would have declined by about 25 percent since 1972, but the combined effects of the secular trend and of changes in social background have reduced those odds by more than 40 percent. In the case of Hispanics and of other racial/ethnic groups, there has been no consistent effect of students changing residential location and social background. Population change has neither improved nor reduced the chances of dropping out in those groups.

DISCUSSION

Our analysis has identified three major sources of trends and differentials in dropout rates.[14] The first—about which we have said very little, despite its great importance—is the state of the economy. This issue affects the dropout rate in a

FIGURE 7 Trends in High School Dropout by Race/Ethnicty: Observed and Adjusted for Social Background

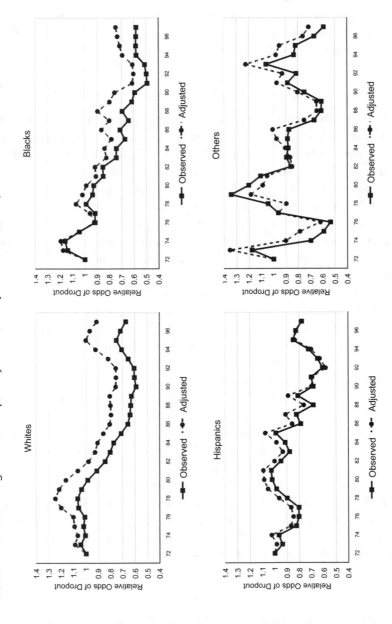

Note: Trends are shown as odds of dropping out relative to 1972.

number of ways. For one thing, changes in the economy, especially as they affect the demand for labor among youth with varying levels of education and skill, also have a bearing on students' decisions to stay in school or drop out, and on what happens to them once they make those decisions. One possible reason blacks are less likely to drop out than whites with the same socioeconomic background is that blacks have fewer opportunities outside of school than whites.

The second source of trends and differentials in dropout rates is the variable geographic and social composition of high school populations. Major changes include not only the growth of African American, Hispanic, and other minority groups, but also the changing residential location, family structure, and socioeconomic standing of those groups. These changes are only expected to accelerate in the next few decades, and as they do they are likely to continue to affect the likelihood that students will remain in school through graduation.

The third major source of change is education policy. To be sure, the present public discussion focuses on changes in education standards and in the implementation of those standards, especially through high-stakes testing and grade retention. But other policies—such as discipline policies—could also affect the dropout rate.

We think that our analysis provides a strong factual basis for discussions about the sources of the high school dropout problems and policies that may affect the future trajectory of dropout rates. To be sure, this analysis does not tell the whole story. We have necessarily left out the all-important factor of academic achievement and glossed over the more proximate school characteristics and social processes associated with leaving school. At the same time, our work does provide a long-term perspective on current policies and—unlike the larger share of dropout research—it applies consistent, if imperfect, methods and standards to the measurement of dropout rates across time and place.

NOTES

1. However, the operational definition of 90 percent high school completion has varied from time to time (Hauser, 1997).
2. NCES reports provide time-series and one-time survey observations of an array of high school dropout measures (Frase, 1989; Kaufman, McMillen, Germino-Hausken, & Bradby, 1992; Kaufman, McMillen, & Whitener, 1991; Kaufman & Frase, 1990; McMillen & Kaufman, 1997, 1996; McMillen, Kaufman, & Whitener, 1994; McMillen, Kaufman, Germino-Hausken, & Bradby, 1993; Kaufman, Kwon, Klein, & Chapman, 2001, 1999; McMillen 1997; Kaufman, Klein, & Frase, 1999).

3. To identify students repeating the tenth grade, one would have to know the grade in which students were enrolled in the year preceding the survey, as well as the highest grade completed. This problem occurs only at the tenth-grade level, not at grades 11 or 12.

4. The NCES reports distinguish among event, status, and cohort dropout rates. The measure used herein is an event rate. A status rate pertains to the share of persons at a given age, for example, 18 and 19 years old, who have neither completed the twelfth grade nor are currently enrolled in high school at the survey date. A cohort rate is similar conceptually to an event rate, but the NCES reports use the former term for dropout over a single year and the latter for dropout over a longer time period in a cohort that has been followed longitudinally. For further discussion of the conceptualization and measurement of high school dropout, see Kominski (1990), Pallas (1989), and Hauser (1997).

5. There were two major changes in the October CPS that affected dropout rates in the early 1990s. First, the new Census educational attainment measure was introduced in 1992. It distinguished high school graduation (including completion of the GED) from completion of the twelfth grade. This new measure led to a sharp increase in estimated dropout rates in the twelfth grade (McMillen & Kaufman, 1996). Second, the CPS shifted from paper and pencil to computer assisted interviewing in 1994, and this tended to improve the quality of responses by reducing branching errors by interviewers.

6. But recall that, because of methodological changes in the CPS, the rates of the 1990s have been overestimated relative to those in earlier decades.

7. For convenience in the analysis, and because it makes little difference in the findings, we have partly ignored the official convention that "Hispanics may be of any race." All blacks, regardless of other ethnic origin, are classified as black. Hispanic refers to persons who would otherwise be classified as white or other.

8. Number of children in the household is a proxy for the student's number of (biological or social) siblings, but it is far from a perfect measure. The main issue is that students of high school age may well have older siblings who no longer live in the parental household.

9. Because of our definition of household headship, the growth of schooling among African American household heads reflects both the increasing schooling of parents and the increasing prevalence of female headship. Historically, black women have been more likely to complete high school than black men.

10. Because of the small number of Hispanics in the sample, the trend data fluctuate more than one could reasonably believe, and we are not sure whether this trend is reliable.

11. Occupational status is based on the Duncan scale, as updated by Stevens and Featherman (1981) and Stevens and Cho (1985). It is a weighted average of the share of occupational incumbents with high education and with high earnings, where the weights were chosen to predict survey-based ratings of occupational prestige.

12. This may be an artifact of the low placement of farmers on the Duncan scale of occupational status. That is, the negative effect of farm occupations on high school dropout may be read as a contrast between the effect of the low education and income of farm occupations and the actual dropout behavior of farm youth.

13. We estimated household income by taking the antilogarithms of mean log incomes; thus, on the assumption that the log of income is distributed symmetrically, the reported figures are rough estimates of median household income.

14. We ignore methodological changes in survey measurement and population coverage; these have also certainly affected our findings in the 1990s.

REFERENCES

Astone, N. M., & McLanahan, S. (1991). Family structure, parental practices, and high school completion. *American Sociological Review, 56,* 309–320.

Ekstrom, R. B., Goertz, M. E., Pollack, J. M., & Rock, D. A. (1986). Who drops out of high school and why? Findings from a national study. *Teachers College Record, 87,* 356–373.

Frase, M. J. (1989). *Dropout rates in the United States: 1988* (National Center for Education Statistics, Analysis Report 89-609). Washington, DC: Government Printing Office.

Haney, W. (1993). Testing and minorities. In L. Weis & M. Fine (Eds.), *Beyond silence: Class, race and gender in United States schools* (pp. 45–73). Albany: State University of New York Press.

Haney, W. (2000). The myth of the Texas miracle in education. *Educational Policy Analysis Archives, 41.*

Hauser, R. M. (1993). Trends in college entry among blacks, Hispanics, and whites. In C. Clotfelter & M. Rothschild (Eds.), *Studies of supply and demand in higher education* (pp. 61–104). Chicago: University of Chicago Press.

Hauser, R. M. (1997). Indicators of high school completion and dropout. In R. M. Hauser, B. V. Brown, & W. R. Prosser (Eds.), *Indicators of children's well-being* (pp. 152–84). New York: Russell Sage Foundation.

Hauser, R. M. (2001). Should we end social promotion? Truth and consequences." In G. Orfield & M. L. Kornhaber (Eds.), *Raising standards or raising barriers? Inequality and high-stakes testing in public education* (pp. 1–78). New York: Century Foundation Press.

Hauser, R. M., & Hauser, T. S. (1993). *Current population survey, October person-household files, 1968–90: Cumulative codebook.* Madison: University of Wisconsin–Madison, Department of Sociology, Center for Demography and Ecology.

Hauser, R. M., Jordan, L., & Dixon, J. A. (1993). *Current population survey, October person-household files, 1968–90.* Madison: University of Wisconsin–Madison, Department of Sociology, Center for Demography and Ecology.

Hauser, R. M., Pager, D. I., & Simmons, S. J. (2004). Race-ethnicity, social background, and grade retention. In H. Walberg, R. J. Reynolds, & M. C. Wang (Eds.), *Can unlike students learn together? Grade retention, tracking, and grouping* (pp. 97–114). Greenwich, CT: Information Age.

Haveman, R., Wolfe, B. L., & Spaulding, J. (1991). Educational achievement and childhood events and circumstances. *Demography, 28,* 133–157.

Kaufman, P., Klein, S., & Frase, M. (1999). *Dropout rates in the United States: 1997* (National Center for Education Statistics, Analysis Report 1999-082). Washington, DC: Government Printing Office.

Kaufman, P., McMillen, M. M., Germino-Hausken, E., & Bradby, D. (1992). *Dropout rates in the United States: 1991* (National Center for Education Statistics, Analysis Report 92-129). Washington, DC: Government Printing Office.

Kaufman, P., Alt, M. N., & Chapman, C. D. (2001). *Dropout rates in the United States: 2000* (National Center for Education Statistics, Analysis Report 2002-114). Washington, DC: Government Printing Office.

Kaufman, P., & Frase, M. J. (1990). *Dropout rates in the United States: 1989* (National Center for Education Statistics, Analysis Report 90-659). Washington, DC: Government Printing Office.

Kaufman, P., Kwon, J. Y., Klein, S., & Chapman. C. D. (1999). *Dropout rates in the United States: 1998* (National Center for Education Statistics, Analysis Report 2000-022). Washington, DC: Government Printing Office.

Kaufman, P., Kwon, J. Y., Klein, S., & Chapman, C. D. (2001). *Dropout rates in the United States: 1999* (National Center for Education Statistics, Analysis Report 2001-022). Washington, DC: Government Printing Office.

Kaufman, P., McMillen, M. M., & Whitener, S. (1991). *Dropout rates in the United States: 1990* (National Center for Education Statistics, Analysis Report 91-053). Washington, DC: Government Printing Office.

Kominski, R. (1990). Estimating the national high school dropout rate. *Demography, 27,* 303–311.

Kominski, R., & Adams, A. (1993). *School enrollment—social and economic characteristics of students: October 1992* (Current Population Reports, Series P-20, No. 474). Washington, DC: U.S. Census Bureau.

Krein, S. F., & Beller, A. H. (1988). Educational attainment of children from single-parent families: Differences by exposure, gender, and race. *Demography, 25,* 221–234.

McLanahan, S. (1985). Family structure and the reproduction of poverty. *American Journal of Sociology, 90,* 873–901.

McMillen, M. M. (1997). *Dropout rates in the United States: 1996* (National Center for Education Statistics, Analysis Report 98-250). Washington, DC: Government Printing Office.

McMillen, M. M., & Kaufman, P. (1996). *Dropout rates in the United States: 1994* (National Center for Education Statistics, Analysis Report 96-863). Washington, DC: Government Printing Office.

McMillen, M. M., & Kaufman, P. (1997). *Dropout rates in the United States: 1995* (National Center for Education Statistics, Analysis Report 97-473). Washington, DC: Government Printing Office.

McMillen, M. M., Kaufman, P., Germino-Hausken, E., & Bradby, D. (1993). *Dropout rates in the United States: 1992* (National Center for Education Statistics, Analysis Report 93-464). Washington, DC: Government Printing Office.

McMillen, M. M., Kaufman, P., & Whitener, S. (1994). *Dropout rates in the United States: 1993* (National Center for Education Statistics, Analysis Report 94-669). Washington, DC: Government Printing Office.

Murphy, K., & Welch, F. (1989). Wage premiums for college graduates: recent growth and possible explanations. *Educational Researcher, 18*(4), 17–26.

Pallas, A. M. (1989). Conceptual and measurement issues in the study of school dropouts. In K. Namboodiri & R. Corwin (Eds.), *Research in the sociology of education and socialization* (vol. 8, pp. 87–116). Greenwich, CT: JAI Press.

Sandefur, G. D., McLanahan, S., & Wojtkiewicz, R. A. (1992). The effects of parental marital status during adolescence on high school graduation. *Social Forces, 71,* 103–121.

Stevens, G., & Cho, J. H. (1985). Socioeconomic indexes and the new 1980 census occupational classification scheme. *Social Science Research, 14,* 142–168.

Stevens, G., & Featherman, D. L. (1981). A revised socioeconomic index of occupational status. *Social Science Research, 10,* 364–395.

U.S. Department of Education. (1990). *National goals for education.* Washington, DC: Author.

CHAPTER 5

The National Dropout
Data Collection System: History and
the Search for Consistency

PHILLIP KAUFMAN*

THE APPEARANCE OF PROGRESS

One of the oldest series of data collected by the federal government is the proportion of the population that has completed high school. These data suggest that there has been remarkable progress in the last half-century in high school completion rates. In one data series, rates increased from 38 percent of all 25- to 29-year-olds in 1940, to around 86 percent in the early 1980s, and have remained constant since (U.S. Department of Education, 2000). As a consequence of this progress, high school completion has become an expectation for young people in this country (Dom, 1996). There is a growing concern, however, that recently adopted policies, such as ending social promotion and imposing high school exit exams, will greatly increase the number of high school dropouts (Bonsteel & Rumberger, 1999; Heubert & Hauser, 1999).

The Weakness of the Data

Obviously, measuring the impact of promotion and exit exams requires reliable statistics on recent trends in high school completion and dropout rates. Unfor-

*Phillip Kaufman was the lead author of a number of the U.S. government's official dropout reports and worked for many years with dropout data. His chapter describes the difficulties and inconsistencies among the various traditional ways of computing dropout numbers in federal reports and data series. It does not discuss the newer measures presented in the book by Robert Balfanz and Christopher Swanson. It does discuss the very low priority and low investment by the federal government in obtaining valid data. Unfortunately, Mr. Kaufman passed away before this book could be published. His analysis will help readers understand the confusion in various historical reports, the reason why the numbers in the Hauser chapter differ so sharply from those in the newer measures, and the reason why a much larger investment should be made to obtain high-quality data. Inserts in [brackets] in this chapter are by the editor and update the discussion from the original draft.

tunately, after decades of collecting data on completers and dropouts, this still remains no easy task. The relatively limited resources that go into the collection of high school completion and dropout data at the federal level produce data that provide more heat than light on some rather basic questions on high school completion—how many students drop out in any given year and how many students complete high school.

A chief reason for the lack of certainty is the different methods used to collect data on completion and graduation. Simply put, completion and dropout rates can vary dramatically depending on the data source. As I show below, these differences in rates arise because

- different rates are based on different populations;
- different rates are derived from different methods;
- rates based on survey methods generally have large sampling errors.

After briefly describing the national data and the state-by-state breakouts of the national data, I will compare the different rates derived from these various data sources and attempt to reconcile some of the differences in reported rates.

In the discussion, I have two specific recommendations to improve data collection on high school completion. My first recommendation is to support the development of the new American Community Survey—a new household survey that has the potential to give much more accurate estimates of high school dropouts and completers at the state and local levels. As these estimates will be derived from the same survey instrument, they will provide comparisons across states (and within states) based on common definitions of dropping out and completion.

My second recommendation is to supplement existing data systems with longitudinal surveys of students. Not only do longitudinal data have the potential to provide more accurate estimates of dropouts and completers, but they also provide the context in which one can understand the changes in the process of dropping out (perhaps due to changes in graduation policies).

Data Sources

Currently, the federal government relies on three sources of data on high school dropouts and completers: the October supplement to the Current Population Survey (CPS) collected by the U.S. Census Bureau, the Common Core of Data (CCD) compiled by the National Center for Education Statistics (NCES), and data from the NCES Longitudinal Studies Program.

DATA FROM THE CURRENT POPULATION SURVEY

The great advantage of the CPS data is that it has been collected in a reasonably uniform manner every year for several decades. It is the only source of long-term trends in dropout and completion rates. It is thus the backbone of the annual dropout report that has been published by NCES every year since 1988 (Kaufman, 2000; see also ch. 4).

Dropout Rates

A variety of dropout rates can be calculated from the CPS data. NCES uses the October Supplement to CPS to calculate two basic dropout rates (Kaufman, Kwon, Klein, & Chapman, 2000). These are the *event* dropout rate and the *status* dropout rate; they measure slightly different phenomena. Event rates describe the proportion of students age 15 to 24 that leave school each year without completing a high school program. This is an annual measure of high school dropouts. Status rates provide cumulative data on dropouts among all young adults within a specified age range; in other words, the total number of students in a given age range who have dropped out of school. Status rates are higher than event rates because they include all dropouts age 16–24, regardless of when they last attended school.

Trends in Event and Status Rates

The CPS data have been collected for well over three decades. In this section I briefly present some of the historical data in event and status rates. There was a general decline in the status and event rates from the early 1970s to around 1990. Since 1990, while there is an appearance of a slight upward trend in both rates, the trend is not statistically significant and may be due simply to sampling error. Our best guess based on the data is that the rates have been flat during the 1990s.

Completion Rates

There are also a variety of completion rates that can be calculated with the CPS data. These rates represent ratios that compare the number of students who completed high school to the number who attended. The major distinctions among these rates are which age group was covered and who was in the denominator. For most federal reports, the age group covered is 18- to 24-year-olds. This age group is chosen because it provides a completion measure that gives the educational community an "early warning system" on the possible effect of current educational policies.[1] The main issue in the choice of a denominator is whether to include those still enrolled in high school. For most federal reports, these students are not included. Since those still enrolled in high school obviously have not completed high school, including them would decrease the completion rate.

Stability of CPS Estimates over Time

While the figures on high school dropout and completion rates look simple, they conceal a great deal of ambiguity in the data and make the trends look more clear-cut than they are in fact. Numerous changes over the years in the CPS questionnaire design make year-to-year comparisons difficult. The most important changes occurred in 1992 and 1994. Furthermore, completion and dropout statistics are complicated by how General Educational Development (GED) certificates or equivalency credentials have been measured in CPS.

Changes Introduced in 1992

Before 1992, educational attainment was based on the control card questions on highest grade attended and completed. Identification as a high school graduate was based on highest grade attended and whether or not that grade was completed. After 1992, educational attainment was measured directly by asking the respondent about actual degrees and diplomas awarded. Identification of a high school graduate was from an answer to one of the following categories:

- High school graduate—high school diploma or the equivalent (e.g., GED)
- All categories indicating some postsecondary education—from some college, no degree, through doctorate degree

The net effect of these changes was an increase in the event dropout rate. The estimated event rate for 1992 was 4.0 percent, compared with a rate of 4.4 percent in 1992, using the new educational attainment item. The status rate in 1992 rose to 11.4 percent from 11.0 percent, based on the new educational attainment item.

Changes Introduced in 1994

During the 1994 data collection and processing, two additional changes were implemented in the CPS. Computer-assisted personal interviewing (CAPI) was introduced, resulting in higher completion rates for each individual data item and thus less reliance on adjustment for missing responses. If the adjustment procedures yielded a distribution different from the 1994 reported patterns, there is the potential for a change in the distribution of the high school completion status.

A second change in 1994 was a change in the benchmark year for these survey estimates, from the 1980 Census to the 1990 Census. In addition, adjustments for undercounting in the Census were also included, which had not been done before. Thus, any age, sex, or racial/ethnic groups that were found to be underrepresented in the 1990 Census were given increased weights. Analysis using 1993 data on the effect of the changes in the benchmark year and adjustments for undercounting indicate that the change especially affected the weights assigned to Hispanic young adults. The change in the benchmark year had a larger impact on status rates than on event rates. Using the 1990-based weights increased the event rate by 1.3 percent, but raised the status rate by 3.2 percent.

Thus while it appears as though there may be an increase in dropout rates in the mid- to late-1990s, these increases may be just an artifact of changes in the way data are collected. While it is almost certain that these changes were needed and that we are getting more accurate numbers now than in the past, it does make comparisons across time more difficult.

The Role of the GED

The latest high school completion rates are very close to the goal of 90 percent set by the president and the nation's governors in 1991. However, Goal 2 actually states, "By the year 2000, the high school *graduation rate* will increase to at least 90 percent" (emphasis added).

Dropout and completion rates indicate the proportion of young people who have or have not completed high school regardless of *how* they completed. That is, some portion of completers did not receive a diploma but an equivalency certificate of some kind (most likely awarded by their state after they passed the GED).

Graduation from high school usually connotes receiving a diploma and not an equivalency certificate. Unfortunately, at the time the national goal was set, the CPS did not collect data on equivalency certificates. If a person was reported to have finished 12 years of school, they were considered to have completed high school—distinctions over how they completed were not made. Since then, the CPS has added an item that tries to disentangle diplomas from certificates. Specifically, in 1988 the Census Bureau added an item explicitly asking if the person finished high school by way of a GED.[2] Figure 1 shows the percentage of 18- through 24-year-olds who completed high school and the percentage who graduated with a diploma.

The difference between the completion rate (which looks steady) and the graduation rate (which looks like it has dropped dramatically over the last decade) is the estimated percentage of young people getting alternative credentials. From these data, it appears there has been a remarkable increase in the last few years in the proportion of young people getting a GED. The alternative completion rate was 4.9 percent in 1993; it rose to 7.0 percent in 1994 and to 9.8 percent in 1996, then reached 10.1 in 1998, and fell back to 9.2 in 1999. Although the standard errors on these estimates are fairly large, the absolute change is also quite large.

There is other evidence that there has indeed been an increase in the number of persons getting GED-based credentials. The GED Testing Service (2000) reports that during the late 1990s, more than 500,000 adults had earned a high school credential based on passing the GED tests. This was about an 18 percent increase over the number of credentials awarded in 1990. Furthermore, other researchers have commented on the increased function of the GED in high school completion (Murnane & Tyler, 2000).

However, as with dropout rates, the changes that have occurred in the CPS data collection methodology make it difficult to come to any unambiguous conclusions about any increase in the percentage of young people getting GEDs. For example, the largest increase in the GED rate (between 1993 and 1994) came in 1994, at the time when CPS instituted computer-assisted personal interviewing. It is possible that some if not all of this increase was due to more accurate reporting of high school completion due to the use of CAPI.

Furthermore, the American Council on Education (ACE), which administers the GED, produces annual reports on the number of people taking the GED and the number who were issued a GED credential. From these reports, it is possible to calculate the number of 18- through 24-year-olds who received a GED in each year for 1990 through 1998. It is also possible to estimate the same quantity from the CPS data for 1990 through 1998 by looking at only those who were reported to have completed a GED in the last year and using this to calculate how many 18- through 24-year-olds obtained GEDs each year. The CPS estimates of the number of GED recipients from 1990 through 1993 were lower than the ACE estimates in each of these years. For 1994 through 1999, the CPS estimates are much closer to the estimates from the ACE and generally are not statistically different from the estimates for the ACE in these years.

Thus, while the GED Testing Service shows a rise in the number of GED recipients, the increase is nowhere near the increases implied in Figure 1. While it is possible that there has been some increase in the proportion of 18- to 24-year-olds getting an equivalency credential, it is unlikely that the increase is as large as is shown in Figure 1. It seems more likely to me that the CPS is now re-

FIGURE 1

High School Completion and Graduation Rates of 18-
through 24-Year-Olds Not Currently Enrolled in High School or Below,
October 1972 through October 1999

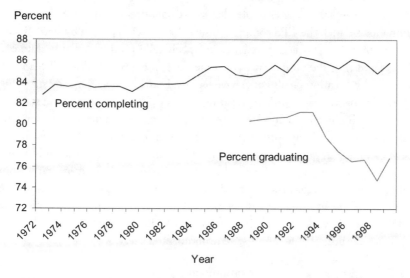

Percent

Source: U.S. Department of Commerce, Census Bureau, Current Population Survey, October (various years).

cording a more accurate graduation rate. Rather than witnessing a decrease in graduation rates over the last few years (as Figure 1 would suggest), I think it is more likely that the graduation rate has always been as low as we are now seeing. Errors in the measurement of the number of GED recipients in the past have masked the "true" graduation rate.

ACCURACY OF RATES FROM CPS

Data from surveys like the CPS are subject to two broad sources of variability or error—sampling and nonsampling error. Sampling errors occur because the data are collected from a sample of a population rather than from the entire population. Estimates based on a sample will differ somewhat from the values that would have been obtained from a universe survey using the same instruments, instructions, and procedures. Nonsampling errors come from a variety of sources and affect all types of surveys, universe as well as sample. Both types of error have an impact on the CPS estimates of dropout and completion rates.

Sampling Error

The sampling errors for national estimates in the CPS are generally within the accepted range for large surveys. However, the CPS was not designed to provide estimates of small subpopulations, and the sampling errors for subgroups can become rather large. For example, due to the data needs of the National Education Goals Panel, the CPS completion rates have been reported by state. Recognizing that the CPS is not designed to specifically produce reliable state estimates and thus the sample sizes for some states are quite small, NCES and the National Education Goals Panel have reported three-year averages by state (Figure 2). However, even with aggregating across three years of data, the standard errors on the state estimates are quite large, so large that state-to-state comparisons are difficult. I have presented error bars (representing the 95% confidence level) along with point estimates for the state completion rates shown in Figure 2. As one can see from this figure, the confidence intervals for most states' completion rates overlap, making any distinctions among states' completion rates unreliable. For example, the difference between Mississippi's completion rate (82%) and Nebraska's rate (93%) is not statistically significant.[3] Survey data of this sort cannot reliably report state dropout rates.

Nonsampling Error

Nonsampling error can occur when members of the target population are excluded from the sampling frame or when sampled members of the population fail to participate in the survey or some part thereof. One of the most important types of error for the discussion here is coverage error.

Coverage errors in CPS can occur for a variety of reasons. For example, CPS is based on a sample of households in which a person within the household (the reference person) is asked to provide information on other members of the household. If the list of households is incomplete (and the separate area frame also misses units), whole households can be missed. If for some reason the reference person does not give a full enumeration of their household members, or misses whole household units within their housing unit, individuals can be omitted from the survey. It is estimated that the CPS survey misses about 7 persons out of 100 because of such coverage errors (U.S. Department of Commerce, 2000). That is, the coverage ratio is about 93 percent. However, for some subgroups this ratio is much lower.

Historically, black and Hispanic males have had low coverage ratios. In 1996, the coverage ratio for black males age 20 to 29 was about 66 percent— one in three were missed in the survey. [This seriously threatens the reliability of minority estimates, which has important civil rights implications for the use of this data.]

FIGURE 2
High School Completion Rates of 18- through 24-Year-Olds
Not Currently Enrolled in High School or Below by State, October 1998

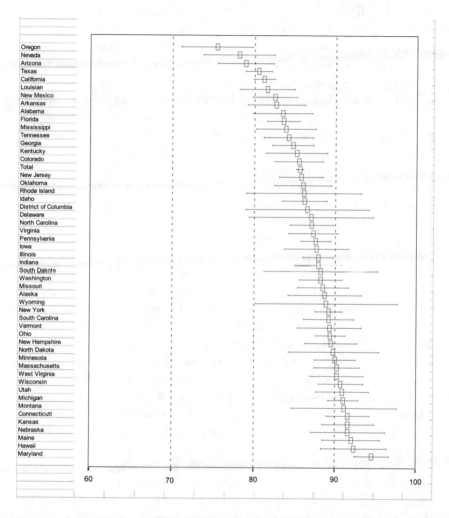

CPS uses independently derived population estimates to modify the sampling weights to adjust for the undercounting of various subpopulations. These adjustments are made within weighting cells based on age, race, and gender. To oversimplify, if black males age 20 to 29 are undercovered by 50 percent, then the first stage sampling weights for black males age 20 to 29 are doubled to properly sum to known population totals. However, this weighting will introduce bias into the estimates of dropout rates if those people missed by CPS drop out at higher rates than do those not missed by CPS; for example, if black males age 20 to 29 missed in the survey drop out at higher rates than those not missed.

While the size of this bias will never be known (you cannot interview people who are not in your survey), it is possible to make some assumptions and estimate what the *potential* bias may be. I have tried to do this in Table 1. Using the age-, gender-, and race-specific coverage ratios provided by the Census Bureau, I have calculated what the status and completion rates might be under different assumptions about the dropout status of those persons missed by the CPS sampling frame.

The second column of Table 1 shows the status and completion rates calculated directly from the 1999 CPS. For the data in the third and fourth columns, I start with the assumption that those undercovered by the survey, regardless of their age, race, and gender, are more likely to be dropouts than others. Under this assumption, undercovered white males are more likely to be dropouts than covered white males, etc. I do not claim to be any expert on this aspect of CPS, but from what I have read about who is likely to be undercovered, this seems like a reasonable assumption. The third column shows the status and completion rates assuming that 50 percent of those undercovered dropped out. In the fourth column, I have assumed a "worst-case scenario" in which all of those undercovered dropped out. I know that this assumption is almost certainly wrong, but it does give an upper boundary to the effect of undercoverage on these rates.

Using these assumptions, adjusting for the undercoverage raises the status rate from 11 to 12 percent for the 50 percent scenario. The black rate rises from 13 to 17 percent under the worst-case scenario. The undercoverage has the potential to have more of an effect on the completion rate, lowering the overall rate from 85 to 80 percent (using the 50% dropout assumption). The black rate falls from 82 to 73 percent. I must emphasize again, however, that the assumption that 50 percent of those missed by CPS are dropouts may not be true. The truth lies somewhere between the extreme of not accounting for bias due to undercoverage and that of assuming all of the undercounted dropped out.

TABLE 1

Status and Completion Rates Adjusted for Undercoverage,[1] October 1999

		Assuming That of Those Not Counted:	
	Rate	50% Dropped Out	100% Dropped Out
		Status Rates	
Total	11.2	12.1	13.0
White, non-Hispanic	11.1	11.8	12.5
Black, non-Hispanic	13.2	15.1	17.0
Hispanic	23.7	25.9	28.1
Other	4.4	4.7	5.0
		Completion Rates	
Total	85.8	80.4	74.9
White, non-Hispanic	86.2	81.4	76.7
Black, non-Hispanic	82.4	73.3	64.2
Hispanic	68.2	62.4	56.6
Other	93.6	88.2	82.8

[1]Based on undercoverage ratios by age, sex, and race, 1996.

Source: U.S. Department of Commerce, Census Bureau, Current Population Survey, October 1999.

DATA FROM THE LONGITUDINAL STUDIES PROGRAM

[The CPS is also a survey of the civilian non-institutionalized population. By definition it excludes those incarcerated and in military service, a population disproportionately non-white and male.]

The NCES Longitudinal Studies Program has periodically surveyed high school students in an attempt to understand the dynamics of high school. Data from studies within this program, such as High School and Beyond (HS&B) and the National Education Longitudinal Study (NELS:88), can be used to look at dropout and completion rates by following students over time (Kaufman, McMillen, & Sweet, 1996). Rather than surveying students and asking them (or a household respondent) about their current and past enrollment patterns, the longitudinal studies survey students in one year and then follow them up at a later time to determine their actual enrollment and completion status.

NELS:88 began with an eighth-grade cohort in 1988. The surveys were administered to an average of 23 students within each of a national probability sample of 1,052 schools. The first follow-up to NELS:88 was conducted in

1990, when most of the eighth-grade cohort were enrolled in tenth grade. Questionnaires and cognitive tests were administered to each student in the first follow-up, and a separate questionnaire was administered to dropouts, one that included items specifically designed to examine the students' decision to leave school. Also, complete transcripts for each student in the sample are available.

Cohort Dropout Rates in 1990–1992

[Note that our most recent national sample entered high school in the fall of 1988, about 15 years ago, before the reported decline in receipt of high school diplomas.]

Students who drop out of school between the eighth and twelfth grades can be defined as those students who were enrolled in the spring of their freshman year who, four years later, were not enrolled in school and had not completed school. With the longitudinal data, one can also calculate the proportion of eighth graders who dropped out of school at *any time* during the next four years, regardless of whether they were enrolled at the time of the survey.

About 12 percent of the eighth-grade class of 1988 were dropouts in the spring of 1992, when most of their classmates were graduating from high school. About 18 percent of Hispanic and 15 percent of black eighth graders were dropouts at that time. In addition, by 1992 almost a quarter of all black and Hispanic eighth graders had dropped out at some time during the four years between their eighth grade and the spring of 1992.

While Table 2 shows dropout rates only by basic demographic variables, the rich data from the longitudinal studies also allow for the examination of other characteristics of students who drop out of school—the wide range of other psychological, sociological, and economic factors that affect students' educational attainment (McMillen & Kaufman, 1996). One can also follow up dropouts with longitudinal data to measure the consequences of dropping out. For example, Rumberger (see chs. 6 and 11) uses NELS data to examine who drops out of school and why they drop out.

The weaknesses of the longitudinal data are that they are designed to provide national estimates of dropout and completion rates and, except for very large states, cannot provide statistically reliable state estimates or any school district estimates. They also are very expensive and labor intensive. Therefore, they are not done often. We have been lucky that NCES has been able to afford to support one high school longitudinal study every ten years or more. Unfortunately, I do not think that the public can afford to wait ten years to see evidence of the results of educational policy.

TABLE 2

NELS:88 Eighth- to Twelfth-Grade Cohort Dropout Rates,
by Sex and Race/Ethnicity, 1992

Characteristics	Dropout in Spring: 1992	Ever Dropped Out: 1988 to 1992
Total	11.6	17.6
Sex		
Male	11.6	17.7
Female	11.6	17.5
Race/Ethnicity		
Asian/Pacific Islander	7.0	7.4
Hispanic	18.3	25.8
Black, non-Hispanic	14.5	23.3
White, non-Hispanic	9.4	15.1
Native American	25.4	42.4

Source: U.S. Department of Education, National Center for Education Statistics, National Education Longitudinal Study of Second Follow-up Survey, 1992, unpublished data.

ACCURACY OF RATES FROM NELS

Since NELS is a sample survey, it is subject to the same potential for bias due to non-response and undercoverage that CPS has. NELS is a two-stage sample survey in which schools are sampled at the first stage and students are then sampled at the second stage. Coverage and response bias in NELS can be introduced when units are excluded at either stage of the sample design. For example, at the first stage bias can occur if the list of schools that is used to make up the sample frame of NELS is incomplete. Presumably, students within schools not on the list are different in some way from those in schools on the list. (Students who are exclusively homeschooled are excluded altogether). This undercoverage may affect dropout rates. The second source of error may occur when schools that are selected in the sample refuse to cooperate with the survey. While these schools are replaced in the sample with schools that are similar to them in terms of basic demographic characteristics of their students, schools that choose not to participate in the survey may be different in unknown ways from schools that participate. For example, a large public urban school with 90 percent minority enrollment that refuses to participate may be different from another large public urban school with 90 percent minority enrollment that agrees to participate. This may bias dropout rates in some unknown manner.

At the second stage of sampling, bias may be introduced due to non-response or exclusion of students *within* schools. In NELS, some students were in fact excluded from the survey by design. Students who were judged unable to complete the questionnaires due to some sort of disability or due to their limited English ability were excused from the survey (Ingels & Quinn, 1996). Assuming that these students were more likely to drop out than others, this introduces some bias into the core sample. However, NCES conducted a follow-up of the excluded students in the base year to determine their dropout status and basic demographic information. (The rates shown in Table 2 include these excluded students.) Indeed, rates for excluded students were higher than for other students. The eighth- to tenth-grade rate rose from 6.0 percent for the core sample to 6.8 percent for the sample, including those originally excluded.

COMMON CORE OF DATA[4]

As seen above, while the CPS and the longitudinal datasets provide national and regional estimates of dropout and completion rates, the sample sizes for most states are not large enough to reliably report on rates for most state education agencies. The Common Core of Data, as a universe survey, has the potential to be used to provide such local estimates. The CCD, also administered by the NCES, is an annual survey of the state-level education agencies in the 50 states, the District of Columbia, and the outlying areas. Through this survey, statistical information is collected on public schools, staff, students, and finances.

There are a variety of rates that can be calculated using the CCD data (Bose & Hoffman, 1997; Winglee, Marker, Henderson, Young, & Hoffman, 2000). I will talk about only a few of the more commonly used: the event dropout rate and two measures of the on-time graduation rate.

Event Dropout Rates

In the late 1990s, CCD universe collection at NCES included a dropout component in the agency-level nonfiscal data collection. NCES, through the National Cooperative for Elementary and Secondary Statistics and the CCD collection, worked with states and school districts to develop this national database of public school dropout rates.

In the 1997–1998 school year collection, 50 states, the District of Columbia, and outlying areas were asked to submit dropout data to the CCD from the 1996–1997 school year. Data from 38 of these states and the District of Columbia met the quality and comparability levels necessary for publishing state-level estimates that support valid cross-state comparisons.[5] Event dropout rates among these states ranged from 2.7 percent in North Dakota and South Carolina to 11.6 percent in Louisiana.

Completion and Graduation Rates

One can also calculate several completion rates with the CCD. One that has been used in the past has been the "on-time" graduation rate. This rate is calculated by taking the ratio of the high school graduates in a state to the number of ninth graders three years earlier. [This is similar to the Balfanz analysis.] Some states also report to NCES the number of alternative credentials that are granted each year in their jurisdiction. This allows one to calculate an on-time completion rate similar to the on-time graduation rate that includes all completers.

These ratios can be calculated by state from numbers submitted to NCES by each state. The on-time graduation rate was routinely reported in the 1970s and 1980s by the U.S. Department of Education and was a central part of Secretary of Education Terrel H. Bell's "Wall Chart" in the early 1980s. This rate has also recently been reported in the annual *Kids Count Data Book* from the Annie E. Casey Foundation (1995; NCES, 1975),

ACCURACY OF RATES FROM CCD

While the CCD is based on administrative records and is essentially a census of public schools, it is still subject to the potential for undercoverage and nonresponse bias that exists in sample surveys.

Event Rates

Reporting dropout statistics accurately can pose challenges for many school districts. This is not to say that education officials in the states do not make efforts to ensure that schools accurately report their students. However, resources are such that many schools cannot track all of their dropouts. While some schools may indeed engage in the "shell game" that their detractors accuse them of—moving dropouts to alternative programs and letting them slip away—many schools just did not know what happened to all of their "no shows." For example, the principal at Oak Ridge High School in California was as mystified as others were by the discrepancies in the graduation and dropout rates (79.5% and 2%, respectively; Kollers, 1998). The principal asked the school psychologist to do further research into what happened to the "missing" students. After some research they found that 388 students had left the school between ninth grade and twelfth grade. These students broke down into:

- Alternative school, 147
- District outside El Dorado County, 109
- Other regular high school in the district, 61
- Adult education, 43
- Private school, 13
- Nongraduates (students who came within a few credits of graduating), 8
- Dropout, 4
- Expelled, 2
- Deceased, 1

Many of these students may have graduated later, many may not have (especially those who transferred into the alternative programs); however, except for the identified four dropouts, none of these students was counted in the official dropout statistics for the school. As the principal said, "Schools are more willing to claim graduates, but nobody wants to claim dropouts" (Kollars, 1998).

Transfer students pose a particularly difficult problem for local school districts. For example, if a student is transferred to an alternative program (such as an adult or continuation high school) and the student drops out before he or she actually enrolls in that program, it is unclear whether the local educational agency (LEA) will report that student as a dropout or ever really know that that student is a dropout. Furthermore, with some states using local dropout rates in accountability measures, some commentators have speculated that schools and LEAs have an incentive to minimize the number of dropouts in their schools.

Several states, including Florida, Texas, and Louisiana, have systems to track students using individual identification numbers. However, most of these systems are not sophisticated enough to track students who leave the state, let alone leave the country. Furthermore, while the most sophisticated systems can locate up to 90 percent of all students in a state, this is about the same coverage rate as the CPS, and we have seen above that such undercoverage has the potential for large bias in estimates. Also, these administrative record systems do not weight for undercoverage as sample surveys do.

Completion Rates

While not as reliant on tracking students as event rates, both the on-time graduation and on-time completion rates also have some well-documented flaws (Pallas, 1990). The problems involve

- how to count students in ungraded or special education programs, who might be counted by the state as graduates or completers, but not as ninth graders;

- how to account for out-migration or immigration in a state over the three years.

While attempts were made to adjust the denominator of the on-time graduation rate for ungraded and special education students, these adjustments were imperfect, especially when attempting to create a time series that would allow for state-by-state comparisons over time. No good adjustments were available to adjust for net out-migration in the numerator or the denominator.

Due to these problems and the potential for misinterpreting the data, NCES no longer publishes this rate—although some of the components to the rate are published in CCD reports (NCES, 2000).[6]

COMPARISON OF RATES

One of the problems with discussing high school completion and dropout rates is the seemingly inconsistent and often conflicting rates reported. Indeed, each of the various sources of data considered in this chapter has yielded different estimates of "the" dropout and completion rate. Part of these discrepancies is due to differences in the target populations and the data collection methods of the various data sources.

There are some noteworthy differences in dropout collection procedures between CCD, CPS, and NELS. The CCD dropout rate represents the number of students who have dropped out over the total number of students enrolled in the state. This differs from the CPS and NELS dropout counts in a few ways. First, the CCD represents a state's public school dropout counts; the CPS and NELS counts include students who were enrolled in either public or private schools. Second, the CCD collection includes dropouts in grades 7 through 12 (although CCD event rates are reported for grades 9 through 12), while the CPS considers only grades 10 through 12, and NELS considers grades 8 through 12. One other difference in the CCD collection is that it counts anyone receiving a GED outside of a regular (approved) secondary education program as a dropout. This is different from CPS and NELS, [so there is no commonality in the definition of a dropout or a graduate or even in the number of school years considered in these various federal data sources.]

Given these and other differences in methods and target populations, it is not surprising that these data sources should produce different estimates of high school dropout rates. Different methods with different populations produce different results.

The status rate for those 17 through 19 years old in 1994 corresponds very roughly with the NELS eighth- to twelfth-grade dropout rate. The NELS rate represents the proportion of eighth graders in 1988 that were dropouts in the spring of 1994 (when most were 17 to 19 years old). Again, these rates are only roughly comparable and the alert reader should be able to develop a long list of differences in these two estimates. (One significant difference is that the CPS estimate includes all young adults regardless of whether they were ever enrolled in U.S. schools.) However, despite these potential biases, it is noteworthy that both data sources result in similar rates—for both the nation and for Texas. About 12 percent of all 17- to 19-year-olds were dropouts in 1993, according to CPS, and about the same percentage of the eighth-grade class of 1988 were dropouts in the spring of 1992.

The event rate for 15- to 19-year-olds for the nation and Texas represents the proportion of people in this age group who dropped out of grades 10 through 12 between October 1992 and October 1994. Conceptually, this rate is closest to the CCD dropout rate, which purports to measure the proportion of ninth though twelfth graders who dropped out in the 1993–1994 school year. While there is no national rate from CCD, the rate for Texas from CCD is substantially lower than the estimate from CPS (the CCD estimate is also beyond the 95% confidence bands for the CPS estimate).

An estimate from CPS of the proportion of 19- to 20-year-olds that have graduated high school with a diploma, restricting the sample to just native-born young people, shows the on-time graduation rate for the eighth-grade class of 1988 from NELS (graduation defined as receiving a diploma, not a GED-based equivalency certificate). The estimate of 76 percent is within the confidence bands of the CPS estimate of 74 percent. Furthermore, both the NELS measure and the CPS measure are roughly analogous to the on-time graduation statistic calculated from the CCD (71%). Again, the three estimates give similar results, although the rate based on CPS and NELS is slightly greater. This difference may reflect simple sampling error, or it may reflect the fact that the NELS survey followed students across time—even if they moved out of state—and the CPS captures 19- and 20-year-olds in their current residence.

The graduation rate for the eighth-grade class of 1988 in 1994—two years after their "normal" graduation—shows that an additional 5 percent had graduated with a diploma in those two years. I use 20- to 22-year-olds as a surrogate sample of high school cohort two years after their "normal" graduation date. Again, the estimate from CPS is lower than the rate from NELS.

DISCUSSION

What can one draw from these comparisons? One conclusion is that the various datasets give approximately similar answers when asked similar questions. That is, differences in published dropout and completion rates from these data sources are due more to differences in definitions and target populations than to differences in their methods. This does not mean that all of these sources do not have serious flaws in their methods. For example, NELS and CPS may both have serious coverage problems in their realized samples. Minority students and schools may be so seriously underrepresented in their sampling frames that it leads to great systematic bias in both surveys. Nevertheless, they do yield similar results—or at least results that are generally within sampling error of one another.

The exception to this general rule of correspondence among data sources is the dropout data generated by the CCD. For Texas, compared to the CPS estimates, the CCD dropout numbers appear to underestimate the proportion of students dropping out in 1994. While it may be that the CPS data are overestimates and the CCD data are closer to reality, the fact that other CPS estimates appear to be consistent with NELS estimates argues in favor of the CPS estimates.

Another lesson one can draw is that no matter how one measures dropout and completion rates, with present survey data there is a great deal of sampling error associated with the estimates. Error is fairly large at the national level and very large at the state level (even after using three-year averages). Great apparent differences are not statistically reliable.

Therefore, while most of the datasets point in a single direction, none of them can reliably give precise answers to some rather basic questions about school dropouts and completers beyond rather broad "ballpark" answers. Certainly, none give the kind of detail that policymakers need to track the impact of current reforms on high school completion rates. For example, using the CPS one would have to have an increase of two percentage points at the national level to conclude that there was a statistically significant change in graduation rates from one year to the next. Even for relatively large states like Texas, it would take almost a ten percentage point change in the graduation rate from year to year to conclude that this change was "real" and not just due to sampling error.

CONCLUSIONS AND RECOMMENDATIONS

The differences among the three major data sources for completion and dropout information have generated confusion, rather than illuminating some basic questions of vital interest to policymakers and the public. This confusion is even more acute when people misinterpret the data by failing to acknowledge the underlying assumptions of each statistic. For example, as seen above, NELS and CCD give approximately the same answers to the question of what proportion of young people graduate "on time." However, as we have also seen, reporting that 70 percent of ninth graders graduated on time does not mean that 30 percent dropped out. Too often, though, the 30 percent number is what seeps into the political discourse.

The American Community Survey

The Census Bureau has developed a new sample survey, The American Community Survey (ACS), based on the idea of continuous measurement of the U.S. population. It is a separate and independent sample of households in the United States each month that provides information on an annual sample of three million housing units. Rolling up data over 12 months allows statistically reliable estimates of the population characteristics of the nation, each state, and towns and cities of 65,000 or more. Providing that the appropriate items are on the ACS, one could then get comparable data on high school completion and dropout rates from all of the states and from most towns and cities to monitor the success of our educational system.[7]

However, like the CPS, the ACS can provide only simple statistics of the number of students who complete or drop out of school. Given that it is a household survey and not an individual interview, it is unrealistic to think that it will provide much detail on the school, community, or family experiences that contributed to an individual's persistence and attainment in school. We may know how many students drop out in any particular year, but will not know what led to their dropping out.

Longitudinal Studies

The best way to provide that kind of contextual information is with longitudinal studies—studies that follow an actual cohort of students for some period of time. As seen above, NELS provided a great deal of information on why students dropped out of school in the early 1990s. Besides merely asking dropouts why they dropped out of school, NELS also has a great deal of contextual data on the prior in-school experiences of dropouts. While cross-sectional surveys could ask individuals about their reasons for dropping out, retrospective responses in a cross-sectional survey can be inaccurate or biased in some unknown way. For example, it would be difficult for cross-sectional surveys to rely on retrospective answers to questions about prior achievement levels or attitudes about schools. These responses may be colored by the respondent's present situation or opinions about school.

Hence, longitudinal studies are the only way to provide the contextual information that begins to make sense of the reported dropout and completion rates from CPS or ACS. Fortunately, on the national level, a new longitudinal study has just begun that will provide information on the context of dropping out of school in the early 2000s. The Educational Longitudinal Study of 2002 (ELS:02) is surveying a new tenth-grade cohort and is following up with them in 2004. While ELS is a general-purpose survey and not targeted specifically at dropouts, we will [in 2005] be able to compare the dropout rates of the tenth-grade classes of 1980, 1990, and 2002 [over a two-year period]. We will also know a little about the characteristics of the students dropping out.

Unfortunately, these large national longitudinal studies are very expensive to conduct—several million dollars for one cohort followed for just two years. Because of the cost, they are only done every ten years or so. However, it may be possible to conduct smaller-scale longitudinal studies that just target issues of high school completion and dropping out. That is, unlike the general-purpose surveys like HS&B, NELS, and ELS, one may be able to design a survey that would focus solely on this issue at a much lower overall cost, thus allowing more frequent surveying. One possibility would be to attach a longitudinal component to the National Assessment of Education Progress (NAEP). That is, NAEP could survey a subset of the sample of students assessed in the fourth, eighth, and twelfth grades and follow up with them in a year or two. If this were done every couple of years, data would be available in a timely manner that would give context to the ongoing collection of dropout statistics from the ACS or CPS.

This approach could also be done within the states. Most states assess their students each year. It may be feasible to sample some portion of those students each year and follow up with them the following year. Like the national longitudinal studies, these follow-ups would track individual students to wherever they may have moved during the year. For example, students who move out of state would still be part of this longitudinal follow-up.

Several states are now developing individual student record systems that purport to track students over time (some use social security numbers to merge the secondary school records with unemployment insurance data systems or college and university data systems). These systems are seen as the "silver bullet" of dropout completion statistics—a way for states once and for all to be able to account for each of their students. However, even these systems will not be perfect: some students will still be no-shows, and no one will be able to say for sure where they are; some students will change states; and some will receive different numbers from different schools. Students will continue to transfer from state to state, and highly mobile students will still be more likely to drop out. Until there is a national system to track students by a common identification number, these students will be more likely to be missed by official statistics. Even if states can match 80 to 90 percent of their students, a significant portion of students will be lost to the system. Those lost may be different in some way from those who are not, thus introducing some unknown bias into the remaining data. [Disadvantaged students tend to be the most difficult to trace. In survey research, such nonresponse would be partially addressed by adjusting the sample weights. I am not aware of any student data system that tries to adjust for this.]

Unfortunately, while a great deal of time and resources are being devoted to measuring one educational outcome—the academic achievement of students in school—less is being devoted to measuring the complementary outcome—how many students complete high school. While the federal government spends more than $40 million on the National Assessment of Educational Progress, it probably spends less than $1 million on dropout statistics.[8] This seems out of balance. As important as the measurement of academic achievement may be, we must make as much effort to measure how many students complete school. If nothing else, without knowing how many students drop out of school we cannot properly interpret any assessment data. But beyond that question of validity, we need accurate information about a significant educational outcome. As with testing data, it is not enough to report just the raw number; we must look behind the numbers as well. Only by understanding high school completion and dropout rates can we begin to do something about them.

NOTES

1. See Kaufman (2000) for a more complete discussion of this issue.
2. The exact wording is, "Did [the subject] complete high school by means of an equivalency test, such as the GED?"
3. Beyond the question of statistical reliability, there is a question of the validity of these rates for evaluating states' educational systems. Because the rate uses 18- to 24-year-olds as the base, some of these young people may not have been to school in the state in which they currently reside. For example, states with a large number of out-of-state college students will have a high completion rate that may have little to do with their secondary educational system. Likewise, states with large numbers of migrant workers who never attended school in that state (or even this country) may have low completion rates also partially unrelated to the performance of their secondary educational system.
4. Much of the following discussion is based on text from Kaufman et al. (2000) and was written in part by Lee Hoffman and Marilyn M. McMillen of the National Center for Education Statistics.
5. However, 12 states reported on an alternative July through June cycle, rather than the standard October through September.
6. A recent publication from NCES recommends yet another graduation rate based on the CCD (Winglee, Marker, Henderson, Aronstamm, & Young, 2000). However, this rate has not been widely adopted and will not be discussed here.

7. The form of the final ACS questionnaire is still under review.
8. It is difficult to calculate exactly how much the federal government spends on dropout statistics, since the collection of these data is imbedded in other data collection efforts, like the CCD and the CPS.

REFERENCES

Annie E. Casey Foundation. (1999). *Kids count data book: 1994*. Baltimore: Author.

Bonsteel, A., & Rumberger, R. W. (1999, May 16). Get ready for dropout shock. *Los Angeles Daily News.*

Bose, J., & Hoffman, L. (1997) *Developing a high school graduation rate using CCD data.* Unpublished manuscript.

Cameron, S. V., & Heckman, J. (1991) *The nonequivalence of high school equivalents.* (Working Paper No. 3804). Cambridge, MA: National Bureau of Economic Research.

Council of Chief State School Officers. (1998). *Trends in state student assessment programs.* Washington, DC: Author.

Dorn, S. (1996). *Creating the dropout: History of school failure.* Westport, CT: Praeger.

Groves, R. M. (1991). Measurement errors across the disciplines. In P. B. Biemer, R. M. Groves, L. E. Lyberg, N. A. Mathiowetz, & S. Sudman (Eds.), *Measurement errors in surveys* (pp. 1–25). New York: John Wiley and Sons.

Hauser, R. M. (1997). Indicators of high school completion and dropout. In R. M. Hauser, B. V. Brown, & W. R. Prosser (Eds.), *Indicators of children's well-being.* New York: Russell Sage Foundation.

Heubert, J., & Hauser, R. M. (1999). *High stakes testing for tracking, promotion and graduation.* Washington DC: National Academy Press.

Ingles, S. J., & Quinn, P. (1996). *Sample exclusion in NELS:88.* Washington, DC: U.S. Government Printing Office.

Kaufman, P. (2000). *Calculating high school dropout and completion rates: The complexities of data and definitions.* Paper presented at the National Academies' workshop on School Completion in Standards-Based Reform: Facts and Strategies, Washington, DC.

Kaufman, P., McMillen, M. M., & Sweet, D. (1996). *A comparison of high school dropout rates in 1982 and 1992* (NCES 96-893). Washington, DC: U.S. Department of Education, Office of Educational Research and Improvement, National Center for Education Statistics.

Kaufman, P., Kwon, J. Y., Klein, S., & Chapman, C. D. (2000). *Dropout rates in the United States: 1998* (NCES 2000-022). Washington, DC: U.S. Department of Education, Office of Educational Research and Improvement, National Center for Education Statistics.

Kominski, R. (1990). Estimating the national high school dropout rate. *Demography, 27,* 303–311.

Kominski, R., & Adams, A. (1993). *School enrollment—social and economic characteristics of students: October 1992* (Current Population Reports, Series P20-474). Washington, DC: U.S. Government Printing Office, U.S. Census Bureau.

Murnane, R. J., Willett, J. B., & Tyler, J. H. (1999). *Who benefits from obtaining a GED? Evidence from high school and beyond* (NBER Working Paper 7172). Unpublished manuscript.

National Center for Education Statistics. (1975). *Statistics of state school systems: 1971–72.* Washington, DC: U.S. Department of Health, Education, and Welfare, Education Division.

Pallas, A. M. (1989). Conceptual and measurement issues in the study of school dropouts. In K. Namboodiri & R. G. Corwin (Eds.), *Research in sociology of education and socialization* (vol. 8). Greenwich, CT: JAI Press.

Singleton, C. (1985). Let there be F's. In B. Gross & R. Gross (Eds.), *The great school debate: Which way for American education?* New York: Simon and Schuster.

U.S. Department of Education. (2000). *Digest of education statistics: 1999 (table 8)* (NCES 2000-031). Washington, DC: U.S. Department of Education, Office of Educational Research and Improvement, National Center for Education Statistics.

U.S. Department of Commerce, U.S. Census Bureau. (2000). *Current population survey design and methodology* (Technical Paper #63). Unpublished manuscript.

Winglee, M., Marker, D., Henderson, A., Aronstamm, B., & Young, L. H. (2000). *A recommended approach to providing high school dropout and completion rates at the state level* (NCES 2000-305). Washington, DC: U.S. Department of Education, Office of Educational Research and Improvement.

CHAPTER 6

Why Students Drop Out of School

RUSSELL W. RUMBERGER

Reducing the number of high school dropouts has become a national policy concern. One of the National Education Goals adopted in 1990 was to increase the high school graduation rate to 90 percent by 2000, with a related objective to eliminate the existing gap in high school graduation rates between minority and nonminority students (U.S. Department of Education, 1990). More recently, the federal No Child Left Behind (NCLB) Act of 2001 requires states to incorporate graduation rates in their accountability systems for schools and districts (U.S. Department of Education, 2004). As a result of this policy focus, numerous programs at the federal, state, and local levels have been established to help reduce the number of students who drop out of school.

Understanding why students drop out of school is the key to addressing this major educational problem. Yet identifying the causes of dropping out is extremely difficult to do because, like other forms of educational achievement (e.g., test scores), it is influenced by an array of proximal and distal factors related to both the individual student and to the family, school, and community settings in which the student lives.

This chapter examines why students drop out of school; a later chapter (Chapter 11) addresses what can be done about it. This research review focuses on both individual and institutional factors, and how these factors can or cannot explain differences in dropout rates among social groups.

The complexity of this phenomenon is illustrated by the variety of reasons that dropouts report for leaving school. Dropouts from the National Education Longitudinal Study of students who were in eighth grade in 1988 reported a wide variety of reasons for leaving school: school-related reasons were mentioned by 77 percent, family-related reasons were mentioned by 34 percent, and work-related reasons were mentioned by 32 percent (see Figure 1). The most specific reasons were "did not like school" (46 percent), "failing school" (39 percent), "could not get along with teachers" (29 percent), and "got a job" (27

FIGURE 1

Reasons Given for Dropping Out of School:
Dropouts from the High School Graduating Class of 1992*

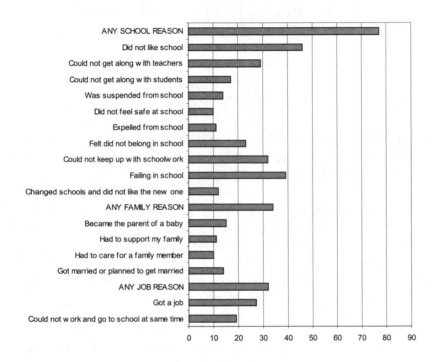

*Reasons are reported as the percentage of respondents who indicated that reason. Respondents could re-
port as many reasons as they wanted.
Source: Berktold, Geis, and Kaufman (1998, Table 6).

percent). But these reasons do not reveal the underlying causes of why students
quit school, particularly those causes or factors from long ago that may have
contributed to students' attitudes, behaviors, and school performance immediately preceding their decision to leave school. Moreover, if many factors contribute to this phenomenon over a long period of time, it is virtually impossible
to demonstrate a causal connection between any single factor and the decision
to quit school. Instead, scholars are limited to developing theories and testing
conceptual models based on a variety of social science disciplines and using a variety of qualitative and quantitative research methods.

A number of theories have been advanced to understand the specific phenomenon of dropping out (e.g., Finn, 1989; Wehlage, Rutter, Smith, Lesko,
& Fernandez, 1989). Other theories have been used to explain dropping out as

part of the larger phenomenon of student achievement (e.g., Coleman, 1988; Newmann, Wehlage, & Lamborn, 1992; Ogbu, 1992).[1] These theories come from a number of social science disciplines—including psychology, sociology, anthropology, and economics—and identify a range of specific factors related to dropping out.[2] Drawing on these theories, I present two conceptual frameworks that focus on two different perspectives for understanding this phenomenon. One framework is based on an individual perspective that focuses on individual factors associated with dropping out; the other is based on an institutional perspective that focuses on the contextual factors found in students' families, schools, communities, and peers. Both frameworks are useful and, indeed, necessary to understand this complex phenomenon. After presenting each framework and reviewing briefly some empirical evidence that highlights some of the most important factors within each framework, I will discuss the extent to which these frameworks can be used to explain differences in dropout rates among social groups, particularly racial and ethnic minorities. In most cases, the factors identified in this review are derived from multivariate statistical models that control for a number of other predictive factors, suggesting that the identified factor has a direct, causal connection with dropping out independent of other causal factors. Yet statistical models can only suggest causal connections, not prove them, so it is better to think of these factors as predictive of dropping out or increasing the risk of dropping out.

INDIVIDUAL PERSPECTIVE

The first framework is based on an individual perspective that focuses on the attributes of students—such as their values, attitudes, and behaviors—and how these attributes contribute to their decisions to quit school. The conceptual framework, illustrated in Figure 2, views the attitudes and behaviors of students through a particular concept—student engagement (Fredricks, Blumenfeld, & Paris, 2004). Several theories have been developed in recent years that suggest that dropping out of school is but the final stage in a dynamic and cumulative process of disengagement (Newmann et al., 1992; Wehlage et al., 1989) or withdrawal (Finn, 1989) from school. Although there are some differences among these theories, they all suggest that there are two dimensions to engagement: academic engagement, or engagement in learning, and social engagement, or engagement in social dimensions of schooling (Wehlage refers to this as school membership). Engagement is reflected in students' attitudes and behaviors with respect to both the formal aspects of school (e.g., classrooms and school activities) and the informal ones (e.g., peer and adult relationships). Both dimensions of engagement can influence the decision to withdraw from

FIGURE 2

Conceptual Framework for Studying Student Educational Performance

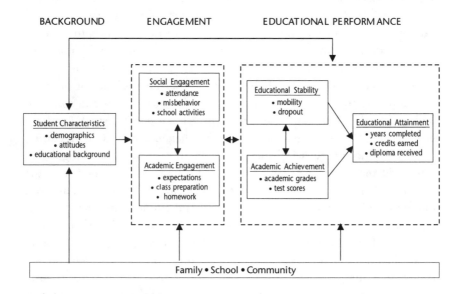

Source: Rumberger and Larson (1998).

school. For example, students may withdraw from school because they quit doing their schoolwork (academic engagement), or because they do not get along with their peers (social engagement).[3]

The framework also suggests that dropping out represents one aspect of three interrelated dimensions of educational achievement: 1) academic achievement, as reflected in grades and test scores; 2) educational stability, which reflects whether students remain in the same school (school stability) or remain enrolled in school at all (enrollment stability); and 3) educational attainment, which is reflected by years of schooling completed and the completion of degrees or diplomas. The framework suggests that educational attainment is dependent on both educational stability and academic achievement. That is, students who either interrupt their schooling by dropping out or changing schools, or who have poor academic achievement in school, are less likely to graduate or complete that segment of schooling.

The framework also posits that engagement and educational achievement are influenced by students' backgrounds prior to entering school, including their educational aspirations and past achievement. Finally, the framework suggests reciprocal relationships among these factors that change over time. Changes in engagement, stability, and achievement as students progress through school affect later attitudes, social relationships, and school experiences. Thus within this framework, student stability is viewed as both a cause and a consequence of engagement in school.

A large body of empirical research has identified many individual predictors of dropping out that are consistent with this framework. Only some of the most important ones will be reviewed here.

The first group of factors has to do with the relationship between dropping out and other dimensions of educational achievement. Numerous studies have found that poor academic achievement is a strong predictor of dropping out (Ekstrom, Goertz, Pollack, & Rock, 1986; Goldschmidt & Wang, 1999; Rumberger, 1995; Rumberger & Larson, 1998; Swanson & Schneider, 1999; Wehlage & Rutter, 1986).

Student engagement has also been shown to predict dropping out even after controlling for the effects of academic achievement and student background. Absenteeism, the most common indicator of overall student engagement, and student discipline problems are both associated with dropping out (Bachman, Green, & Wirtanen, 1971; Carbonaro, 1998; Ekstrom et al., 1986; Goldschmidt & Wang, 1999; Rumberger, 1995; Rumberger & Larson, 1998; Swanson & Schneider, 1999; Wehlage & Rutter, 1986). These studies support the idea that dropping out is influenced by both the social and academic experiences of students. In other words, dropping out is not simply a result of academic failure.

Student mobility is also associated with dropping out of school. A growing body of research suggests that both residential mobility (changing residences) and school mobility (changing schools) increases the risk of dropping out of high school (Astone & McLanahan, 1994; Haveman, Wolfe, & Spaulding, 1991; Rumberger, 1995; Rumberger & Larson, 1998; Swanson & Schneider, 1999; Teachman, Paasch, & Carver, 1996). Some scholars have argued that student mobility represents a less severe form of student disengagement or withdrawal from school (Lee & Burkam, 1992; Rumberger & Larson, 1998). In fact, one study found that the majority of high school dropouts changed high schools at least once before withdrawing, while the majority of high school graduates did not (Rumberger, Larson, Palardy, Ream, & Schleicher, 1998).

Other experiences in high school are also associated with dropping out. One of them is high school employment. Several studies have found that working long hours (more than 20 hours) during high school can increase the likelihood of dropping out and does not vary among gender, race, or socioeconomic status (SES) groups (Goldschmidt & Wang, 1999; Marsh, 1991; Warren & Lee, 2003), although the impact of working in high school depends on the type of job held and on the student's gender (McNeal, 1997a). But although these studies control for other predictors of dropping out, there is still the possibility that the relationship between high school employment and dropping out is not causal, but rather could reflect a reduced interest and disengagement from school and increased interest in work (Shanahan & Flaherty, 2001; Warren, 2002).

Another activity associated with dropping out is teenage pregnancy. Several studies have examined the relationship between teenage pregnancy and school dropouts. Studies that consider teenage pregnancy an exogenous decision independent of the decision to drop out generally show that childbearing has a negative effect on high school completion (e.g., Mott & Marsiglio, 1985; Pirog & Magee, 1997), whereas studies that consider teenage pregnancy as an endogenous factor—such that both teenage pregnancy and dropping out are influenced by a set of unobservable factors—find childbearing has no independent effect on high school completion (Evans, Oates, & Schwab, 1992; Ribar, 1994; Upchurch & McCarthy, 1990).

Finally, a number of student background characteristics have been shown to predict withdrawal from school. Several demographic variables have been examined in the literature: gender, race and ethnicity, immigration status, and language background (Fernandez, Paulsen, & Hirano-Nakanishi, 1989; Fry, 2003; Goldschmidt & Wang, 1999; Rumberger, 1983, 1995; Rumberger & Larson, 1998; Steinberg, Blinde, & Chan, 1984; Swanson & Schneider, 1999; Velez, 1989). These factors are discussed in more detail below. Other individual attributes have also been shown to predict dropping out, including disabilities and low educational and occupational aspirations (Ekstrom et al., 1986; Kortering, Haring, & Klockars, 1992; Newmann et al., 1992; Rumberger, 1995; Rumberger & Larson, 1998; Swanson & Schneider, 1999; Wehlage & Rutter, 1986).

As mentioned earlier, the framework is based on the idea that student disengagement and withdrawal from school is a long-term process that can be influenced by students' early school experiences. Several studies, based on long-term studies of cohorts of students, have examined the predictors of dropping out from as early as early childhood (Alexander, Entwisle, & Horsey, 1997; Alexander, Entwisle, & Kabbini, 2001; Barrington & Hendricks, 1989; Cairns, Cairns, & Necherman, 1989; Ensminger & Slusacick, 1992; Gamier, Stein, & Jacobs, 1997; Jimerson, Egeland, Sroufe, & Carlson, 2000; Morris, Ehren, & Lenz, 1991; Roderick, 1993). These studies found that early academic achievement and engagement (e.g., attendance, misbehavior) in elementary and middle school predicted eventual withdrawal from high school. One longitudinal study of 143 at-risk children found that the quality of caregiving at 12 and 40 months of age could significantly discriminate between dropouts and graduates even after controlling for other early predictors, such as problem behaviors in first grade (Jimerson, et al., 2000). Studies also show that early risk factors are compounded, such that the more risk factors the students experience over their schooling careers, the greater their likelihood of dropping out (Alexander et al., 2001).

One additional indicator of prior school performance has received considerable attention of late—retention. Historically, a large number of students are retained in school each year. Data from the National Education Longitudinal Study suggest that about one in five eighth graders in 1988 had been retained at least once since first grade (Rumberger, 1995, Table 1). As more states end social promotion and institute high school exit examinations, this number will no doubt rise. Already in Texas, which has instituted both policies, one out of every six ninth-grade students in 1996–1997 was retained (Texas Education Agency, 1998, Appendix A). Although some recent studies have suggested that retention may have some positive effects on academic achievement (Alexander, Entwisle, & Dauber, 1994; Roderick, Bryk, Jacob, Easton, & Allensworth, 1999), virtually all the empirical studies to date suggest that retention, even in lower elementary grades, significantly increases the likelihood of dropping out (Goldschmidt & Wang, 1999; Grisson & Shepard, 1989; Jimerson, 1999; Kaufman & Bradby, 1992; Roderick, 1994; Roderick, Nagaoka, Bacon, & Easton, 2000; Rumberger, 1995; Rumberger & Larson, 1998). For example, Rumberger (1995) found that students who were retained in grades 1 to 8 were four times more likely to drop out between grades 8 and 10 than students who were not retained, even after controlling for socioeconomic status, eighth-grade school performance, and a host of background and school factors. A recent literature review of seventeen studies confirms these findings (Jimerson, Anderson, & Whipple, 2002). Yet one recent study suggests that grade retention may also be an endogenous factor that does not exert an independent influence on dropping out (Eide & Showalter, 2001).

INSTITUTIONAL PERSPECTIVE

While the first framework can provide a way to understand dropping out from an individual perspective, individual attitudes and behaviors are shaped by the institutional settings where people live. This latter perspective is common in such social science disciplines as economics, sociology, and anthropology. Historically it has been less common in psychology, which has focused more on human behavior itself and less on the social environment in which behavior takes place. But over the last decade a new paradigm has emerged in the field of developmental psychology called developmental behavioral science (Jessor, 1993). This paradigm, illustrated in Figure 3, recognizes that the various settings or contexts in which students live—families, schools, and communities—all shape their behavior. This framework was used by the National Research Council Panel on High-Risk Youth (1993), which argued that too much emphasis has been placed on high-risk youth and their families, and not enough on the high-risk settings in which they live and go to school. It was also used by the National Research Council Committee on Increasing High School Students' Engagement (2004), which showed how schools, families, communities, and peers all contributed to students' engagement in learning. This view reflects the new emphasis on contexts and not simply individuals.

Empirical research on dropouts has identified a number of factors within students' families, schools, and communities (and peers) that predict dropping out. Again for brevity, only some of the most important ones are reviewed below.

Family Factors

Family background is widely recognized as the single most important contributor to success in school. Ever since early work by Coleman, Jencks, and others found that family background alone could explain much of the variation in educational outcomes (Coleman et al., 1966; Jencks et al., 1972), virtually all research has found that family background still exerts a powerful, independent influence on student achievement. But what aspects of family background matter and how do they influence student achievement?

Much of the empirical research has focused on the *structural* characteristics of families, such as socioeconomic status and family structure. Research has consistently found that socioeconomic status, most commonly measured by parental education and income, is a powerful predictor of school achievement and dropout behavior (Bryk & Thum, 1989; Ekstrom et al., 1986; McNeal, 1999; Pong & Ju, 2000; Rumberger, 1983, 1995; Rumberger & Larson, 1998). Research has also demonstrated that students from single-parent families and stepfamilies are more likely to drop out of school than students from two-parent families (Astone & McLanahan, 1991; Ekstrom et al., 1986; Goldschmidt & Wang, 1999; McNeal, 1999; Rumberger, 1983, 1995; Rumberger & Larson, 1998; Teachman et al., 1996). However, one recent study found that the dissolution of two-parent families did not increase the likelihood of dropping out, apart from its effects on income loss (Pong & Ju, 2000).

Until recently, there has been relatively little research that has attempted to identify the underlying processes through which family structure influences dropping out. The powerful effects of parental education and income are gener-

FIGURE 3

The Influence of Context on Adolescent Development over Time

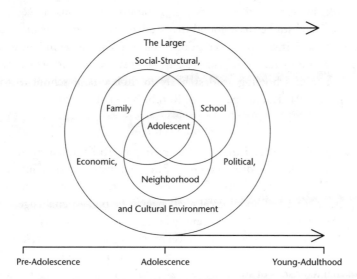

Source: Jessor (1993, Figure 2).

ally thought to support human capital theory. According to human capital the-ory, parents make choices about how much time and other resources to invest in their children based on their objectives, resources, and constraints, which in turn affect their children's tastes for education (preferences) and cognitive skills (Haveman & Wolfe, 1994). Parental income, for example, allows parents to provide more resources to support their children's education, including access to better quality schools, afterschool and summer school programs, and more support for learning within the home.

Sociologist James Coleman (1988) argued that human capital (parental ed-ucation) and financial capital (parental income) were insufficient to explain the connection between family background and school success. He argued that so-cial capital, which is manifested in the relationships parents have with their children, other families, and the schools, also influences school achievement in-dependent of the effects of human and financial capital. Although Coleman re-lied on indirect measures of social capital (e.g., family structure) in his research, some recent studies with more direct measures of family relationships have con-firmed that strong relationships between students and parents reduce the odds of dropping out of school (McNeal, 1999; Teachman et al., 1996).[4] Social capi-tal actually represents part of a larger research literature on the role of families in promoting student achievement, including parental involvement in schools

(Epstein, 1990; Sui-Chu & Willms, 1996) and types of parental practices known as "parenting style" (Baumrind, 1991; Dornbusch, Ritter, Leiderman, Roberts, & Fraleigh, 1987; Steinberg, Lamborn, Dornbusch, & Darling, 1992). Empirical studies have found that students whose parents monitor and regulate their activities, provide emotional support, encourage independent decisionmaking (known as authoritative parenting style), and are generally more involved in their schooling are less likely to drop out of school (Astone & McLanahan, 1991; Rumberger, 1995; Rumberger et al., 1990).

School Factors

It is widely acknowledged that schools exert powerful influences on student achievement, including dropout rates. But demonstrating the influence of schools and identifying the specific school factors that affect student achievement present some methodological challenges. The biggest challenge is disentangling the effects of student and family background from the effects of school factors. Recent developments in statistical modeling have allowed researchers to estimate school effects more accurately after controlling for the individual background characteristics of students (Lee, 2000; Raudenbush & Willms, 1995).

The overall influence of schools on dropping out is illustrated in Figure 4. The left panel shows the estimated tenth grade dropout rates for a sample of 247 urban and suburban high schools in 1990. The median dropout rate is 4.2 percent, which means about four out of every 100 tenth-grade students dropped out of the "average" high school in the sample. However, the dropout rate for individual schools varied from less than 2 percent to over 40 percent. At least some of that variability, however, is due to differences in the background characteristics of students. The right panel shows tenth-grade dropout rates after adjusting for differences in the background characteristics of students. Although less variable than the unadjusted rates, the adjusted dropout rates still show widespread differences among schools. This suggests that schools influence dropout rates.

But what factors account for these differences? Four types of school characteristics have been shown to influence student performance: 1) student composition, 2) resources, 3) structural characteristics, and 4) processes and practices. The first three factors are sometimes considered as school inputs by economists and others who study schools because they refer to the "inputs" into the schooling process that are largely "given" to a school and therefore not alterable by the school itself (Hanushek, 1989). The last factor refers to practices and policies that the school does have control over and thus can be used to judge a school's effectiveness (Shavelson, McDonnell, Oakes, & Carey, 1987). Yet all the characteristics of schools could be altered through policy.

FIGURE 4

Distribution of Estimated and Adjusted Two-Year Dropout Rates
for 247 Urban and Suburban High Schools, 1990–1992

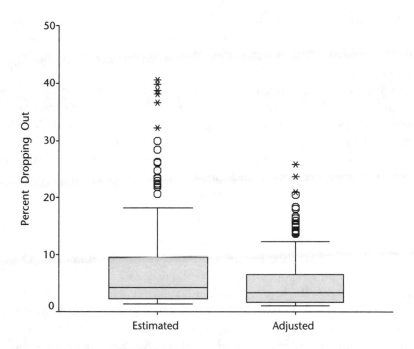

Note: The distributions are represented by box plots, where the bottom edge of the box represents the bottom 25th percentile of the distribution, the solid line within the box represents the 50th percentile or median of the distribution, and the top of the box represents the 75th percentile of the distribution. Hence the middle 50 percent of the values lie within the box. The line extending from the bottom edge of the box marks the lowest value in the distribution and the line extending from the top edge of the box represents 1.5 times the length of the box (which is referred to as the interquartile range). The circles above the top line represent individual outlier values that are outliers (more than 1.5 box lengths and less than 3 box lengths) and the stars (*) represent individual extreme values (more than 3 box lengths). Estimated rates were derived from an HLM one-way ANOVA model and unit-specific empirical Bayes residual estimates for each school. Adjusted rates were derived from a fixed coefficient model controlling for student background characteristics and student composition centered on the grand mean and unit-specific empirical Bayes residual estimates for each school.

Source: Rumberger and Thomas (2000, Figure 2).

Student Composition: Student characteristics not only influence student achievement at an individual level, but also at an aggregate or social level. That is, the social composition of students in a school can influence student achievement apart from the effects of student characteristics at an individual level (Gamoran, 1992; Jencks & Mayer, 1990). Several studies have found that the social composition of schools predicts school dropout rates even after controlling for the individual effects of student background characteristics (Bryk & Thum, 1989; Mayer, 1991; McNeal, 1997b; Rumberger, 1995; Rumberger & Thomas, 2000).

School Resources: There is currently considerable debate in the research community about the extent to which school resources contribute to school effectiveness (Hanushek, 1994, 1997; Hedges, Lame, & Greenwald, 1994). Several studies suggest that resources influence school dropout rates. Three studies found that the pupil/teacher ratio had a positive and significant effect on high school and middle school dropout rates even after controlling for a host of individual and contextual factors that might also influence those rates (McNeal, 1997b; Rumberger, 1995; Rumberger & Thomas, 2000). One of those studies found that the higher the quality of the teachers as perceived by students, the lower the dropout rate, while the higher the quality of teachers as perceived by the principal, the higher the dropout rate (Rumberger & Thomas, 2000).

School Structure: There is also considerable debate in the research community about the extent to which structural characteristics (e.g., size, location), particularly type of control (public, private), contribute to school performance. This issue has been most widely debated with respect to one structural feature—public and private schools (Bryk, Lee, & Holland, 1993; Chubb & Moe, 1990; Coleman & Hoffer, 1987). Although widespread achievement differences have been observed among schools based on structural characteristics, what remains unclear is whether structural characteristics themselves account for these differences or whether they are related to differences in student characteristics and school resources often associated with the structural features of schools. Most empirical studies have found that dropout rates from Catholic and other private schools are lower than dropout rates from public schools, even after controlling for differences in the background characteristics of students (Bryk & Thum, 1989; Coleman & Hoffer, 1987; Evans & Schwab, 1995; Neal, 1997; Rumberger & Thomas, 2000; Sander & Krautmann, 1995). Yet empirical studies have also found that students from private schools typically transfer to public schools instead of or before dropping out, meaning that student turnover rates in private schools are not statistically different than turnover rates in public schools (Lee & Burkam, 1992; Rumberger & Thomas, 2000). School size also appears to influence dropout rates both directly (Lee & Burkam, 2003; Rumberger & Palardy, 2004; Rumberger & Thomas, 2000) and indirectly (Bryk & Thum, 1989), although the largest direct effect appears to be in low-SES schools (Rumberger, 1995). This latter finding is consistent with case studies of schools with effective dropout-prevention programs, which suggest that small schools are more likely to promote the engagement of both students and staff (Wehlage et al., 1989).

School Policies and Practices: Despite all the attention and controversy surrounding the previous factors associated with school effectiveness, many people believe that the area of school processes holds the most promise for understanding and improving school performance. Several studies found academic and social climate—as measured by school attendance rates, students taking advanced courses, and student perceptions of a fair discipline policy—predict school dropout rates, even after controlling for the background characteristics of students and the resource and structural characteristics of schools (Bryk & Thum, 1989; Rumberger, 1995; Rumberger & Palardy, 2004; Rumberger & Thomas, 2000). Another study using one of the same datasets but different sets of variables and statistical techniques found no effect of academic or social climate on high school dropout rates, after controlling for the background characteristics of students, social composition, school resources, and school structure (McNeal, 1997b). Two more recent studies found that school social capital—as reflected in positive relationships between students and teachers—reduced the risk of dropping out, especially among high-risk students (Croninger & Lee, 2001; Lee & Burkam, 2003).

Current research literature on school dropouts suggests two ways that schools affect student withdrawal. One way is indirectly, through general policies and practices that are designed to promote the overall effectiveness of the school. These policies and practices, along with other characteristics of the school (student composition, size, etc.), may contribute to *voluntary* withdrawal by affecting conditions that keep students engaged in school. This perspective is consistent with several existing theories of school dropouts and departure that view student disengagement as the precursor to withdrawal (Finn, 1989; Wehlage et al., 1989).

Another way that schools affect turnover is directly, through explicit policies and conscious decisions that cause students to *involuntarily* withdraw from school. These rules may concern low grades, poor attendance, misbehavior, or being over age, which can lead to suspensions, expulsions, or forced transfers.[5] This form of withdrawal is school initiated and contrasts with the student-initiated form mentioned above. This perspective considers a school's own agency, rather than just that of the student, in producing dropouts and transfers. One metaphor that has been used to characterize this process is discharge: "students *drop out* of school, schools *discharge* students" (Riehl, 1999, p. 231). Several studies, mostly based on case studies, have demonstrated how schools contribute to students' involuntary departure from school by systematically excluding and discharging "troublemakers" and other problematic students (Bowditch, 1993; Fine, 1991; Riehl, 1999).

One specific practice that schools can use to influence dropout rates is the requirement that students pass a test in order to receive a diploma (National Research Council, 1999). Such requirements can be set by high schools themselves, but more typically they are set by school districts and states. Historically, some schools and districts required students to pass a so-called minimum competency exam. More recently, many states have instituted high school exit exams that test students' proficiency in a number of state-mandated academic standards. A number of studies have examined the impact of such testing policies on the likelihood of dropping out (Catteral, 1989; Griffin & Heidorn, 1996; Jacob, 2001; Lillard & DeCicca, 2001; Muller, 1998). The results of these studies are quite mixed: some found that such requirements increased the likelihood of dropping out (Catteral, 1989; Lillard & DeCicca, 2000); some found no impact on dropping out (Muller, 1998); and some found differential effects — one finding that they only increased dropout rates among better students (Griffin & Heidorn, 1996) and another finding that they only increased dropout rates among lowest-ability students (Jacob, 2001).

Community and Peers

In addition to families and schools, communities and peer groups can influence students' withdrawal from school. Several studies have shown that having friends or siblings who have dropped out increases the likelihood of dropping out (Carbonaro, 1998; Ellenbogen & Chamberland, 1997; Rumberger & Thomas, 2000). Research has also shown that having high-achieving friends can reduce the likelihood of dropping out of school (Kasen, Cohen, & Brook, 1998).

There is at least some empirical evidence that differences in neighborhood characteristics can help explain differences in dropout rates among communities apart from the influence of families (Brooks-Gunn, Duncan, & Aber, 1993; Clark, 1992; Crane, 1991; Ensminger, Lamkin, & Jacobson, 1996; South, Baumer, & Lutz, 2003). Crane (1991) further argues that there is a threshold or tipping point on the quality of neighborhoods that results in particularly high dropout rates in the lowest-quality neighborhoods. But Clark (1992), using more recent data, found no evidence of a tipping point, but did find that the odds of a boy dropping out of school increased substantially as the neighborhood poverty rate increased from zero to 5 percent. Moreover, two studies found that living in a high-poverty neighborhood was not necessarily detrimental to completing high school, but rather that living in an affluent neighborhood was beneficial to school success (Brooks-Gunn et al., 1993; Ensminger, Lamkin, & Jacobson, 1996)

While these studies find that communities do influence dropout rates, they are unable to explain how they do so. Poor communities may influence child and adolescent development through the lack of resources (playgrounds and parks, afterschool programs) or negative peer influences (Brooks-Gunn et al., 1997; Hallinan & Williams, 1990; Wilson, 1987). Community residence may also influence parenting practices over and above parental education and income (Klebanov, Brooks-Gunn, & Duncan, 1994). Finally, students living in poor communities may also be more likely to be exposed to negative peer influences, such as having dropouts as friends, which increase the likelihood of dropping out of school (Carbonaro, 1998; South, Baumer, & Lutz, 2003). Yet the impact of peers varies among youth, depending on both family circumstances and their own characteristics (Crowder & South, 2003; Farmer et al., 2003).

Another way that communities can influence dropout rates is by providing employment opportunities both during and after school. Relatively favorable employment opportunities for high school dropouts, as evidenced by low neighborhood unemployment rates, appear to increase the likelihood that students will drop out, while more favorable economic benefits of graduating, as evidenced by the higher salaries of high school graduates compared to dropouts, tend to lower dropout rates (Bickel & Papagiannis, 1988; Clark, 1992; Rumberger, 1983).

EXPLAINING RACIAL AND ETHNIC DIFFERENCES IN DROPOUT RATES

One of the most challenging educational issues facing the United States is understanding and solving the persistent disparities in achievement among racial and ethnic groups. While much of the focus on this issue has centered on student achievement as measured by grades and test scores (e.g., Jencks & Phillips, 1998; Steinberg, Dombusch, & Brown, 1992), there has been considerable attention to understanding and explaining differences in dropout rates as well (Fernandez, Paulsen, & Hirano-Nakanishi, 1989; Ogbu, 1989).

Two general approaches have been used to explain differences in dropout rates among racial and ethnic groups. The first approach is based on the idea that differences in dropout rates and other measures of educational achievement can be explained largely by differences in resources and by human and social capital frameworks that suggest that these factors affect achievement similarly for all groups. Those groups that lack these resources, in this approach, are more at risk for poor outcomes. This approach was used by the National Research Council Panel on High-Risk Youth, which used its study on the high-risk settings of family, school, and community to explain the poor outcomes of high-risk and minority students (National Research Council, 1993). Indeed, the family, school, and community conditions for racial and ethnic minorities in the United States are generally much worse than for the white majority. To take but one example, child poverty rates for blacks and Hispanics are more than twice as high as child poverty rates for whites (U.S. Department of Education, 2003, Table 21). As a result, minority students are more likely to attend high-poverty schools that have fewer resources and poorer learning environments (U.S. Department of Education, 1997).[6] Several empirical studies of dropouts have found that at least half of the observed differences in dropout rates between racial groups can be attributed to differences in family and community characteristics (Fernandez et al., 1989; Rumberger, 1983; Velez, 1989). Another study found that up to half of the observed differences in dropout rates between whites and minorities would be reduced if racial groups attended schools with similar racial and socioeconomic compositions (Mayer, 1991).

The second approach is based on the idea that differences in resources and conventional theories are insufficient to explain differences in achievement among racial and ethnic groups. In particular, critics of the first approach argue that it fails to explain why some minority groups with similar levels of socioeconomic background succeed, while other groups do not. Instead, they argue that sociocultural factors—particularly cultural differences in values, attitudes, and behaviors—help explain why some racial and ethnic minorities are successful in U.S. schools and others are not.

Ogbu (1989, 1992), one of the best-known proponents of the sociocultural perspective, argues that minorities can be classified into two groups: 1) voluntary minorities, who came to the United States by their own choosing (e.g., European Americans and Asian Americans); and 2) involuntary minorities, who were brought into the United States against their will, either through immigration or domination (e.g., African Americans and early Mexican Americans). Voluntary and involuntary minorities view school success very differently: "Voluntary minorities do not perceive learning the attitudes and behaviors required for school success as threatening their own culture, language, and identities, [while] . . . involuntary minorities do not seem to be able or willing to separate attitudes and behaviors that result in academic success from those that may result in linear acculturation or replacement of their cultural identity with white American cultural identity" (Ogbu, 1992, pp. 9–10). Although Ogbu's perspective offers an appealing explanation of minority groups' differences in achievement, empirical support for this perspective is limited (Ainsworth-Darnell & Downey, 1998; Cook & Ludwig, 1997; Farkas, Grobe, Sheehan, & Shuan, 1990; Gibson, 1997; Matute-Bianchi, 1986; Mickelson, 1990).

Other sociocultural perspectives also suggest that differences in attitudes and behaviors of students, peers, and families help explain racial and ethnic differences in achievement. For example, Steinberg, Dombusch, and Brown (1992) demonstrate that Asians are more successful in school than other ethnic groups because of two cultural beliefs: 1) a belief that not getting a good education will hurt their chances for future success (rather than a belief that a good education will help their chances); and 2) a belief that academic success comes from effort rather than ability or the difficulty of the material.[7] They also find that the contexts of families, schools, and peers influence the achievement of racial and ethnic groups differently. Other studies have also shown differences among racial and ethnic groups (e.g, Jordon, Lara, & McPartland, 1996; Rumberger, 1995). Steele (1997) and Steele and Aronson (1998) demonstrate that the social stigma of intellectual inferiority among certain cultural minorities (and women in quantitative fields)—referred to as the stereotype threat—contributes to their lower academic achievement. What has yet to be demonstrated empirically is whether these more recent sociocultural perspectives can help explain racial and ethnic differences in dropout rates.

Despite limited empirical evidence, both socioeconomic and sociocultural perspectives may help explain racial and ethnic differences in dropout rates by emphasizing different causal mechanisms. Socioeconomic perspectives focus on the fiscal, human, and social resources of families, schools, and communities and their similar influence on the development of students' values and cognitive abilities across all racial and ethnic groups. Sociocultural perspectives focus on cultural differences in the attitudes and behaviors among racial and ethnic groups that influence school success in both the social and academic arenas.

CONCLUSION

Understanding why students drop out of school is a difficult if not impossible task because, as with other forms of educational achievement, it is influenced by an array of individual and institutional factors. Nonetheless, a review of the theoretical and empirical literature does yield some useful insights into the nature of this problem and what can be done about it. First, dropping out is not simply a result of academic failure, but, rather, often results from both social and academic problems in school. Second, these problems often appear early in students' school careers, suggesting the need for early intervention. Third, these problems are influenced by a lack of support and resources in families, schools, and communities. These findings suggest that reducing dropout rates will require comprehensive approaches both to help at-risk students address the social and academic problems that they face in their lives and to improve the at-risk settings that contribute to these problems. Does the United States have the capacity and political will to reduce dropout rates and eliminate disparities in dropout rates among racial and ethnic groups?

(For the second part of this research review, see ch. 11.)

NOTES

1. The extent to which general theories of student achievement can be used to explain the specific phenomenon of school dropouts is rarely questioned. Yet theories that may be useful in explaining differences in achievement outcomes, such as test scores or grades may not necessarily be useful in explaining why some students drop out of school, especially to the extent that dropping out is unrelated to academic achievement, as dropout theories suggest.

2. Often the factors associated with dropping out are identified as "risk factors" because they denote characteristics of the individual or environment associated with an increased risk of dropping out. But some scholars have pointed out the need to also identify "protective factors" that promote successful development and buffer the effects of risk factors (e.g., Jessor, 1993; National Research Council, 1993).

3. Because engagement concerns both the academic and social aspects of schooling, it provides a more comprehensive concept than some others, such as motivation or effort, that focus on only the academic aspect of schooling. For an in-depth discussion of these two concepts, see National Research Council (2004, ch. 2).

4. As Portes (1998) points out, in using the concept of social capital, it is important to distinguish between the relationships themselves and the access to resources that such relationships provide.

5. One specific example is the growth of "zero tolerance" (automatic discharge) for violations of school safety rules (Skiba & Peterson, 1999).

6. Recent reforms may be exacerbating these differences. For example, California's class-size reduction program has increased the disparities in the proportion of fully credentialed teachers between high- and low-poverty schools (Stecher & Bohrnstedt, 2000, Figure 3.4).

7. Other scholars have also found cultural differences in achievement motivation (Kao & Tienda, 1995; Suárez-Orozco & Suárez-Orozco, 1995).

REFERENCES

Ainsworth-Damell, J. W., & Downey, D.B. (1998). Assessing the oppositional culture explanation for racial/ethnic differences in school performance. *American Sociological Review, 63,* 536–553.

Alexander, K . K., Entwisle, D. R., & Horsey, C. (1997). From first grade forward: Early foundations of high school dropout. *Sociology of Education, 70,* 87–107.

Alexander, K. L., Entwisle, D. R., & Dauber, S. L. (1994). *On the success of failure: A reassessment of the effects of retention in early grades.* New York: Cambridge University Press.

Alexander, K. L., Entwisle, D. R., & Kabbini, N. S. (2001). The dropout process in life course perspective: Early risk factors at home and school. *Teachers College Record, 103,* 760–882.

Astone, N. M., & McLanahan, S. S. (1991). Family structure, parental practices and high school completion. *American Sociological Review, 56,* 309–320.

Astone, N. M., & McLanahan, S. S. (1994). Family structure, residential mobility, and school dropout: A research note. *Demography, 31,* 575–584.

Bachman, J. G., Green, S., & Wirtanen, I. D. (1971). Dropping out: Problem or symptom? In *Youth in transition* (Vol. 3). Ann Arbor: University of Michigan, Institute for Social Research.

Barrington, B. L., & Hendricks, B. (1989). Differentiating characteristics of high school graduates, dropouts, and non-graduates. *Journal of Educational Research, 82,* 309–319.

Baumrind, D. (1991). Parenting styles and adolescent development. In R. Lerner, A. C. Petersen, & E. Brooks-Gunn (Eds.), *Encyclopedia of adolescence* (pp. 758–772). New York: Garland.

Bickel, R., & Papagiannis, G. (1988). Post-high school prospects and district-level dropout rates. *Youth and Society, 20,* 123–147.

Bowditch, C. (1993). Getting rid of troublemakers: High school disciplinary procedures and the production of dropouts. *Social Problems, 40,* 493–509.

Brooks-Gunn, J., Duncan, G. J., & Aber, J. L. (1997). *Neighborhood poverty.* New York: Russell Sage Foundation.

Brooks-Gunn, J., Duncan, G. J ., Klebanov, P. K., & Sealand, N. (1993). Do neighborhoods influence child and adolescent development? *American Journal of Sociology, 99,* 353–395.

Bryk, A. S., Lee, V. E., & Holland, P. B. (1993). *Catholic schools and the common good.* Cambridge, MA: Harvard University Press.

Bryk, A. S., & Thum, Y. M. (1989). The effects of high school organization on dropping out: An exploratory investigation. *American Educational Research Journal, 26,* 353–383.

Cairns, R. B., Cairns, B. D., & Necherman, H. J. (1989). Early school dropout: Configurations and determinants. *Child Development, 60,* 1437–1452.

Carbonaro, W. J. (1998). A little help from my friend's parents: Intergenerational closure and educational outcomes. *Sociology of Education, 71,* 295–313.

Catterall, J. S. (1989). Standards and school dropouts: A national study of tests required for high school graduation. *American Journal of Education, 98,* 1–34.

Chubb, J. E., & Moe, T. M. (1990). *Politics, markets, and America's schools.* Washington, DC: Brookings Institution.

Clark, R. L. (1992). *Neighborhood effects on dropping out of school among teenage boys* (Discussion paper). Washington, DC: Urban Institute.

Coleman, J. S., Campbell, E., Hobson, C., McPartland, J., Mood, F., Weinfeld, F., & York, R. (1966). *Equality of educational opportunity.* Washington, DC: U.S. Government Printing Office.

Coleman, J. S. (1988). Social capital in the creation of human capital. *American Journal of Sociology, 24,* 595–5120.

Coleman, J. S., & Hoffer, T. (1987). *Public and private high schools: The impact of communities.* New York: Basic Books.

Cook, P. J., & Ludwig, E. (1997). Weighing the "burden of 'acting white'": Are there race differences in attitudes toward school. *Journal of Policy Analysis and Management, 16,* 256–278.

Crane, J. (1991). The epidemic theory of ghettos and neighborhood effects on dropping out and teenage childbearing. *American Journal of Sociology, 96,* 1226–1259.

Croninger, R., & Lee, V. (2001). Social capital and dropping out of high school: Benefits to at-risk students of teachers' support and guidance. *Teachers College Record, 103,* 548–581.

Crowder, K., & South, S. J. (2003). Neighborhood distress and school dropout: The variable significance of community context. *Social Science Research, 32,* 659–698.

Dornbusch, S. M., Ritter, P. L., Leiderman, P. H., Roberts, D. F., & Fraleigh, M. J. (1987). The relation of parenting style to adolescent school performance. *Child Development, 58,* 1244–1257.

Eide, E. R. & Showalter, M. H. (2001). The effect of grade retention on educational and labor market outcomes. *Economics of Education Review, 20,* 563–576.

Ekstrom, R. B., Goertz, M. E., Pollack, J. M., & Rock, D. A. (1986). Who drops out of high school and why? Findings from a national study. *Teachers College Record, 87,* 356–373.

Ellenbogen, S., & Chamberland, C. (1997). The peer relations of dropouts: A comparative study of at-risk and not at-risk youths. *Journal of Adolescence, 20,* 355–367.

Ensminger, M. E., Lamkin, R. P., & Jacobson, N. (1996). School leaving: A longitudinal perspective including neighborhood effects. *Child Development, 67,* 2400–2416.

Ensminger, M. E., & Slusacick, A. L. (1992). Paths to high school graduation or dropout: A longitudinal study of a first-grade cohort. *Sociology of Education, 65,* 95–113.

Epstein, J. L. (1990). School and family connections: Theory, research, and implications for integrating sociologies of education and family. *Marriage and Family Review, 15,* 99–126.

Evans, W. N., Oates, W. E., & Schwab, R. M. (1992). Measuring peer group effects: A study of teenage behavior. *Journal of Political Economy, 100,* 966–991.

Evans, W. N., & Schwab, R. M. (1995). Finishing high school and starting college: Do Catholic schools make a difference? *Quarterly Journal of Economics, 110,* 941–974.

Farkas, G., Grobe, R. P., Sheehan, D., & Shuan, Y. (1990). Cultural resources and school success: Gender, ethnicity, and poverty groups within an urban district. *American Sociological Review, 55,* 127–142.

Farmer, T. W., Estell, D. B., Leung, M.-C., Trott, H., Bishop, J., & Cairns, B .D. (2003). Individual characteristics, early adolescent peer affiliations, and school dropout: An examination of aggressive and popular group types. *Journal of School Psychology, 41,* 217–232.

Fernandez, R. M., Paulsen, R., & Hirano-Nakanishi, M. (1989). Dropping out among Hispanic youth. *Social Science Research, 18,* 21–52.

Fine, M. (1991). *Framing dropouts: Notes on the politics of an urban public high school.* Albany: State University of New York Press.

Finn, J. D. (1989). Withdrawing from school. *Review of Educational Research, 59,* 117–142.

Fry, R. (2003). *Hispanic youth dropping out of U.S. schools: Measuring the challenge.* Washington, DC: Pew Hispanic Center.

Gamier, H. E., Stein, J. A., & Jacobs, J. K. (1997). The process of dropping out of high school: A 19-year perspective. *American Educational Research Journal, 34,* 395–419.

Gamoran, A. (1992). Social Factors in Education. In M. C. Alkin (Ed.), *Encyclopedia of Educational Research* (pp. 1222–1229). New York: Macmillan.

Gibson, M.A. (1997). Complicating the immigrant/involuntary minority typology. *Anthropology and Education Quarterly, 28,* 431–454.

Goldschmidt, P., & Wang, J. (1999). When can schools affect dropout behavior? A longitudinal multilevel analysis. *American Educational Research Journal, 36,* 715–738.

Griffin, B. W., & Heidorn, M. H. (1996). An examination of the relationship between minimum competency test performance and dropping out of high school. *Educational Evaluation and Policy Analysis, 18,* 243–252.

Grisson, J. B., & Shepard, L. A. (1989). Repeating and dropping out of school. In L. A. Sheppard & M. L. Smith (Eds.), *Flunking grades: Research and policies on retention* (pp. 34–63). New York: Falmer Press.

Hallinan, M. T., & Williams, R. A. (1990). Students' characteristics and the peer-influence process. *Sociology of Education, 63,* 122–132.

Hanushek, E. A. (1989). The impact of differential expenditures on school performance. *Educational Researcher, 18,* 45–51, 62.

Hanushek, E. A. (1994). Money might matter somewhere: A response to Hedges, Laine, and Greenwald. *Educational Researcher, 23,* 5–8.

Hanushek, E. A. (1997). Assessing the effects of school resources on student performance: An update. *Educational Evaluation and Policy Analysis, 19,* 141–164.

Haveman, R., & Wolfe, B. (1994). *Succeeding generations: On the effects of investments in children.* New York: Russell Sage Foundation.

Haveman, R., Wolfe, B., & Spaulding, J. (1991). Childhood events and circumstances influencing high school completion. *Demography, 28,* 133–157.

Hedges, L. V., Lame, R. D., & Greenwald, R. (1994). Does money matter? A meta-analysis of studies of the effects of differential school inputs on student outcomes. *Educational Researcher, 23,* 5–14.

Jacob, B. (2001). Getting tough? The impact of high school graduation exams. *Educational Evaluation and Policy Analysis, 23,* 99–121.

Jencks, C., Smith, M., Bane, M. J., Cohen, D., Gintis, H., Heyns, B., & Michelson, S. (1972). *Inequality: A reassessment of the effects of family and schooling in America.* New York: Basic Books.

Jencks, C., & Mayer, S. E. (1990). The social consequences of growing up in a poor neighborhood. In L. Lynn Jr. & M. G. H. McGeary (Eds.), *Inner-city poverty in the United States* (pp. 111–186). Washington, DC: National Academy Press.

Jencks, C., & Phillips, M. (1998). *The Black-White test score gap.* Washington, DC: Brookings Institution.

Jessor, R. (1993). Successful adolescent development among youth in high-risk settings. *American Psychologist, 48,* 117–126.

Jimerson, S. R. (1999). On the failure of failure: Examining the association between early grade retention and education and employment outcomes during late adolescence. *Journal of School Psychology, 37,* 243–272.

Jimerson, S., Anderson, G. E., & Whipple, A. D. (2002). Winning the battle and losing the war: Examining the relation between grade retention and dropping out of high school. *Psychology in the Schools, 39,* 441–457.

Jimerson, S., Egeland, B., Sroufe, L. A., & Carlson, B. (2000). A prospective longitudinal study of high school dropouts: Examining multiple predictors across development. *Journal of School Psychology, 38,* 525–549.

Jordan, W. J., Lara, J., & McPartland, J. M. (1996). Exploring the causes of early school dropout among race-ethnic and gender groups. *Youth and Society, 28,* 62–94.

Kao, G., & Tienda, M. (1995). Optimism and achievement: The educational performance of immigrant youth. *Social Science Quarterly, 76,* 1–19.

Kasen, S., Cohen, P., & Brook J. S. (1998). Adolescent school experiences and dropout, adolescent pregnancy, and young adult deviant behavior. *Journal of Adolescent Research, 13,* 49–72.

Kaufman, P., & Bradby, D. (1992). *Characteristics of at-risk students in the NELS: 88.* Washington, DC: U.S. Government Printing Office.

Klebanov, P. K., Brooks-Gunn, J., & Duncan, G. J. (1994). Does neighborhood and family poverty affects mother's parenting, mental health and social support. *Journal of Marriage and Family, 56,* 441–455.

Kortering, L., Haring, N., & Klockars, A. (1992). The identification of high-school dropouts identified as learning disabled: Evaluating the utility of a discriminant analysis function. *Exceptional Children, 58,* 422–435.

Lee, V. E. (2000). Using hierarchical linear modeling to study social contexts: The case of school effects. *Educational Psychologist, 35,* 125–141.

Lee, V. E., & Burkam, D.T. (1992). Transferring high schools: An alternative to dropping out? *American Journal of Education, 100,* 420–453.

Lee, V. E., & Burkam, D.T. (2003). Dropping out of high school: The role of school organization and structure. *American Educational Research Journal, 40,* 353–393.

Lillard, D. R., & DeCicca, P. P. (2001). Higher standards, more dropouts? Evidence within and across time. *Economics of Education Review, 20,* 459–473.

Marsh, H. W. (1991). Employment during high school: Character building or a subversion of academic goals? *Sociology of Education, 64,* 172–189.

Matute-Bianchi, M. E. (1986). Ethnic identities and patterns of school success and failure among Mexican-descent and Japanese-American students in a California high school: An ethnographic analysis. *American Journal of Education, 95,* 233–255.

Mayer, S. (1991). How much does a high school's racial and socioeconomic mix affect graduation and teenage fertility rates? In C. Jencks & P. Peterson (Eds.), *The urban underclass* (pp. 321–341). Washington, DC: Brookings Institution.

McNeal, R. B. (1997a). Are students being pulled out of high school? The effect of adolescent employment on dropping out. *Sociology of Education, 70,* 206–220.

McNeal, R. B. (1997b). High school dropouts: A closer examination of school effects. *Social Science Quarterly, 78,* 209–222.

McNeal, R. B. (1999). Parental involvement as social capital: Differential effectiveness on science achievement, truancy, and dropping out. *Social Forces, 78,* 117–144.

Mickelson, R. A. (1990). The attitude-achievement paradox among black adolescents. *Sociology of Education, 63,* 44–61.

Morris, J. D., Ehren, B. J., & Lenz, B. K. (1991). Building a model to predict which fourth through eighth graders will drop out of high school. *Journal of Experimental Education, 59,* 286–293.

Mott, F., & Marsiglio, W. (1985). Early childbearing and completion of high school. *Family Planning Perspectives, 17,* 234–237.

Muller, C. (1998). The minimum competency exam requirement, teachers' and students' expectations and academic performance. *Social Psychology of Education, 2,* 199–216.

National Education Goals Panel. (1999). *National Education Goals report: Building a nation of learners, 1999.* Washington, DC: U.S. Government Printing Office.

National Research Council, Panel on High-Risk Youth. (1993). *Losing generations: Adolescents in high-risk settings.* Washington, DC: National Academy Press.

National Research Council, Committee on Appropriate Test Use. (1999). *High stakes: Testing for tracking, promotion, and graduation* (J. P. Heubert & R. M. Hauser, eds.). Washington, DC: National Academy Press.

National Research Council, Committee on Increasing High School Students' Engagement and Motivation to Learn. (2004). *Engaging schools: Fostering high school students' motivation to learn.* Washington, DC: National Academies Press.

Neal, D. (1997). The effects of Catholic secondary schooling on educational achievement. *Journal of Labor Economics, 15,* 98–123.

Newmann, F. M., Wehlage, G. G., & Lamborn, S. D. (1992). The significance and sources of student engagement. In F. M. Newmann (Ed.), *Student engagement and achievement in American secondary schools* (pp. 11–39). New York: Teachers College Press.

Ogbu, J. U. (1989). The individual in collective adaptation: A framework for focusing on academic underperformance and dropping out among involuntary minorities. In L. Weis, E. Farrar, & H. G. Petrie (Eds.), *Dropouts from school: Issues, dilemmas, and solutions* (pp. 181–204). Albany: State University of New York Press.

Ogbu, J. U. (1992). Understanding cultural diversity and learning. *Educational Researcher, 21,* 5–14.

Pirog, M. A., & Magee, C. (1997). High school completion: The influence of schools, families, and adolescent parenting. *Social Science Quarterly, 78,* 710–724.

Pong, S. L., & Ju, D. B. (2000). The effects of change in family structure and income on dropping out of middle and high school. *Journal of Family Issues, 21,* 147–169.

Portes, A. (1998). Social capital: Its origins and applications in modern sociology. *Annual Review of Sociology, 24,* 1–24.

Raudenbush, S. W., & Willms, J. D. (1995). The estimation of school effects. *Journal of Educational and Behavioral Statistics, 20,* 307–335.

Ribar, D. C. (1994). Teenage fertility and high school completion. *Review of Economics and Statistics, 76,* 413–424.

Riehl, C. (1999). Labeling and letting go: An organizational analysis of how high school students are discharged as dropouts. In A. M. Pallas (Ed), *Research in sociology of education and socialization* (pp. 231–268). New York: JAI Press.

Roderick, M. (1993). *The path to dropping out.* Westport, CT: Auburn House.

Roderick, M. (1994). Grade retention and school dropout: Investigating the association. *American Educational Research Journal, 31,* 729–759.

Roderick, M., Bryk, A. S., Jacob, B. A., Easton, J. Q., & Allensworth, E. (1999). *Ending social promotion: Results from the first two years.* Chicago: Consortium on Chicago School Research.

Roderick, M., Nagaoka, J., Bacon, J., & Easton, J. Q. (2000). *Update: ending social promotion.* Chicago: Consortium on Chicago School Research.

Rumberger, R. W. (1983). Dropping out of high school: The influence of race, sex, and family background. *American Educational Research Journal, 20,* 199–220.

Rumberger, R. W. (1995). Dropping out of middle school: A multilevel analysis of students and schools. *American Educational Research Journal, 32,* 583–625.

Rumberger, R. W., Ghatak, R., Poulos, G., Ritter, P. L., & Dornbusch, S. M. (1990). Family influences on dropout behavior in one California high school. *Sociology of Education, 63,* 283–299.

Rumberger, R. W., & Larson, K. A. (1998). Student mobility and the increased risk of high school dropout. *American Journal of Education, 107,* 1–35.

Rumberger, R. W., Larson, K. A., Palardy, G. A., Ream, R. K., & Schleicher, N. A. (1998). *The hazards of changing schools for California Latino adolescents.* Berkeley, CA: Chicano/ Latino Policy Project.

Rumberger, R. W., & Palardy, G. J. (2004, April 1–5). *Test scores, dropout rates, and transfer rates as alternative indicators of school performance.* Revised paper originally presented at the annual meeting of the American Educational Research Association, New Orleans.

Rumberger, R. W., & Thomas, S. L. (2000). The distribution of dropout and turnover rates among urban and suburban high schools. *Sociology of Education, 73,* 39–67.

Sander, W., & Krautmann, A. C. (1995). Catholic schools, dropout rates and educational attainment. *Economic Inquiry, 33,* 217–233.

Shanahan, M. J., & Flaherty, B. P. (2001). Dynamic patterns of time use in adolescence. *Child Development, 72,* 385–401.

Shavelson, R., McDonnell, L., Oakes, J., & Carey, N. (1987). *Indicator systems for monitoring mathematics and science education.* Santa Monica, CA: RAND.

Skiba, R., & Peterson, R. (1999). The dark side of zero tolerance: Can punishment lead to safe schools? *Phi Delta Kappan, 80,* 372–376, 381–382.

South, S. J., Baumer, E. P., & Lutz, A. (2003). Interpreting community effects on youth educational attainment. *Youth and Society, 35,* 3–36.

Stecher, B. M., & Bohrnstedt, G. W. (Eds.). (2000). *Class size reduction in California: The 1998–99 evaluation findings.* Sacramento: California Department of Education.

Steele, C. (1997). The threat in the air: How stereotypes shape intellectual identity and performance. *American Psychologist, 52,* 613–629.

Steele, C. M., & Aronson, J. (1998). Stereotype threat and the test performance of academically successful African Americans. In C. Jencks & M. Phillips (Eds.), *The black-white test score gap* (pp. 401–427). Washington, DC: Brookings Institution Press.

Steinberg, L., Blinde, P. L., & Chan, K. S. (1984). Dropping out among language minority youth. *Review of Educational Research, 54,* 113–132.

Steinberg, L., Dombusch, S. M., & Brown, B. B. (1992). Ethnic differences in adolescent achievement. *American Psychologist, 47,* 723–729.

Steinberg, L., Lamborn, S. D., Dombusch, S. M., & Darling, N. (1992). Impact of parenting practices on adolescent achievement: Authoritative parenting, school involvement, and encouragement to succeed. *Child Development, 63,* 1266–1281.

Suárez-Orozco, M. M., & Suárez-Orozco, C. E. (1995). The cultural patterning of achievement motivation: A comparison of Mexican, Mexican immigrant, Mexican American, and non-Latino White American students. In R. G. Rumbaut & W. A. Cornelius (Eds.), *California's immigrant children: Theory, research, and implications for educational policy* (pp. 161–190). San Diego: University of California, San Diego, Center for U.S.-Mexican Studies.

Sui-Chu, E. H., & Willms, J. D. (1996). Effects of parental involvement on eighth-grade achievement. *Sociology of Education, 69,* 126–141.

Swanson, C. B., & Schneider, B. (1999). Students on the move: Residential and educational mobility in America's schools. *Sociology of Education, 72,* 54–67.

Teachman, J. D., Paasch, K., & Carver, K. (1996). School capital and dropping out of school. *Journal of Marriage and the Family, 58,* 773–783.

Texas Education Agency. (1998). *1996–97 report on grade level retention.* Austin: Author.

U.S. Department of Education. (1990). *National goals for education.* Washington, DC: U.S. Department of Education.

U.S. Department of Education. (2004). *No child left behind.* Washington, DC: U.S. Department of Education. Retrieved June 16, 2004, from http://www.ed.gov/nclb/landing.jhtml?src=pb.

U.S. Department of Education, National Center for Education Statistics. (1997). *The condition of education, 1997.* Washington, DC: U.S. Government Printing Office.

U.S. Department of Education, National Center for Education Statistics. (2003). *Digest of education statistics, 1999.* Washington, DC: U.S. Government Printing Office. Retrieved June 16, 2004, from http://nces.ed.gov/programs/digest/d02/list_tables1.asp#c1_4.

Upchurch, D., & McCarthy, J. (1990). The timing of a first birth and high school completion. *American Sociological Review, 55,* 224–234.

Velez, W. (1989). High school attrition among Hispanic and non-Hispanic white youths. *Sociology of Education, 62,* 119–133.

Warren, J. R. (2002). Reconsidering the relationship between student employment and academic outcomes: A new theory and better data. *Youth & Society, 33,* 366–393.

Warren, J. R., & Lee, J. C. (2003). The impact of adolescent employment on high school dropout: Differences by individual and labor-market characteristics. *Social Science Research, 32,* 98–128.

Wehlage, G. G., & Rutter, R. A. (1986). Dropping out: How much do schools contribute to the problem? *Teachers College Record, 87,* 374–392.

Wehlage, O. G., Rutter, R. A., Smith, G. A., Lesko, N., & Fernandez, R. R. (1989). *Reducing the risk: Schools as communities of support.* New York: Falmer Press.

Wilson, W. J. (1987). *The truly disadvantaged: The inner city, the underclass, and public policy.* Chicago: University of Chicago Press.

CHAPTER 7

Graduation and Dropout Rates after Implementation of High-Stakes Testing in Chicago's Elementary Schools: A Close Look at Students Most Vulnerable to Dropping Out

ELAINE M. ALLENSWORTH

Beginning with the 1995–1996 eighth-grade class, Chicago Public Schools (CPS) initiated a high-stakes testing policy that required students to meet a minimum score on the Iowa Tests of Basic Skills (ITBS) before being promoted to high school. This initiative was at the forefront of a national trend in grade promotion linked to performance on standardized tests, and has been repeatedly cited as a model program for other places.[1] Such policies are politically popular because they are seen as decisively dealing with problems of low achievement. There often is hope that the threat of retaining students will spur students to try harder in school, and motivate parents and teachers to address more effectively the educational needs of poorly performing students. But high-stakes tests also raise concerns that students who do not meet the promotion standard and are held back in grade will be more likely to drop out of school. Of particular concern are the effects on subgroups of students who are most likely to drop out of school, including racial/ethnic minority students, students who are older than others in their grade, and English-language learners. Because students in these subgroups are also more likely than average to have low achievement-test scores, they are especially at risk of not meeting the promotion standard and being retained. Therefore, high-stakes tests are likely to aggravate the dropout rates of students already most vulnerable to dropping out. The Chicago policy has been touted as a model for other cities. Therefore, the effects of this policy on the most vulnerable students need to be carefully examined.

THE CHICAGO PROMOTION POLICY

Beginning in spring 1996, the Chicago Public Schools attempted to end the social promotion of students. In the first year, eighth-grade students were required to meet a minimum score on the Iowa Tests of Basic Skills in both reading and mathematics in order to be promoted into ninth grade. The test-score cutoff for promotion was set using the grade-equivalent metric, which is based on national norms.[2] The cutoff score in the first year was two years below grade level, or 6.8 grade equivalents (GEs). The district increased the eighth-grade cutoff score each subsequent year, to 7.0 in 1997, 7.2 in 1998, 7.4 in 1999, and 7.7 GEs in 2000. Students who did not meet the cutoff score in both reading and math were required to participate in a summer-school program called Summer Bridge, where they received instruction in reading and math aimed at helping them to pass the test. At the end of the summer, students took the ITBS again. Those who did not pass the second time were retained in eighth grade or moved into a transition center. Transition centers were new schools designed specifically for students who failed the eighth-grade standards but were too old to remain in elementary school.[3] Between 40 and 50 percent of students held back by the eighth-grade standard enrolled in transition centers each year, beginning in the 1997–1998 school year.

Two groups of students—those in special education and those in bilingual education for three years or less—were not held to the promotion criteria in the same ways as other students. The promotion decisions for special education students were based on criteria outlined in their Individual Education Plans (IEP). At the start of the policy, bilingual students were excluded if they had been enrolled in a bilingual education program for fewer than three complete years as of the beginning of the school year. In 1999, the criterion was changed from three to four years. By the time they were in eighth grade, however, few students had been enrolled in the bilingual program for fewer than four years.

About 1,800 eighth graders were held back from entering ninth grade in the first year of the promotion policy. Even more students were held back from entering ninth grade each of the following three years: about 3,000 students repeated eighth grade or entered a transition center in the fall of 1997; 3,900 students in the fall of 1998; and 3,300 students in the fall of 1999.[4] In spring 1997, promotion standards were also implemented in the third and sixth grades. Unfortunately, it is too early to know the effects of the promotion standards in the early grades on students' eventual likelihood of dropping out or graduating because these students are still too young to graduate from high school.[5]

THE DEBATE ABOUT HOLDING STUDENTS BACK

There is a great deal of research on grade retention resulting from individual decisions of teachers and parents, and this work is the primary basis for concerns about the effects of promotional standards on dropout rates. Research on teacher-initiated retention has consistently shown that retained students are much more likely to drop out than students at the expected grade for their age (e.g., Alexander, Entwisle, & Kabbani, 2001; Grissom & Shepard, 1989; Roderick, 1994; Rumberger, 1995). There may be many reasons this relationship exists. Dropping out has been characterized as resulting in part from weak attachment to school developed through years of poor school performance and feelings of failure (see Alexander, Entwisle, & Horsey, 1997; Finn, 1989). From this perspective, holding students back in grade could increase the likelihood of dropping out by lowering students' self-efficacy, compounding feelings of failure, and bringing about negative attitudes toward school.[6] From a developmental perspective, retention also produces the stigma of being older than classmates and a dislocation from age-specific responsibilities (Grissom & Shepard, 1989; Holmes & Saturday, 2000; Roderick, 1994). In the 1980s, New York City tried holding back seventh graders who were not at standards, but gave up the practice because so many of the retained students dropped out of school (House, 1998). Therefore, when Chicago's policy was implemented, there was substantial concern that the city's already high dropout rate would get worse.

Despite these concerns, the promotion policy was initiated as a means of helping low-achieving students. School districts do not necessarily adopt high-stakes testing policies because they believe retention is good in itself, but because they believe the *threat* of retention is beneficial.[7] They think it will motivate students to work harder and encourage teachers and parents to pay more attention to children who most need extra help. Implementing stricter standards should prompt better ongoing assessment of students that have fallen behind and teachers who need support, so that resources can be allocated to those students and teachers who need them most.[8] All of this should bring increases in achievement and reductions in dropout rates, especially among the lowest-achieving students.[9] In fact, after the promotion policy was implemented, students in Chicago did report trying harder in school so that they would meet the eighth-grade standard, and low-performing students reported receiving more academic support from their teachers and parents (Roderick & Engel, 2001).

Furthermore, while there is a strong relationship between teacher-initiated retention and dropping out, its applicability to the high-stakes testing environment is not clear cut. There are three issues that could be argued by proponents of high-stakes testing (HST) to discount the results of studies on traditional, teacher-initiated retention. First, the context of retention is different under HST than with traditional retention, and so its effects are not necessarily the same.[10] Second, some of the relationship that has been found between dropping out and teacher-initiated retention is likely spurious—occurring because some students who are held back are already in the process of disengagement from school (e.g., showing high absence rates) and would drop out regardless of whether retained or not. Finally, efforts to end social promotion are rarely implemented without considering the risk of elevated dropout rates. There is often an effort to "get it right" by accompanying grade retention with programs to get students over the threshold. In Chicago, for example, the policy to end social promotion included summer school for all students who failed the promotion cutoffs, multiple chances to pass, and afterschool tutoring programs.

Some Subgroups of Students Are at Particular Risk under High-Stakes Testing Policies

Because of the contradictory effects expected from high-stakes testing, there has been substantial debate about whether its overall effects would be adverse or beneficial for students' likelihood of eventually graduating from school. Yet even if the policy had beneficial effects on student achievement, the policy would not be experienced in the same way among all students. Chicago's policy was intended to help raise the achievement of the lowest-performing students in the system, yet very low-achieving students would have a difficult time passing the promotion standard even if they showed substantial improvements. In May 1996, 18 percent of students in seventh grade in CPS were more than a year and a half behind the standard they would need to pass at the end of the next year in order to be promoted into high school (Roderick, Bryk, Jacob, Easton, & Allensworth, 1999). To meet the standard, these students would need to show learning gains that were 150 percent higher than the average student. This would prove difficult; most would fail, half would be retained. Even if they did not meet the standard, these students could have shown substantial improvements in achievement in eighth grade, and this could have improved their attachment to school. However, unless the positive effects of improving achievement were enough to counter any adverse effects of retention, students who failed the test-score cutoff and were retained in school would be less likely to graduate.

Low-achieving students are most vulnerable to the adverse effects of retention policies, therefore those groups of students who tend to have the lowest achievement are most at risk of being adversely affected by HST. In Chicago, almost all students that were retained by the promotion standards were African American or Latino. Not only do African American and Latino students comprise the majority of students in Chicago's public schools, but Asian and non-Hispanic white students were much less likely to have achievement that put them at risk of failing the promotion standard (Roderick et al., 1999).

One group of students was at particular risk from this policy—those who had been held back in school previously, or those who entered school late and were already older than most students in their class. Without this kind of policy, few teachers would recommend holding a student back a second time, making the student more than two years older than his classmates. However, the strict criterion of the policy required that students be held back despite their age or previous experience with grade retention.

High-stakes testing policies also raise concern for students who have difficulty performing well on standardized tests because of disabilities or limited English proficiency. In Chicago, most students classified as learning disabled and students with fewer than four years in bilingual education were exempt from the test score cutoff for promotion. The policy still could have had adverse effects for these students if instructional resources were shifted to students at risk of being retained by the promotion standard. Unfortunately, because inclusion in bilingual and special education programs changed across the decade, it is difficult to study changes in dropout rates among these students without introducing selection bias into the comparisons. The evidence that does exist suggests that students exempt from the test score cutoff for promotion were not adversely affected by the policy.[11] However, students who had completed more than four years of bilingual education but were not yet proficient in English faced a more difficult standard than other students because the test was given in English.[12]

SYSTEMWIDE GRADUATION AND DROPOUT RATES AFTER IMPLEMENTING EIGHTH-GRADE PROMOTION STANDARDS

Methodology for Studying Trends

To study the effects of the promotion policy on graduation and dropout rates, cohorts of students who were subject to the promotion policy were compared to earlier cohorts of students who passed through eighth grade before the promotion standard was implemented. Cohorts were defined as students who were 13 years old on September 1 of each year from 1991 to 1998. For students at the expected grade for their age, this was the fall of their eighth-grade year. This allowed for four prepolicy and four postpolicy cohorts.[13] Cohorts were defined by age rather than grade, so that comparisons across cohorts were not biased by changes in grade progression through elementary school. Each cohort was followed for at least five years, until age 18, and those that had turned 19 by the end of September 2003 were followed for six years. At the end of each period, administrative records were used to determine whether students had dropped out, were still enrolled, or had graduated. Students were classified as dropouts if they were no longer active for any of the following reasons: lost could not be located; transferred to an evening school; lost undeclared; exited IEP (rather than graduated); dropout self-declared; dropout for absences; did not arrive at school; received alternative school certificate (GED, alternative diploma); left an alternative school (unless transferred to a regular CPS school); still enrolled in an alternative school at age 19; no leave code recorded.[14] There is always uncertainty as to whether students who drop out may have been misclassified as transfer students. However, over the period studied, transfer rates in Chicago public schools remained fairly steady, suggesting no substantial change in misclassification rates that would affect the trends in dropout or graduation rates.

Graduation and Dropout Trends

In the early 1990s, graduation rates were improving in the Chicago Public Schools. As shown in Figure 1, 42.5 percent of students who were 13 years old in 1994 graduated by the time they were 18 in 1999, compared to just 37.6 percent of those who had been thirteen years old in 1991. This was partly due to a decline in dropout rates, from 41.2 to 39.9 percent, but it also occurred because more students were getting through school by age 18 so they were less likely to still be enrolled in school. Graduation rates at age 19, which allow students an extra year to move through school, were almost three percentage points higher in the 1994 cohort than the 1991 cohort.[15]

With the first cohort subject to the eighth-grade promotion policy, the 1995 cohort, the improvements in dropout and graduation rates stopped. Graduation and dropout rates were similar to those in the previous cohort. The trend reversed with the second cohort subject to the gate, so that graduation rates at age 18 were lower than for the previous three cohorts, and graduation rates at age 19 were lower than for the previous two cohorts. With the third and fourth cohorts, both dropout and graduation rates began to improve again, although from the inferior levels. Graduation rates at age 18 were set back more than dropout trends, because students were not only more likely to drop out among the first two cohorts subject to the promotion standard, but those who stayed in school were also less likely to finish by age 18. Graduation trends also improved less with the last two cohorts than did dropout rates. Students were

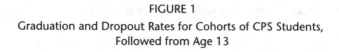

FIGURE 1

Graduation and Dropout Rates for Cohorts of CPS Students,
Followed from Age 13

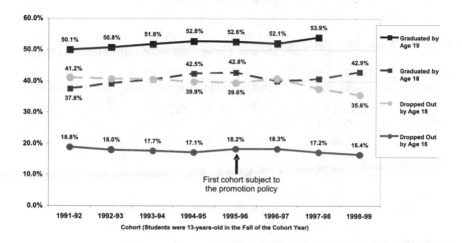

Graduation and dropout rates at age 18 are calculated with students still enrolled in the denominator. The difference between their sum and 100% is the percentage of students still enrolled at age 18. Graduation rates at age 19 are calculated without students still enrolled in either the numerator so that dropout rates at age 19 are the difference from 100%. Transfer students are not included in any calculations, and there is no evidence that dropouts were increasingly hidden as transfer students. Transfer rates declined slightly over this period.

taking longer to graduate, on average, because many students' entry to high school had been delayed by the eighth-grade promotion standard.

Looking at trends across the cohorts, it appears that the promotion policy set back improvements that were occurring in the schools since the early 1990s. If not for the policy, dropout and graduation rates might have been even better among the most recent cohorts. However, it could also be argued that the policy had a beneficial effect on dropout and graduation rates. Dropout rates worsened only with the first two cohorts through the policy, and then improved substantially with the fourth cohort subject to the standard. It could be argued that the policy was not yet fully implemented when the first two cohorts encountered it, and that is why dropout rates showed an initial setback. Only the latter two cohorts had access to the full range of services for low-achieving students, including positively received afterschool and summer school programs.[16] Proponents of promotion standards have argued that improved achievement should offset the adverse effects of higher rates of retention. That is what happened in Chicago, beginning with the third cohort through the promotion standard.

After the policy was implemented in 1995, achievement improved dramatically among Chicago's eighth graders (Rosenkranz, 2002). Some of these improvements were a result of changes in the testing environment postpolicy—students were trying harder on the test, and teachers were putting more time into preparing students to take the test. However, even if adjustments are made for potential testing effects, the improvements in achievement were substantial. Adjusted for testing effects, students scoring in the 50th percentile who were in the fourth cohort to pass through the promotional gate would have scored at the 70th percentile if they were part of a pre-policy cohort.[17] These improvements in achievement explain almost all of the decline in dropout rates when estimated by statistical models.[18] Students were leaving elementary school better prepared to do high school work, and their high school outcomes reflect this, including their graduation and dropout rates.[19]

However, it is doubtful that the improvements in achievement were fully attributable to the promotion policy. There are many reasons achievement could have improved in this period. In the early 1990s, Chicago's elementary schools underwent substantial changes due to unprecedented decentralization reforms enacted in 1988. In the early 1990s, following the introduction of the reform act, most elementary schools showed significant improvements in students' test scores on the ITBS. Students who were in the primary grades during this time of improving test scores would have moved into eighth grade during the latter part of the decade, around the same time that the promotion gates were put into place. Therefore, at least some of the rise in achievement and the decline in dropout rates are likely due to earlier school reforms.[20] Furthermore, in 1995, the mayor of Chicago took over control of the schools and appointed a CEO of schools. For the first time in years there was stability in CPS leadership, conflict with the teachers union subsided, and there was an influx of money for substantial capital improvements. These changes also should have improved conditions for student learning.

A final appraisal of the systemwide effects of the promotion policy on dropout rates depends on the extent to which one believes that the improvements in achievement were a result of the promotion policy. Given the rise in achievement, dropout rates should have fallen with the 1995 and 1996 cohorts. That did not happen because the rise in eighth-grade retentions had a countervailing effect on dropout rates. Dropout rates declined dramatically with the 1998 cohort because it had the highest achievement of any cohort, and because substantially fewer students in this cohort were retained than in the preceding postpolicy cohort.[21]

Whether or not the policy was good for *systemwide* dropout trends, those students held back by the high-stakes test had a greater risk of dropping out than they would have had without the policy. Retention by the standard was, in fact, related to higher dropout rates. Furthermore, retention increased the risk of dropping out more than higher achievement decreased the risk for very low-achieving students who did not meet the promotion cutoff. Statistical models estimate that retention by the promotional standard increased students' probability of dropping out by age 17 from 30.8 to 38.8 percent for a typical retained student, and from 44 to 57 percent by age 19 (for details, see Allensworth, 2004).[22] This retention effect is not as large as that seen with traditional teacher-initiated retention, and it suggests either that spurious factors account for much of the relationship with traditional retention or that the context of retention under Chicago's high-stakes testing program moderated the effect of retention.[23] This is one reason dropout rates did not show the sharp rise that was anticipated by opponents to the policy. Still, retention by the standard did increase students' probability of dropping out by age 17 by 8 percentage points, which is a *26 percent* increase from the base rate of 31 percent. Rising achievement mitigated this effect to some degree, but the effect of rising achievement was not as large as the effect of retention. Improvements in achievement account for a decline of 1.2 percentage points among retained students in the 1995 cohort, and between 3.5 and 6.1 percentage points in the 1998 cohort.[24] For students retained under high-stakes testing, the adverse effects on dropping out from retention outweighed any beneficial effect of rising achievement. Even if the policy was responsible for all of the improvements in achievement, those improvements came at the expense of higher dropout rates among students held back by the policy. Dropout rates among students with very low achievement remained high postpolicy while falling among all other students.

POLICY EFFECTS BY RACE/ETHNICITY AND GENDER
Retention Rates

Almost all students held back by the promotion standard were African American or Latino. As shown in Figure 2, eighth-grade retention rates rose dramatically among African American and Latino girls and boys with implementation of the promotion standard. While white and Asian students were also more likely to be retained after the policy was implemented, the changes were much more modest than among Latino or African American students. Controlling for achievement, there did not seem to be a racial or gender bias in implementation of the eighth-grade standard (Roderick et al., 1999). However, because the standard was based on achievement and there were large differences in achieve-

FIGURE 2

Percentage of Students Retained in Eighth Grade by Race/Ethnicity, Gender, and Cohort

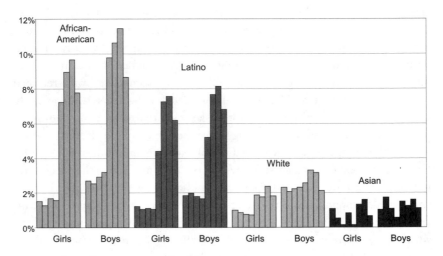

Cohorts are represented left to right, from the 1991 cohort through the 1998 cohort, within each race and gender. The fifth cohort is the first to pass through the eighth-grade promotional standard.

ment by race/ethnicity across the school district, unbiased implementation of the policy still meant unequal policy outcomes across racial and ethnic groups. These racial/ethnic differences in retention contributed to a widening gap in graduation rates by race across the decade.

Among Latino students, those who had been English-language learners were especially likely to be held back by the gate. Because there is limited information on bilingual program participation in the early 1990s, English-language learners can only be distinguished in the 1998 cohort, preventing a cross-cohort comparison of bilingual students.[25] However, students in the 1998 cohort who had participated in the bilingual program, about half of all Latino students, were almost twice as likely to be retained in eighth grade as other Latino students—9.6 percent of formerly bilingual Latino students were retained in eighth grade, compared to 5.0 percent of those who were never in the bilingual program. Adjustments for students' economic status explain only a small part of this difference.[26] Students whose native language was not English were less likely to do well on the test, especially on the reading section. On average, Latino students who had been in the bilingual program scored 0.4 GEs lower than students never in the bilingual program. Students who had been in the bilingual program were also more likely to be retained because they were less likely to be exempt from the promotion standard than Latino students who had not been part of the bilingual program.[27]

Dropout Rates

African American students were held back at higher rates by the policy than students of any other race, and their postpolicy graduation rates reflect this. In the first part of the 1990s, prior to the promotion policy, graduation rates were improving among both African American boys and girls, as shown in Figures 3 and 4. Improvements in graduation rates occurred mostly because African American students were more likely to graduate by age 18, not because they were less likely to drop out. Dropout rates were not improving among African American students in the first part of the 1990s, but graduation rates were improving because more students were completing the courses they needed to graduate. With the first cohort subject to the promotion standard, dropout rates increased, and they rose even further with the next cohort. Graduation rates also fell substantially with the second cohort through the policy. Dropout rates then resumed a downward trend with the third cohort through the policy, and continued to decline with the fourth cohort. Improvements in graduation rates were much slower to recover than dropout rates, however, because fewer students were able to graduate by age 18. The final two cohorts of African American students showed improving dropout and graduation rates. Still, even with these improvements, dropout rates were no better, and graduation rates were worse, than among the last two cohorts of African American students to pass through eighth grade before the standard was implemented.

Among Latino students, graduation and dropout trends were also improving in the early 1990s, and these improvements were even stronger than those seen among African American students. Graduation rates improved by almost nine percentage points from the 1991 to the 1994 cohort among Latino girls, and by more than seven percentage points among Latino boys. Latino students were more likely to accumulate the credits they needed to graduate, and they were less likely to drop out of school.[28] These improvements slowed with the first cohort subject to the promotion policy, and graduation rates fell considerably with the second postpolicy cohort. Graduation and dropout rates started to improve again with the third and fourth cohorts through the policy and showed stronger recovery than among African American students. As a result, graduation rates among Latino girls surpassed those of African American girls by the end of the decade, while graduation rates of Latino boys improved much more than those of African American boys.

FIGURE 3

Graduation Rates at Age 18 and Dropout Rates at Age 16
for Cohorts of CPS Girls by Race/Ethnicity

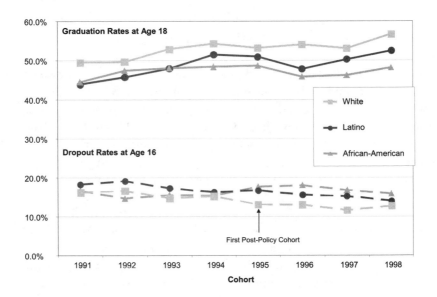

There were also improvements in graduation and dropout rates through the 1991–1994 cohorts and the 1997–1998 cohorts of white students. While not as strong as the improvements seen among Latino students, the trends were stronger than those for African American students. More importantly, instead of reversing with the promotion standard policy, graduation and dropout trends simply remained flat for the first two cohorts of white students subject to the policy. As a result, the gaps between graduation rates of white students, compared to Latino and African American students, were larger at the end of the decade than in pre-policy years.

Dropout and graduation rates improved substantially among all but African American students over the latter part of the 1990s, resulting in larger racial inequities in school completion by the end of the decade than at the beginning. It could be argued that this was a good result—graduation rates improved among most racial/ethnic groups. Certainly this is better than having racial gaps grow because graduation rates among some groups declined. Furthermore, dropout rates among African American students were improving again by the end of the decade. Yet, while dropout and graduation rates among African American students were improving by the fourth cohort, achievement was also at a record high. On average, the 1998 cohort of African American students had

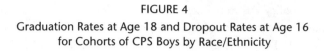

FIGURE 4

Graduation Rates at Age 18 and Dropout Rates at Age 16
for Cohorts of CPS Boys by Race/Ethnicity

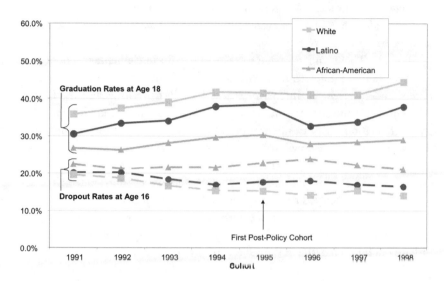

achievement, adjusted for testing effects, that was almost half a standard deviation higher than pre-policy cohorts. However, dropout and graduation rates were still at pre-policy levels. For African American students, substantial gains in achievement did not result in declining dropout rates because the beneficial effects of higher achievement were countered by the adverse effect of so many African American students being retained in eighth grade.

STUDENTS ESPECIALLY VULNERABLE TO MANDATORY GRADE RETENTION: THOSE ALREADY OLD-FOR-GRADE

The promotion policy was intended to end social promotion. But even before its implementation, teachers often held students back in grade. In each cohort, about 15 percent of the students who were subject to the test score cutoff for promotion had not yet made it to eighth grade by the time they were 13 years old. Most of these students had been retained in grade at an earlier point in school, so they were in sixth or seventh grade at age 13. Others had entered school after age five. While most educators would be concerned about making a student two years older than expected for their grade, the promotion standard made no exceptions for these students.

Once the policy was implemented, these students were much more likely to be retained by the promotion standard than students who had reached eighth grade by age 13. They were at high risk of failing the standard because their achievement, on average, was very low. In addition, some students already old for their grade at age 13 never even had the opportunity to pass the promotion standard because they were moved into transition centers before reaching the eighth grade. These students were too old to remain in elementary school and they were no longer allowed to move directly into high school. In the transition centers students received intensive remedial study in reading and math, but they took few courses that would allow them to accumulate credits for high school graduation. Prior to the promotion-standard policy, students who were too old to remain in elementary school moved directly into high school and could begin taking some courses for high school credit. Across the four postpolicy cohorts, nearly a quarter (24%) of students old-for-grade at age 13 were in some way delayed from entering high school because of the promotion gate—either they were retained in eighth grade or they enrolled in a transition center instead of a high school.[29] In comparison, fewer than one percent of the students old for their grade in the 1992 cohort were held back in eighth grade.

Many of the old-for-grade students who were retained by the standard would have dropped out regardless of the policy, but retention at the promotion standard made it almost certain that they would do so.[30] By age 19, 78 percent of the students already old for their grade at age 13 who were retained by the promotion standard had dropped out of school, and only 11 percent had graduated. Of the remaining students, one-third were enrolled in alternative schools that do not grant CPS diplomas, so these students would likely leave school without a diploma, or with an alternative diploma or GED. At most, only about 15 percent of the students already old for their grade before being retained by the promotion standard likely ever received a regular diploma.[31]

Graduating from high school would be extremely difficult for students who were retained in eighth grade despite already being old-for-grade. Because they were too old to remain in elementary school, these students went to transition centers after failing the promotion gate. But transition centers were problematic for several reasons. Students faced an extra school transition, a stressful event for many students. In addition, transition centers concentrated very low-achieving students together in one school, which produced a compositional effect that increased each student's likelihood of dropping out.[32] Furthermore, by the time they entered high school, these students were at least 16 years old. It would be impossible for them to accumulate enough credits to graduate by age 18. Even graduating by age 20 would be difficult, since these students would have more than the typical difficulty passing their courses, and course failure rates in CPS high schools are high.[33] The promotion standard was supposed to ensure that students would have the skills needed to succeed in high school. However, its implementation made it unlikely that the lowest-achieving students would have the opportunity to complete their education at a regular high school.

SUMMARY

In the first part of the 1990s, graduation and dropout rates were improving in the Chicago Public Schools. When the school system started holding back large numbers of eighth-grade students, these positive trends stopped and then fell back with the first two cohorts through the policy. Improvements began again with the third and fourth cohorts. Proponents of promotion standards may look at the positive trends among the latter cohorts as evidence that the promotion gates had no adverse effects on students' likelihood of completing school and were even beneficial. However, improvements in graduation and dropout rates stopped when the policy was implemented and only resumed after being set back to earlier levels. If the trends seen in the early 1990s had continued without this setback, graduation and dropout rates might have been even better by the end of the decade. Chicago has extremely high dropout rates, so any policy that decreases students' likelihood of school completion should be of great concern.

The policy most adversely affected students who were already most likely to drop out before the policy—those with very low achievement—yet these are the students the policy was intended to help. Students who failed the standard and were retained were less likely to graduate than they would have been without the policy. Students who had been held back in school before encountering the standard were particularly vulnerable to failing it, and almost all of those who did fail eventually dropped out of school. The policy to end social promotion resulted in students beginning high school two or more years behind their agemates. These students could not graduate in a reasonable time.

Racial gaps in school completion grew as a result of this policy, especially between African American and other students. By the fourth cohort through the policy, graduation rates among African American students were no better than among pre-policy cohorts, even though achievement had improved dramatically. The improvements in graduation rates that had been occurring prior to the policy resumed only after being set back considerably. Graduation rates among Latino students also declined dramatically with the implementation of the policy and might have been higher without it. English-language learners were especially likely to be held back in school by the promotion standard.

Only white and Asian students showed no decline in graduation rates after the policy was implemented, because few of these students faced the threat of retention. While the policy was equally implemented across racial groups, it was structured such that its harmful effects would predominantly be borne by African American and Latino students.

Proponents of the promotion standard have argued that the policy was necessary to raise student achievement. There is no denying that achievement improved dramatically after the promotion standard was implemented. Others have disputed whether it was the promotion standard that was responsible, as there were many other changes occurring in Chicago's schools that could have spurred achievement gains. It is likely that some, but not all, of the improvements in student achievement occurred because of the promotion gate. If so, this begs the question of how to encourage the positive motivational effects and teacher responses without harming the most vulnerable children. This requires better understanding of how the promotion standard affects student achievement.

Was it the threat of retention that motivated students to work harder in school and encouraged more support from teachers and parents, or was it something else about the policy? If the threat of retention was responsible for the improvements in achievement, students whose achievement put them at no risk of failing the cutoff should have shown only modest improvements in test scores. However, in eighth grade, even students at the top of their class, who were at no risk of retention, showed higher test scores postpolicy.[34] This starts to suggest that it was more than just the threat of retention that was responsible for improvements in achievement. For example, it could be that emphasis on the promotion standard prompted all students to care more about the academic achievement and encouraged teachers to pay more attention to data on students' academic progress.

Was it necessary to retain large numbers of students to motivate students to work harder? It seems possible that alternative consequences might have motivated students. For example, students could have been threatened with mandatory summer school, and with being retained only if they failed to participate fully. Promoted students could receive additional supports in high school, such as tutoring to help them handle high school–level course work, rather than simply preventing them from attempting it. Many retained students were struggling with health problems or personal/emotional issues that interfered with their performance in school. The promotion standard could act as a screen for targeting assessments and appropriate interventions for struggling students, rather than as a purely motivational mechanism. It is also not clear that the standard needed to be raised each year to continue to motivate students. The standard has been raised regularly since the policy was implemented, yet gains in achievement from seventh to eighth grade have been flat (Rosenkranz, 2002). Currently, students whose reading score is below the 35th percentile in a national sample are at risk of being held back in Chicago. These are very high standards, and many students are retained because the current standard is so high. Yet it is not known whether this high standard increases motivation any more than standards set at a low level.

There is still a great deal that is not known about the effects of this policy on students. Other school districts are following Chicago's lead, but we do not know the extent to which the policy can be credited with raising achievement, what it was about the policy that resulted in higher achievement, and whether promotion policies implemented in different ways and with different populations would show the same dramatic changes. Yet, while we do not know the extent to which the policy affected achievement, we do know that it dramatically affected students' likelihood of being held back in school. Furthermore, holding students back in school made them more likely to drop out, and struggling students were most likely to be adversely affected by the policy. This kind of policy aims to improve systemwide outcomes at the expense of the most vulnerable students. When viewed from the perspective of the most vulnerable students in the system, Chicago's policy to end social promotion is a problematic model.

NOTES

1. For example, in 1999, President Clinton hailed Chicago's policy as a model for the nation in his State of the Union address. Recently, in 2004, New York's Mayor Bloomberg also cited Chicago's success as support for a similar policy in New York's schools. Texas, Florida, and North Carolina, as well as a number of cities, have implemented promotion standards within the last decade.

2. Using this metric, a student is considered on grade level if they obtain a score of their grade plus the number of months in the school year that have passed (e.g., a score of 8.8 would be on grade level for an eighth-grade student taking the exam in the eighth month of the school year).

3. Students who will turn 15 years old by December 1 of the school year are not allowed to enroll in elementary school. These schools were later renamed "Academic Preparation Centers."

4. These numbers include all students who repeated eighth grade or enrolled in a transition center, including double-retainees and students who entered CPS through a transition center.

5. The first cohort of students to pass through the third-grade standard has just turned 15 years old. The first cohort to pass through the sixth-grade standard is the same as the fourth cohort through the eighth-grade standard, and its outcomes can be seen in this chapter. However, I am hesitant to make any conclusions about the effects of the sixth-grade standard based on only one cohort of students.

6. Research on traditional retention suggests it can have negative psychological consequences, such as lowering students' self-efficacy and increasing feelings of failure and negative attitudes toward school that might encourage students to leave school (e.g., Byrnes, 1989; Campbell, 1993).

7. Some proponents of HST do believe that retention itself is beneficial for low-performing students, and favor these policies for that reason. While most studies of grade retention do not show positive academic effects, there have been some exceptions in cases where substantial support is provided for failing students (see Holmes, 1989, for a meta-analysis of this work). Most pertinent to the area of high-stakes testing, analysis of the HST program in Texas (Dworkin et al., 1999), the Texas Assessment of Academic Skills (TAAS), did show improved test scores among retained students, compared to those who were socially promoted. But these gains have been disputed as representing only test-specific effects (Klein, Hamilton, McCaffrey, & Stecher, 2000).

8. See Rabinowitz, Zimmerman and Sherman (2001) and National Research Council (2001) for a summary of the potentially contradictory effects of promotion standards on dropout rates.

9. Just as grade retention has consistently been found to be associated with higher dropout rates, so has poor academic performance (e.g., Alexander et al., 2001; Grissom & Shepard, 1989; Pallas, 1987).

10. A number of differences could be hypothesized, in terms of both the social-psychological effects of retention and the instructional responses of teachers and schools. For example, from the student's perspective, the explicit criteria for promotion under high-stakes testing might lead students to internalize failure more when retained, rather than blaming their school or teacher. Alternatively, students may be less likely to feel singled out or unfairly punished. If retention is relatively common in a school, as it is in some of the lowest-performing schools in Chicago, the stigma associated with being held back may not be as strong. Teachers may react differently to students retained under high-stakes testing than those that have been singled out for retention. For example, they may be more likely to tailor instruction to a group of retained students than they would to a student retained alone. They also may be more likely to view retained students as victims of an external policy, rather than seeing deficits in particular students, and may be more sympathetic in their interactions.

11. Students classified in special education programs were officially held to a promotion standard set in their IEP. In practice, however, retention rates changed little under the policy for students in special education. Slightly more students were held back in the first year of the policy, but retention rates among special education students declined in each subsequent year to below-policy levels by the fourth postpolicy cohort. Dropout rates among special education students who were excluded from the promotion standard showed similar patterns to those of included students—a rise in the first year (when more students were retained), and then declining dropout rates each subsequent year. However, some of these changes could have occurred because of selection effects, as the composition of students in special education changed slightly across the cohorts, and dramatically with the fourth postpolicy cohort.

12. There are a number of reasons the test scores of English-language learners may underestimate their true ability. For a summary of these issues, see Heubert and Hauser (1999).

13. Classifying students as pre- or postpolicy based on cohort results in unbiased estimates of policy effects. However, the classification is not precise at the level of individuals because

not all of the students in postpolicy cohorts were subject to the gate, while some students in the pre-policy cohorts were subject to the gate. Classifying students by whether they were actually subject to the standard would bias estimations of cohort effects. Students in the first three cohorts who were subject to the standard were primarily those who had been retained prior to eighth grade, the lowest-achieving students in their cohorts. Students in the last four cohorts who were not subject to the standard were primarily those who had skipped a grade, generally the highest achieving students in their cohorts. By including the lowest-performing early-cohort students as postpolicy students, and the highest-performing late-cohort students as pre-policy students, the policy effect would appear more negative than it actually was.

14. Students with alternative school diplomas and GEDs were treated as dropouts because the standards for receiving these degrees are lower than for receiving a CPS diploma, and evidence suggests that economic outcomes are similar among dropouts and GED recipients (Cameron & Heckman, 1993).

15. There were several reasons for the improvements in graduation rates over this period. Some of these improvements can be credited to improved economic conditions, although not among African American students. More importantly, there were fewer students who had been held back in school at some point in the later pre-policy cohorts. The largest factor contributing to increased graduation rates was that students were attempting and passing more classes in high school, so they were more likely to accumulate the credits needed to graduate. [To determine why graduation rates improved, net of changes in dropout rates, logistic regression models were run predicting the likelihood of graduating among students who did not drop out by age 18. Models were run separately by race. Variables entered as predictors included cohort, social status, poverty, old-for-grade by age 13, age student began high school, high school credits attempted at age 16, high school credits earned at age 16, whether attended magnet school, adjusted (underlying) ITBS score at the end of eighth grade. Neither ITBS score nor magnet school attendance explained pre-policy cohort improvements in graduation rates. Across all students, changes in economic status explain 5% of the improvement in graduation rates of the 1994 cohort, compared to the 1991 cohort; a decline in pre-eighth-grade retentions explains an additional 36%; the number of courses attempted at age 16 an additional 11%; and credits earned explain an additional 47%.]

16. In general, students and teachers evaluated these programs very positively, and they seem to have been effective in raising students' test scores in the short term (Roderick, Engel, & Nagaoka, 2003).

17. Students may have tried harder on the eighth-grade test than in previous years, and they likely received special instruction in how to take the test, inflating their eighth-grade score. To more accurately represent students' true achievement levels at the end of the eighth grade, each student's history of performance on the ITBS was used to adjust their eighth-grade score for unusually high or low performance, given their performance on previous tests. A two-level HLM, nesting years within students, was used to determine each student's learning trajectory from grade three to grade eight. Before running the HLM, students' test scores were equated through Rasch analysis to remove form and level effects (Bryk, Thum, Easton, & Luppescu, 1998, pp. 13–17). Level 1 in the HLM model included variables representing students' learning trajectory (grade, grade-squared) that were allowed to vary across students. There was also a dummy variable representing a repeated year in the same grade, to adjust for learning that occurred the sec-

ond time in a grade, and a different dummy variable for repeating the eighth-grade year so that additional learning that occurred when eighth grade was repeated could be added into a student's latent score. Separate models were run for each cohort of first-time eighth-grade students in CPS, separately for reading and math. Math and reading achievement were combined into one measure of overall achievement by averaging the latent reading and math scores, after standardizing them across all cohorts. For further details on these models, see Miller, Allensworth, and Kochanek (2002).

18. Some of the decline in dropout rates is explained by changing demographic and economic conditions in Chicago public schools, but the rise in achievement explains most of the decline. Once changes in achievement and retention rates are controlled, there are no significant differences across cohorts in dropout rates. For details, see Allensworth (2004).

19. There were a number of improvements in high school outcomes at the end of the 1990s, including improvements in course failure rates, high school test scores, likelihood of being on-track to graduate at the end of the ninth grade, and graduation and dropout rates. These are largely explained by improvements in incoming achievement among students entering CPS high schools (Miller, Allensworth, & Kochanek, 2002).

20. See Bryk (2003) for elaboration of this theory.

21. Fewer students were retained in the 1998 cohort because ITBS scores were much higher than in preceding cohorts, and because there was an increase in policy waivers and exemptions for special education status.

22. Some postpolicy students would have been retained even without the promotion standard, and their dropout rates would be more similar to those of students retained pre-policy. The estimates of the effect of retention from the promotion standard are adjusted to take out the effects of retention that would have occurred regardless of the standard.

23. Pre-policy, the relationship between retention in the eighth grade (teacher-initiated) and dropping out was 2.4 times the size of the relationship of postpolicy retention (test-based).

24. Because more students in the 1998–1999 cohort were excluded from test reporting (i.e., classified into special education) than in previous cohorts, some of the improvements seen in this cohort's average achievement may be a result of selection bias. Without any adjustments for potential selection bias, the rise in achievement should have produced a decline in dropout rates of 6.1 percentage points among retained students. When adjusted for the maximum possible selection effect, the estimate of the achievement effect is just 3.5 percentage points. The true effect is likely between the two estimates.

25. Students who exit the bilingual program at earlier ages tend to have higher achievement than those who exit later. Therefore, to compare English-language learners to other students, it is necessary to identify students in the bilingual program in the primary grades, before many students exit. Information on bilingual program participation is only available beginning in spring 1994, when most of the 1998 cohort was in third grade and few bilingual students would have exited the program. Most students in earlier cohorts would have completed at least three years of school by spring 1994, and the higher-achieving bilingual students would have exited the program before being identified as English-language learners.

26. The log-odds of being retained in eighth grade were predicted in a logistic regression equation with variables representing social status and poverty. The bilingual coefficient was reduced by 18 percent, compared to a model without control variables. The social

status and poverty variables were constructed from 1990 Census data on block groups. The social status variable used data on 1) the percentage of adults in the block group working as managers, professionals or executives; and 2) the average level of education of adults. The poverty variable used data on: 1) the percentage of males unemployed for the year; and 2) the percentage of families under the poverty line. Variables representing free/ reduced price lunch status were not used as almost all students in CPS are eligible, and this indicator provides no discrimination among them.

27. Most eighth-grade exemptions were based on students' classification as eligible for special education services. Special education classification of bilingual students is often problematic; see Heubert and Hauser (1999) for a review of some of the issues. But differences in special education exemptions in the 1998–1999 cohort might also have occurred because some bilingual-program students were exempt from the sixth-grade standard for bilingual program participation. Students who failed the sixth-grade standard were more likely to be classified into special education than other students. Additionally, even after controlling for social status, test scores, inclusion in test reporting, and age at grade 13, bilingual Latino students still showed a greater likelihood of being held back in eighth grade than nonbilingual Latino students. A number of reasons for this difference could be hypothesized; for example, parents who do not speak English may have had more difficulty requesting waivers from the policy for their children. Additional research is necessary on this issue.

28. As with African American students, these improvements can be explained by a decline in students held back in the elementary grades and by improvements in credit accumulation in high school. In addition, Latino and white students also showed improvements in economic status that contributed slightly to improvements in dropout and graduation rates.

29. The 24 percent figure is calculated only from those students whose scores were included in test reporting, who would have been held to the test score cutoff by the policy.

30. Controlling for race, SES (poverty and social status in students' block groups), achievement adjusted for testing effects, and age, the odds of dropping out by age 18 were 1.54 times higher for students retained at eighth-grade postpolicy than for students who were not retained.

31. Only the 1995 cohort can be followed until age 21 to determine eventual dropout rates. In this cohort, 54 percent of the students still enrolled in school at age 19 received a CPS diploma within the next two years.

32. There are large compositional effects on dropping out, so that a student who goes to a school with large numbers of low-achieving students is more likely to drop out than if the same student went to a school with fewer low-achieving students (Roderick, Allensworth, & Nagaoka, 2004).

33. Only about half of first-time high school students in CPS receive enough credits in their first year to be on-track to graduate in four years (Miller, Allensworth, & Kochanek, 2002).

34. Postpolicy gains in reading scores in eighth grade were highest among students at risk for retention, but the opposite was true in math—gains were highest among students not at risk of retention. In both subjects, students in all risk categories showed higher gains than among pre-policy cohorts (Roderick, Jacob, & Bryk, 2002). Furthermore, the rise in eighth-grade test scores was due not only to gains in the eighth-grade year, but also to gains in test scores in earlier years when students were not immediately at risk of being retained for low test scores.

REFERENCES

Alexander, K. L., Entwisle D., & Kabbani, N. S. (2001). The dropout process in life course perspective: Early risk factors at home and school. *Teachers College Record, 10,* 760–822.

Alexander, K. L., Entwisle D., & Horsey C. S. (1997). From first grade forward: Early foundations of high school dropout. *Sociology of Education, 70,* 87–107.

Allensworth, E. M. (2004). *Ending social promotion: Dropout rates in Chicago after implementation of the eighth-grade promotion gate.* Chicago: Consortium on Chicago School Research. Available online at http://www.consortium-chicago.org/publications/p69.html.

Beatty, A., Neisser, U., Trent, W. T., & Heubert, J. P. (Eds.). (2001). *Understanding dropouts: Statistics, strategies, and high-stakes testing. Committee on educational excellence and testing equity.* Washington, D.C.: National Academy Press.

Bryk, A. S. (2003). No child left behind, Chicago style. In P. E. Peterson & M. R. West (Eds.), *No child left behind? The politics and practice of school accountability.* Washington DC: Brookings Institution.

Bryk, A. S., Thum, Y. M., Easton J. Q., & Luppescu, S. (1998). *Academic productivity of Chicago public elementary schools: A technical report sponsored by the consortium on Chicago school research.* Chicago: Consortium on Chicago School Research.

Byrnes, D. B. (1989). Attitudes of students, parents, and educators toward repeating a grade. In L. A. Shepard & M. L. Smith (Eds.), *Flunking grades: Research and policies on retention* (pp. 108–130). New York: Falmer Press.

Cameron, S. V., & Heckman, J. J. (1993). The nonequivalence of high school equivalents. *Journal of Labor Economics, 11,* 1–47.

Campbell, J R. (1993). Failing students: A qualitative study of the grade retention experience for seventh graders. In *Phi Delta Kappa 1993 outstanding doctoral dissertation awards* (pp. 26–36). Bloomington, IN: Phi Delta Kappa.

Dworkin, A. G., Lorence, J., Toenjes L. A., Hill, A. N., Perez, N., & Thomas, M. (1999). *Elementary school retention and social promotion in Texas: An assessment of students who failed the reading section of the TAAS.* Houston: University of Houston, Sociology of Education Research Group.

Finn, J. D. (1989). Withdrawing from school. *Review of Educational Research, 59,* 117–142.

Grissom, J. B., & Shepard, L. A. (1989). In L. A. Shepard & M. L. Smith (Eds.), *Repeating and dropping out of school. Flunking grades: Research and policies on retention* (pp. 34–63). New York: Falmer Press.

Heubert, J. P., & Hauser, R. M. (Eds.). (1999). *High stakes: Testing for tracking, promotion and graduation.* Washington, DC: National Academy Press.

Holmes, C. T., & Saturday, J. (2000). Promoting the end of retention. *Journal of Curriculum and Supervision, 15,* 300–314.

Holmes, C. T. (1989). Grade level retention effects: A meta-analysis of research studies. In L. A. Shepard & M. L. Smith (Eds.), *Flunking grades: Research and policies on retention* (pp. 16–33). New York: Falmer Press.

House, E. R. (1998). *The predictable failure of Chicago's student retention program.* Boulder: University of Colorado School of Education.

Klein, S. P., Hamilton, L. S., McCaffrey, D. F., & Stecher, B. M. (2000). *What do test scores in Texas tell us?* Rand education issue paper. Available online at http://www.rand.org/publications/IP/IP202/.

Miller, S. R., Allensworth, E. M., & Kochanek, J. R. (2002). *Student performance: Course taking, test scores, and outcomes.* Chicago: Consortium on Chicago School Research.

Pallas, A. M. (1987). *School dropouts in the United States.* Washington, DC: Center for Education Statistics.

Rabinowitz, S., Zimmerman, J., & Sherman, K. (2001). *Do high stakes tests drive up student dropout rates? Myths versus reality.* San Francisco: West Ed.

Roderick, M., & Engel, M. (2001). The grasshopper and the ant: Motivational responses of low-achieving students to high-stakes testing. *Educational Evaluation and Policy Analysis, 23,* 197–227.

Roderick, M. (1994). Grade retention and school dropout: Investigating the association. *American Educational Research Journal, 31,* 729–759.

Roderick, M., Allensworth, E. M., & Nagaoka, J. (2004). *How do we get large urban high schools to care about dropout rates, and will No Child Left Behind help or hurt?* Paper presented at the conference, Developmental, Economic and Policy Perspectives on the Federal No Child Left Behind Act, Center for Human Potential and Public Policy, University of Chicago, Chicago. Available online at http://harrisschool.uchicago.edu/chppp/springconference04/pdf/roderick.pdf.

Roderick, M., Bryk, A. S., Jacob, B. A., Easton, J. Q., & Allensworth, E. (1999). *Ending social promotion: Results from the first two years.* Chicago: Consortium on Chicago School Research.

Roderick, M., Engel, M., & Nagaoka, J. (2003). *Ending social promotion: Results from Summer Bridge.* Chicago: Consortium on Chicago School Research.

Roderick, M., Jacob, B., & Bryk, A. S. (2002). The impact of high-stakes testing in Chicago on student achievement in promotional gate grades. *Educational Evaluation and Policy Analysis, 24,* 333–357.

Rosenkranz, T. (2002). *2001 CPS test trend review: Iowa Tests of Basic Skills.* Chicago: Consortium on Chicago School Research.

Rumberger, R. W. (1995). Dropping out of middle school: A multilevel analysis of students and schools. *American Educational Research Journal, 32,* 583–625.

CHAPTER 8

Accountability and the Grade 9 to 10 Transition: The Impact on Attrition and Retention Rates

LISA ABRAMS

WALT HANEY

Close to 100 years ago, in a book titled *Laggards in Our Schools: A Study of Retardation and Elimination in City School Systems,* Leonard Ayres wrote:

> No standard which may be applied to a school system as a measure of accomplishment is more significant than that which tells us what proportion of the pupils who enter the first grade succeed in reaching the final grade. (1909, p. 8)

Nearly a century later, rates of student progress through elementary and secondary school have continued to be recognized as indicators of the quality of education systems and as measures of student academic achievement. However, the rate at which students progress through the K–12 public school education pipeline may not always be steady or seamless. In the current era of high standards and accountability, a growing number of states tie decisions about grade promotion and graduation to student test performance on state-mandated exams. As a result, student progress through the grades may be slowed or even stalled by failure to meet test-performance requirements. In addition to the push to raise expectations, state education reform policies typically call for the end of social promotion—the practice of allowing students to advance to the next grade without having mastered the prerequisite cognitive skills or subject matter. Although these policies rely on appealing logic, rooted in the belief that students should have the necessary skills before moving on to the next grade, half a decade of research indicates that retaining or holding back students in grade bears little to no academic benefit and contributes to future academic failure by significantly increasing the likelihood that retained students will drop out of high school (Jimerson, 2001; Owings & Magliaro, 1998; Shepard & Smith, 1989).

In this chapter, we present the results of analyses of grade enrollment data for the last several decades, both nationally (1968–2000) and for all 50 states (1984–2000), in an effort to assess the progress public school students are making as they advance through the education pipeline from kindergarten through high school graduation. We focus our discussion in particular on the transition from grade 9 to grade 10. We have relied on enrollment data because state-reported dropout statistics are often unreliable, and most states do not regularly report grade-retention data, that is, data on the rates at which students are held back to repeat grades. Therefore, the only way to study long-term rates of student progress through elementary-secondary education systems is to examine data on grade enrollments over time.

These analyses allow us to examine the education pipeline in the United States in order to identify key transition points through which students progress, or fail to progress, by calculating the percent loss or gain of students from one academic year to the next. This chapter describes the data used and methods by which enrollment data have been analyzed before presenting the results. The results show that over the last 30 years, attrition between grades 9 and 10 has increased, resulting in a growing "bulge" of students in grade 9, especially in the last decade. Taken together, these two trends suggest that progressing from grade 9 to grade 10 is becoming increasingly difficult for substantial numbers of students, particularly those in states that have implemented high-stakes tests. Each of these trends will be discussed in turn. The chapter ends with a discussion of causes and consequences of changes in the education pipeline in the United States over the last three decades, focusing particularly on the influence of test-based accountability programs.

DATA AND METHODS

The data used in the analyses in this chapter are the numbers of students enrolled in public schools by grade for each academic year and the numbers of students graduating each academic year. These data are available from the *Digest of Education Statistics* (DES), a report issued annually by the National Center for Education Statistics (NCES) since 1962, and the Common Core of Data (CCD), a federal repository of education statistics.

To examine patterns of student progress through the education pipeline, we have conducted cohort progression analyses. These analyses are used to address questions such as, Of 1,000 students enrolled in grade 9 in 1990–1991, how many progressed to grade 10 in 1991–1992? We have examined such year-to-year "grade-to-grade" rates of progress for 13 transition points, from kindergarten through grade 12 and to graduation. We conducted cohort progression analyses for such year-to-year transitions, nationally from 1968–1969 to 2000–2001, and for all 50 states from 1984–1985 through 2000–2001. Before presenting results, we provide an example to make the approach we use as clear as possible. Table 1 shows the enrollments for U.S. public schools for kindergarten through grade 12 for 1968–1969 through 1972–1973. The bottom half of Table 1 shows enrollments for grades 1 through 12 for 1969–1970 through 1972–1973 in terms of the percentage increases or decreases as compared with enrollments in the previous grade the previous year. For example, in 1969–1970 there were 3.86 million enrolled in grade 1, or 53 percent more than the 2.53 million enrolled in kindergarten in 1968–1969. We have conducted cohort progression analyses for the U.S. and for all 50 states.

INCREASING ATTRITION BETWEEN GRADES 9 AND 10

The first major finding from our cohort progression analyses is that the rate at which students disappear between grades 9 and 10 has *tripled* over the last 30 years. Figure 1 shows the percent fewer students enrolled nationally in grade 10 than in grade 9 the previous year. As shown, during the first half of the 1970s less than 4 percent fewer students were enrolled in grade 10 than in grade 9 the previous year. Attrition or loss between grades 9 and 10 started increasing in the late 1970s and accelerated from the mid-1980s onward. By the turn of the century there were nearly 12 percent fewer students enrolled in grade 10 than in grade 9 the previous year. To provide some sense of the numbers of students being lost between grades 9 and 10, in 1998–1999 there were 3.86 million students enrolled in grade 9, but in 1999–2000 there were 3.42 million enrolled in grade 10. The difference, 440,000 students, means that 11.4 percent of ninth graders in 1998–1999 did not show up as enrolled in grade 10 in 1999–2000. In short, by the end of the century the grade 9 to 10 transition was clearly the largest leak in the education pipeline. This was not the case 30 years ago. As the data in Table 1 indicate, three decades ago far more students were lost between grades 11 and 12 than between 9 and 10. In subsequent sections of this chapter we discuss why students may be leaving or dropping out of high school earlier, but first we summarize the results of state-level analyses of student attrition between grades 9 and 10.

Analyses of enrollment data at the state level reveal that there has long been substantial variation in rates of student attrition between grades 9 and 10. Between 1984–1985 and 1985–1986, when the rate of attrition between grades 9

TABLE 1

U.S. Public School Enrollment, Kindergarten to Grade 12,
1968–1969 to 1972–1973 (in 1000s)

Grade/Year	68–69	69–70	70–71	71–72	72–73
K	2526	2601	2559	2483	2487
1st grade	3923	3858	3814	3570	3352
2nd grade	3765	3714	3654	3587	3383
3rd grade	3694	3721	3662	3612	3533
4th grade	3629	3660	3676	3623	3554
5th grade	3570	3619	3634	3662	3597
6th grade	3556	3565	3599	3622	3639
7th grade	3552	3665	3662	3710	3713
8th grade	3420	3515	3601	3635	3649
9th grade	3508	3567	3652	3781	3779
10th grade	3310	3408	3457	3571	3648
11th grade	2987	3051	3127	3200	3247
12th grade	2655	2733	2774	2862	2871

Percentage increase or decrease from previous grade the previous year

	69–70	70–71	71–72	72–73
1st grade	52.7%	46.6%	39.5%	35.0%
2nd grade	−5.3%	−5.3%	−6.0%	−5.2%
3rd grade	−1.2%	−1.4%	−1.1%	−1.5%
4th grade	−0.9%	−1.2%	−1.1%	−1.6%
5th grade	−0.3%	−0.7%	−0.4%	−0.7%
6th grade	−0.1%	−0.6%	−0.3%	−0.6%
7th grade	3.1%	2.7%	3.1%	2.5%
8th grade	−1.0%	−1.7%	−0.7%	−1.6%
9th grade	4.3%	3.9%	5.0%	4.0%
10th grade	−2.9%	−3.1%	−2.2%	−3.5%
11th grade	−7.8%	−8.2%	−7.4%	−9.1%
12th grade	−8.5%	−9.1%	−8.5%	−10.3%

and 10 nationally stood at a little less than 5 percent, six states had attrition rates of 10 percent or more (Georgia, 16.5%; Texas, 14.9%; Louisiana, 13.2%; South Carolina, 11.5%; Kentucky, 11.2%; Virginia, 10.0%), but ten states showed grade 9 to 10 attrition rates of less than 2 percent (California, Minnesota, Nebraska, Nevada, Utah, Kansas, Wyoming, South Dakota, Hawaii, and Wisconsin).

FIGURE 1

National Public School Enrollment, Percentage Fewer Students in Grade 10
Than in Grade 9 the Previous Year, 1969–1970 to 2000–2001

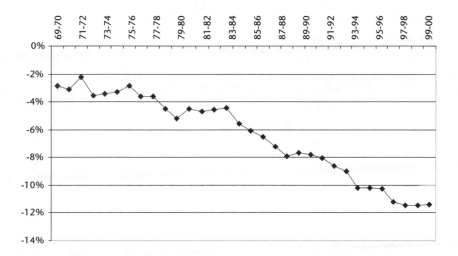

By the end of the century, however, the list of states with grade 9 to grade 10 attrition rates of more than 10 percent had more than tripled. Table 2 lists the 21 states with the highest rates of attrition between 1999–2000 and 2000–2001. Since the number of states with grade 9 to grade 10 attrition rates of more than 10 percent had more than tripled between the mid-1980s and the end of the century, it is hardly surprising that the national rate had more than doubled during the same interval, from less than 5 percent to more than 11 percent.

The Growing Bulge in Grade 9 Enrollment

The increasing rate of attrition between grades 9 and 10 may be explained in part by the second key finding from our analyses of enrollment data—that there has been a sharp increase in the "bulge" of students enrolled in grade 9 during the last 30 years.

Figure 2 shows how enrollments have been "bulging up" in grade 9. As this figure illustrates, during the 1970s there were only 4–6 percent more students enrolled in grade 9 than in grade 8 the previous year. However, beginning in the mid-1980s, this percentage began to climb sharply, so that by the end of the century there were about 13 percent more students enrolled in public schools nationally in grade 9 than in grade 8 the previous year. This means that, in the

TABLE 2

States with the Highest Attrition Rates between Grades 9 and 10,
1999–2000 to 2000–2001

State	Grade 9 to 10 Attrition Rate 1999–2000 to 2000–2001
Florida	–23.8%
South Carolina	–22.7%
Georgia	–20.3%
Texas	–20.0%
Nevada	–18.8%
North Carolina	–18.0%
Louisiana	–17.3%
Hawaii	–15.9%
Alabama	–15.0%
Mississippi	–14.4%
New York	–13.9%
Tennessee	–13.9%
Kentucky	–13.4%
New Mexico	–13.1%
Alaska	–12.6%
Delaware	–12.4%
Maryland	–11.3%
Ohio	–11.0%
Massachusetts	–10.7%
Michigan	–10.6%
Rhode Island	–10.2%

last 30 years, the bulge of students in grade 9 has more than tripled, from around 4 percent to 13 percent.

This combination of increasing attrition of students between grades 9 and 10, and increasingly more students enrolled in grade 9 relative to grade 8, is surely a reflection of the fact that more students nationally were being held back to repeat grade 9. This pattern bodes ill for future graduation rates, because research suggests that retaining students to repeat a grade is not a sound educational strategy and contributes to the likelihood that these students will drop out of high school (Shepard & Smith, 1989). Indeed, recent evidence from Texas and other states indicates that 70–80 percent of students who are required to repeat grade 9 will not persist in high school to graduation (Haney, 2001). Other research suggests that retained students are two to 11 times more

FIGURE 2

Percentage More Students Enrolled in Grade 9 Than in Grade 8 the Previous
Year, U.S. Public Schools, 1969–1970 to 2000–2001

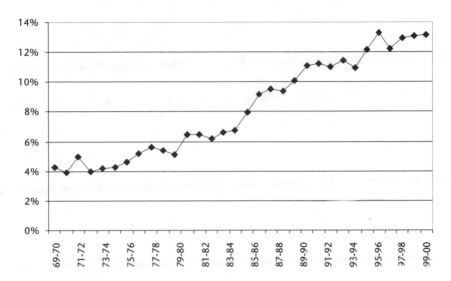

likely to drop out of high school (Roderick, 1994). In the next section we explore the impact of state testing policies on these trends by comparing results among states with high- and low-stakes testing programs, but we first summarize evidence from state-level analyses of the grade 9 "bulge."

Analyses of state-level enrollment data from 1984–1985 to 2000–2001 indicate that the grade 9 bulge, like attrition between grades 9 and 10, has long varied across the states. As of 1985–1986, one state, New York, had 20 percent more students enrolled in grade 9 than in grade 8 the previous year, and seven states (California, Delaware, Florida, Georgia, Hawaii, Michigan, and Wisconsin) had a grade 9 bulge of 10–13 percent. In contrast, in 1985–1986, 22 states had grade 9 bulges of less than 5 percent.

By the end of the century, however, this pattern had changed dramatically. By 2000–2001 more than half the states had 10 percent or more students enrolled in grade 9 than in grade 8 the previous year, and *seven* states had grade 9 bulges of 20 percent or more. Table 3 lists the 26 states with the largest grade 9 "bulges" as of 2000–2001. In contrast, by the end of the century just eight states (Michigan, South Dakota, Montana, North Dakota, Utah, Wyoming, Arkansas, and Maine) had a grade 9 bulge of less than 5 percent. This sharp reversal—more than double the number of states with grade 9 bulges of more

TABLE 3

States with Largest Bulge in Grade 9 Enrollments 2000–2001
Relative to Grade 8 Enrollment 1999–2000

State	Percentage More Students in Grade 9 in 2000–2001 than in Grade 8 in 1999–2000
Florida	32%
South Carolina	24%
Nevada	24%
New York	21%
Hawaii	21%
Kentucky	20%
Texas	20%
Georgia	19%
Delaware	19%
North Carolina	16%
Virginia	16%
Wisconsin	15%
New Mexico	14%
Maryland	14%
Washington	13%
California	13%
Colorado	12%
Ohio	11%
Pennsylvania	11%
Illinois	11%
Rhode Island	11%
Connecticut	10%
Tennessee	10%
Massachusetts	10%
Michigan	10%
Alaska	10%

than 10 percent, and a fall in the number of states with bulges of less than 5 percent from 22 to 8—is a clear sign that far more states were requiring far more students to repeat grade 9 by the end of the century than in the mid-1980s.

COMPARISON AMONG HIGH- AND LOW-STAKES STATES

In this section, we compare the grade 9 to 10 attrition rate and grade 9 "bulge rate" across the states in terms of states' testing programs—specifically, by high-stakes and low-stakes testing policies. Before exploring patterns according to the type of testing program, we summarize the current testing landscape. Current testing policies grew out of standards-based reform begun in the early 1990s. This initiative called for a rigorous and demanding curriculum that, in addition to requiring students to demonstrate their command of basic content knowledge, also asked them to exhibit higher-level cognitive processes (e.g., application, problem-solving, and inquiry). The shift from basic skills to high standards has given rise to the current state-level accountability systems designed to hold schools, administrators, and teachers (and sometimes students) responsible for meeting these raised expectations. These systems have four main components: 1) content standards that communicate the desired content knowledge and skills; 2) tests that measure progress toward achieving the content standards; 3) performance targets that identify criteria used to determine whether schools, students, or both have reached the desired level of achievement; and 4) incentives, such as the consequences (rewards and sanctions), or stakes, that reinforce the attainment of performance targets.

Over the last decade, test-based accountability systems have become widespread; every state except Iowa has instituted curricular standards or frameworks.[1] Moreover, every state uses a test to measure the degree to which students have mastered the knowledge and skills expressed in these standards (Edwards, 2004). While on the surface it might appear that state testing policies are becoming increasingly similar, there are substantial differences in test content, item format, and how test results are used, especially for accountability purposes. For example, Kentucky, Vermont, and Washington use test results to hold schools accountable. In New York, Massachusetts, Texas, Virginia, and Florida, test results are used to make highly consequential decisions at both the school and student levels (Edwards, 2004).

The focus on state assessment requirements was further emphasized in the 2001 reauthorization of the Elementary and Secondary Education Act (ESEA), known more commonly as the No Child Left Behind Act (NCLB). This far-reaching legislation sought to raise the level of achievement for all students and to reduce the gaps in performance between students from different backgrounds. At the heart of NCLB are the assessment and accountability requirements, which will substantially increase the extent to which students are tested. The implementation of NCLB has expanded a majority of current state assessment programs, requiring testing at more grade levels. The federal law requires that states annually administer reading and math tests to all students in grades 3–8, and in one year between grades 9 and 12, starting in 2005–2006. This requirement affects at least 25 million students annually. Arguably, NCLB is one of the most aggressive federal efforts to improve elementary and secondary education and marks a major departure from the traditionally noninterventionist role of the federal government in forming state education policy.

The NCLB law includes school accountability provisions; however, states still retain the authority to determine how, or if, students will be held responsible for test performance. As such, the subsequent discussion focuses on the use of test results for purposes of student accountability. To illustrate the potential impact of high-stakes testing programs on rates of student attrition and retention, we compare grade progression analyses for high- and low-stakes states. Highly consequential, or high-stakes, uses of test results for students include decisions about grade promotion and graduation. Low-stakes states are those that do not use test scores to hold students accountable for test performance.

Of the 21 states with the highest rates of attrition between grades 9 and 10 (see Table 2), all but four (Hawaii, Kentucky, Michigan, and Rhode Island) have high-stakes testing policies and use state test scores to make decisions about grade promotion and high school graduation (Edwards, 2004). Similarly, of the 26 states listed in Table 3 with the largest bulges in grade 9 enrollments relative to grade 8 the previous year, the majority (16) have high-stakes statewide assessments (Edwards, 2004). To identify the most current information about how states are using test results for accountability purposes, we relied on *Education Week*'s annual reports on state education systems, which document state-level student accountability practices (Edwards, 2001, 2002, 2003, 2004).

In order to show how the grade 9 enrollment patterns differ by the severity of sanctions tied to test performance, we report comparisons of grade progression results for high- and low-stakes states. Since it is not possible to present grade-level enrollment analyses for all of the states, we have selected six large states (Florida, Louisiana, New Mexico, New York, North Carolina, and Texas) that have been classified consistently in several studies as having high stakes (Amrein & Berliner, 2002a, 2002b; Clarke et al., 2003; Pedulla et al., 2003). For comparison, the low-stakes states will include five states (Connecticut, Kentucky, Iowa, Oklahoma, and Pennsylvania) having relatively few or no stakes attached to test results (Amrein & Berliner, 2002a; Edwards, 2001). Michigan is a more ambiguous case, but since it did not have high stakes for students as classified by Amrein and Berliner (2002a), Clarke et al. (2003), and Pedulla et al. (2003), we will treat it here as a relatively low-stakes case.

As shown in Table 4, the rates at which students are lost between grades 9 and 10 are much greater for high- than low-stakes states on average. By 2000–2001 the attrition rates for the high-stakes states ranged between −13.07 and −23.8 percent. In contrast, for low-stakes states the rates ranged between −3.5 and −13.45 percent—a rate just slightly higher than that of New Mexico, the state with the lowest rate of attrition among the high-stakes states. In addi-

TABLE 4

High- v. Low-Stakes States: Percentage Loss Between Grade 9 and Grade 10 from One Year to the Next, 1986–1987 to 2000–2001

	1986–87	1988–89	1990–91	1992–93	1994–95	1996–97	1998–99	2000–01
High-Stakes States								
Florida	−7.7%	−8.6%	−7.9%	−8.7%	−10.3%	−11.7%	−15.8%	−23.8%
Texas	−14.3%	−15.6%	−17.0%	−18.0%	−20.9%	−21.3%	−21.5%	−20.0%
North Carolina	−7.6%	−9.1%	−10.7%	−11.1%	−13.5%	−15.3%	−18.4%	−18.0%
Louisiana	−13.8%	−14.3%	−17.4%	−16.5%	−17.4%	−19.9%	−18.6%	−17.3%
New York	−4.3%	−7.4%	−7.5%	−7.8%	−9.9%	−12.1%	−13.6%	−13.9%
New Mexico	−5.1%	−7.7%	−7.2%	−6.7%	−11.9%	−13.4%	−12.1%	−13.1%
Low-Stakes States								
Kentucky	−10.3%	−10.0%	−9.1%	−9.4%	−11.0%	−13.6%	−14.4%	−13.4%
Michigan	−10.3%	−10.8%	−11.5%	−11.6%	−13.5%	−6.6%	−10.3%	−10.6%
Oklahoma	−6.5%	−5.5%	−4.9%	−4.6%	−7.1%	−8.0%	−7.2%	−8.7%
Connecticut	1.8%	−8.3%	−6.0%	−7.1%	−7.4%	−9.1%	−9.7%	−7.7%
Pennsylvania	−5.0%	−6.4%	−6.7%	−7.1%	−8.4%	−9.1%	−8.5%	−7.4%
Iowa	−4.1%	−3.2%	−2.8%	−2.8%	−2.0%	−2.7%	−2.8%	−3.5%

tion, these rates increased more sharply between 1986–1987 and 2000–2001 for high-stakes states than for low-stakes states. Florida and New York had the most dramatic increases in attrition rates from grade 9 to 10 during this interval. In both states, the rate at which students were lost by 2000–2001 had increased to almost four times the 1986–1987 rate (Florida, 7.66% to –23.8%; New York, 4.27% to –13.9%). Furthermore, the attrition rates for North Carolina and New Mexico nearly tripled during this same time period (North Carolina, 7.63% to –17.98%; New Mexico, 5.13% to 13.07%). By comparison, the change in the percent loss between grades 9 and 10 for the low-stakes states was not nearly as striking as for the high-stakes states. In several cases the rate of attrition remained fairly stable, with only minor increases from year to year. If the anomalous results for Connecticut in 1986–1987 are discounted, grade progression analyses indicate that, among the low-stakes states, Kentucky had the greatest change in the attrition rate, with an increase of roughly 3.10 percent between 1986–1987 (–10.35%) and 2000–2001 (–13.45%).

Patterns similar to those found for high- and low-stakes rates of attrition are evident for the grade 9 bulge rates (see Table 5). Compared to low-stakes states, the grade 9 bulge rate is higher and increased more rapidly for high-stakes states between 1986–1987 and 2000–2001. By the end of the twentieth century, enrollment in grade 9 was between 14 percent and 31.5 percent more than in grade 8 the previous year among high-stakes states (excluding the irregular pattern for Louisiana in 2000–2001). In contrast, the bulge rate for low-stakes states ranged between a low of 5.7 percent and a high of 20.4 percent. Although the grade 9 bulge is evident among states without high-stakes testing, it does not exist to the same degree as in high-stakes states. Compared to the grade 9 to 10 attrition rates of high-stakes states, the increase in the bulge rates in low-stakes states from 1986–1987 to 2000–2001 are not as dramatic, yet they are still sizable. For example, the grade 9 bulge rate in Florida almost tripled during this interval—from a low of 11.8 percent in 1986–1987 to a high of 31.5 percent in 2000–2001—indicating that in the 2000–2001 academic year there were almost one-third more students enrolled in grade 9 than were enrolled in grade 8 during 1999–2000. Similar increases are evident in North Carolina, where the grade 9 bulge rate was 7 percent in 1986–1987 and 16.4 percent in 2000–2001. In contrast, the grade 9 bulge rate for New York and Louisiana remained fairly constant throughout this time interval, with periodic fluctuations during the mid-1990s.

With the exception of Michigan, the grade 9 bulge rates among the low-stakes states increased slowly but steadily from 1986–1987 to 2000–2001. Kentucky had the largest increase, with a near tripling of the grade 9 bulge rate in that period. Connecticut had the smallest rate of increase (2.2%) over the same

TABLE 5

High- v. Low-Stakes States' Grade 9 Bulge: Percentage Gain from Grade 8 to Grade 9 from One Year to the Next, 1986–1987 to 2000–2001

	1986–87	1988–89	1990–91	1992–93	1994–95	1996–97	1998–99	2000–01
High-Stakes States								
Florida	11.8%	12.6%	16.1%	14.0%	16.0%	18.1%	23.3%	31.5%
New York	20.8%	17.6%	20.2%	21.1%	20.6%	24.5%	25.8%	21.3%
Texas	11.8%	12.8%	15.1%	17.1%	17.9%	20.7%	19.9%	19.9%
North Carolina	7.0%	7.5%	10.3%	11.6%	13.3%	20.1%	16.9%	16.4%
New Mexico	9.6%	11.6%	13.1%	14.6%	14.7%	15.5%	15.2%	14.3%
Louisiana	16.0%	11.2%	13.5%	15.5%	21.4%	18.0%	14.5%	-3.2%
Low–Stakes States								
Kentucky	7.7%	8.8%	10.2%	9.5%	8.7%	11.8%	11.1%	20.4%
Pennsylvania	8.6%	7.5%	11.5%	14.1%	13.2%	11.8%	9.8%	11.2%
Connecticut	8.3%	6.2%	7.2%	8.6%	9.6%	9.9%	10.4%	10.5%
Michigan	11.9%	11.6%	12.1%	9.8%	10.0%	16.6%	11.2%	9.7%
Iowa	3.4%	4.9%	4.9%	4.8%	5.3%	5.6%	8.3%	7.1%
Oklahoma	1.8%	2.8%	2.8%	4.9%	5.8%	5.5%	4.8%	5.7%

time span, from 8.3 percent to 10.5 percent. On average, the rate of increase among low-stakes states was not nearly as dramatic as for the high-stakes states. In 1986–1987 the grade 9 bulge rate ranged from a low of 1.8 percent (Oklahoma) to a high of 11.9 percent (Michigan). Approximately 15 years later, the rate ranged from a low of 5.7 percent (Oklahoma) to a high of 20.4 percent (Kentucky).

The results in Tables 4 and 5 suggest that clear differences exist between high- and low-stakes states, suggesting that the transition from grade 9 to grade 10 is considerably more difficult in states with high-stakes testing programs than in states that do not use tests scores to make graduation and grade promotion decisions. While the grade 9 bulge patterns indicate that retention is apparent in both low- and high-stakes states, the rate at which students are getting held back is much greater in states with high- rather than low-stakes testing programs.

LIMITATIONS OF GRADE PROGRESSION ANALYSES

Before discussing the causes and consequences of the increasing rates of grade 9 to 10 attrition and grade 9 bulge rates, it is necessary to describe several limitations of the grade-level enrollment-based progression analyses. Cohort progression analyses of the sort discussed so far do not take into account four ways students may disappear from their cohorts or classes from one year to the next, other than being held back in grade or dropping out of school. First, students may die. Second, they may move out of the state or country. Third, they may move out of public schools into nonpublic schools. Fourth, they may be withdrawn from public schools to be schooled at home via what has come to be called homeschooling. In subsequent portions of this section we discuss each of these possibilities.

Mortality

In theory, one possible cause for students disappearing from one grade one year and the next grade the next year is that they may die. However, statistics on mortality rates indicate that deaths of young people could have only a very small impact on results of cohort progression analyses. Death rates in the United States have been falling for some decades. As of 2000, the rate of death for the general population was 873 per 100,000, or 0.87 percent. For school-age populations, however, death rates were much, much lower: for those ages 5–9, it was 16 per 100,000; ages 10–14 years, 21 per 100,000; and ages 15–19, 68 per 100,000. Since the mortality rates for the school-age population are so low—all less than one-tenth of one percent—outright death, even over a four-year period, is clearly not a major source of leaks in the education pipeline. Moreover, given that death rates for school-age children in the United States have dropped substantially over the last 20 years, this decreasing death rate for young people would, if anything, have been *decreasing* the leakage from the education pipeline over this interval.[2]

Migration

A second possible influence on the results of cohort progression analyses is migration. For example, instead of progressing from grade 9 to grade 10, or on to graduation, young people might leave the United States, or in the case of state-level analyses, move from one state to another. We have a special tabulation by the U.S. Census Bureau's 2000 results showing patterns of gross and net migration by age of the U.S. population by region and state. Since results for the total United States are simpler to explain, we start with the nation as a whole before dealing with migration at the state level.

According to Census 2000, the total population age five and older in 2000 was 262 million (U.S. Census Bureau, 2003). Of these, 7.5 million, or 2.9 percent, were immigrants who arrived within the previous five years. Immigration rates vary substantially by age, with the highest rates evident for the young adult age ranges of 20–24 and 25–29 (both more than 6%). For the elementary-secondary school-age ranges of 5–9, 10–14, and 15–20 years, immigrants as percentages of the age-group population were 2.8 percent, 2.5 percent, and 3.9 percent, respectively. We suspect that the latter is slightly higher because it includes 18- and 19-year-olds, many of whom were taking up U.S. residence to attend college.

So let us assume that the 2.5 percent rate is a reasonable estimate for immigration in the elementary-secondary school-age population between 1995 and 2000. Presuming that the immigration for the age group was spread out evenly over the period, this would imply an annual net immigration of 0.5 percent for elementary-secondary school-age children during the last half of the 1990s. What this implies is that immigration would have been contributing to *increases* rather than leakage in the education pipeline over this interval.

Dealing with migration in analyses at the state level is slightly more complex because we must deal not just with international, but also domestic migration; that is, with migration across states. Census 2000 also provides information on the patterns of gross and net migration from abroad and across states for individuals ages 10 to 14 for the high- and low-stakes states discussed in this chapter. Results indicate that most states had a small positive net in-migration of 10- to 14-year-old children between 1995 and 2000. However, two states had in-migrations of more than 5 percent (Florida, +6.8%, North Carolina, +6.3%).

Three states had small percentages of net out-migration, ranging from .4 percent to 1 percent (Louisiana, −.9%; New Mexico, −.4%; New York, −1.0%). The small net out-migration between 1995 and 2000 for these states may explain roughly one percent of the increasing rates of grade 9 retention and grade 9 to10 attrition. Conversely, for the states with positive net in-migration, we would expect that migration would have contributed to *decreases* in the leakage in the education pipeline between 1995 and 2000 (U.S. Census Bureau, 2003).

Private School Enrollments

A third possible cause of increasing leakage from the public education pipeline (specifically, sharp increases in attrition between grades 9 and 10) is that some students might be leaving public schools to enroll in private schools. By private schools we refer to all nonpublic schools, including Catholic schools, other religious schools, and nonsectarian private schools. In 1999, for example, there were about 8,000 Catholic schools, 13,000 other religious schools, and 6,000 nonsectarian schools in the United States (NCES, 2002, Table 59, p. 71).

One way of examining whether flow through the public school pipeline has been affected by patterns of enrollment in nonpublic schools is to look at enrollments in public versus private schools in grades 9 through 12 over the last three decades. The *Digest of Education Statistics 2002* reports the total enrollments in grades 9–12 in all schools, public and private, from 1970 to 2000 (see NCES 2002, Table 56, p. 69). Total enrollments in grades 9–12 have ebbed and flowed somewhat over the last three decades—from close to 15 million in 1970, ebbing to about 12.5 million in 1990, and increasing back up to almost 15 million in 2000. Enrollments in grades 9–12 in public schools have closely paralleled these totals. This is hardly surprising, since over the last three decades 90–92 percent of all students in grades 9–12 have been enrolled in public rather than private schools. In contrast, enrollments in private schools have been remarkably stable over the last 30 years, varying only between 1.15 and 1.40 million. As a percentage of total enrollments in grades 9–12, private school enrollments were at a high of just over 10 percent in the early 1980s and have declined to just under 9 percent in the late 1990s. This means that leakage from the public education pipeline clearly has not been caused by sharp increases in private school enrollments.

Homeschooling

A fourth and final possible way students may leave the public school pipeline is for homeschooling, that is, to be schooled at home instead of in public or private schools. Unfortunately, statistics on the homeschooling phenomenon are hard to find. Rudner (1999) estimates that in 1998 there were between 700,000 and 1.2 million students enrolled in home schools. More recently a homeschooling advocacy organization, the Home School Legal Defense Association, reported that the annual rate of growth in numbers of students being schooled at home in the last decade has been 7 percent to 15 percent. The same source estimates that as of the 2001–2002 school year there were between 1.7 and 2.2 million children in the United States being schooled at home.[3] Independent analysts, however, indicate that these estimates are somewhat inflated. Citing national survey data, Henke, Kaufman, and Broughman (2000) report that the number of homeschooled children in the United States was estimated at 345,000 in 1994 and 636,000 in 1996. Bielick, Chandler, and Broughman (2001) report that in spring 1999 an estimated 850,000 students nationwide were being homeschooled. They noted, however, that about 20 percent of homeschoolers were enrolled in public or private schools part-time. More recently, Bauman (2002) of the U.S. Census Bureau reports that the number of homeschooled children was well under one million in 1999, and that the growth rate from 1996 to 1999 was unlikely to have exceeded 15 percent per year. Both Bauman (2002) and Bielick, Chandler, and Broughman (2001) report data indicating that the number of homeschooled children is relatively evenly divided across the school-age years of 6 to 17.

Thus, it seems clear that fewer than 3 percent of children nationwide are being homeschooled (1 million divided by 42 million enrolled in public schools = 2.4%). There is some evidence that homeschooling increased over the last decade, so as a liberal estimate let us suppose that homeschooling had been increasing by 150,000 per year during the late 1990s. Assuming that this number was evenly distributed across the 13 grade levels of kindergarten through grade 12, this would imply an outflow from the public school system of only about 11.5 thousand per year per grade (150,000/13 = 11,538). Between 1999–2000 and 2000–2001, attrition between grades 9 and 10 was 448,000. This indicates that increases in homeschooling—even given the most liberal estimates—could account for only a tiny share of the attrition between grades 9 and 10 (11,500/ 448,000 = 2.6%).

In sum, it is clear that rates of attrition between grades 9 and 10, as well as the grade 9 bulge (that is, the number of students held back to repeat grade 9), have been increasing over the last two decades. In this section we have reviewed evidence on possible alternative explanations of these trends, namely, mortality, migration, private school enrollments, and homeschooling. None of these possibilities can explain the broad trends in public school enrollments previously recounted.

CAUSES AND CONSEQUENCES

What has been causing these changes in the U.S. education pipeline over the last 30 years, and what are their likely consequences? As to causes, the following questions arise: Why were more students being retained in grade 9 in 2000 than in 1970? Why has attrition between grades 9 and 10 increased in the 1980s and 1990s? Before presenting a discussion of these questions, we offer a disclaimer: Politicians, researchers, and ordinary citizens often try to make judgments about whether a certain change (such as a piece of federal legislation or an increase in atmospheric carbon dioxide) caused a particular development (such as an economic boom or global warming). But as with the two examples just offered, it is often difficult to make cause-and-effect inferences about complex systems, be they social or physical, with absolute certainty. Indeed, there is no way to prove cause and effect regarding historical matters with absolute certainty. Thus, we readily acknowledge that some of what we suggest in this section about probable causes and consequences of changes in the U.S. education pipeline over the last three decades is somewhat conjectural. Nonetheless, we argue, as did Leonard Ayres a century ago, that rates of student progress through elementary and secondary school are one of the best measures of the health of an education system. Our analysis of the education pipeline suggests that constrictions in the secondary school pipeline are likely leading to unfortunate negative consequences, not just for young people but for society as a whole.

Constriction of the High School Pipeline

A dramatic change in the education pipeline over the last three decades is evidence of what might be called constriction in the high school pipeline. By this we refer to the increasing rates of attrition between grades 9 and 10 and the increasing bulge of students in grade 9. As stated previously, proving cause and effect regarding historical developments is no easy matter, but what seems clear is that constriction in the education pipeline has been associated with three waves of education reform over the last three decades, namely, minimum competency testing, the academic standards movement, and high-stakes testing.

As shown in Figure 1, attrition between grades 9 and 10 was low and relatively stable at around 3 percent during the first half of the 1970s. However, during the late 1970s, attrition between grades 9 and 10 increased to around 5 percent. This coincided with the rise of the minimum competency testing movement (Haney & Madaus, 1978). By the late 1980s, studies showed that there was a relationship between state implementation of minimum competency testing and dropout rates (Kreitzer, Madaus, & Haney, 1989). In a study of the effects of grade retention, Shepard and Smith observed that "the percentages of overage students [that is, students older than the modal age for particular grades] began to climb . . . in the late 1970s in response to the minimum competency testing movement" (1989, p. 6).

As shown in Figure 1, attrition between grades 9 and 10 was relatively stable in the early 1980s, but began a steady increase, from less than 5 percent in 1983–1984 to 8 percent in 1988–1989. This happened following publication in 1983 of one of the last century's most publicized education reform reports, *A Nation at Risk*. In this report, the National Commission on Excellence in Education ominously warned that "the educational foundations of our society are presently being eroded by a rising tide of mediocrity that threatens our very future as a Nation and a people" (1983, p. 5). To remedy what it saw as declining academic standards, the commission called for increased academic course requirements in high school and for the use of standardized tests at "major transition points from one level of schooling to another" (p. 8).

In a follow-up study to *A Nation at Risk* entitled *Meeting the Challenge*, the staff of the commission surveyed the 50 states and the District of Columbia's recent efforts to improve education. Though acknowledging that many reform initiatives were underway prior to the release of *A Nation at Risk*, the follow-up report recounted that, among the reform efforts nationwide, "action has been taken or proposals made" with regard to "student evaluation/testing" by 35 states, and with regard to "graduation requirements" by 44 states (p. 6). Thus, it seems clear that what might be called the academic standards movement of the 1980s was a likely cause of the constriction in the high school pipeline during this period.

Referring again to Figure 1, it is apparent that the third period of increase in attrition between grades 9 and 10 started about 1990 and lasted until the end of the decade. During this period, attrition between grades 9 and 10 increased nationally almost 50 percent, from about 8 percent to nearly 12 percent. This further constriction in the high school pipeline has been associated with the rise of so-called standards-based reform and high-stakes testing. Others, such as Shepard (2002), have combined the education reform movement of the 1990s with reforms immediately following *A Nation at Risk*, in what she calls the excellence movement. Nonetheless, we think what happened in the 1990s was fundamentally different from what was going on earlier for one key reason, namely, that in the 1990s test results started being used to make decisions not just about students but also about schools.

As described previously, standards-based reform refers to a process by which states have been encouraged to develop grade-level academic "standards," then to develop tests based on those standards, and finally to use results of those tests to make decisions about both students and schools. For example, it is often advocated that decisions about whether to promote students from one grade to the next or to award them high school diplomas should be made based on results of such standards-based tests. Similarly, it is often recommended that ratings of schools be based on such test results (indeed, such ratings of schools are now mandated in the NCLB law).

Though the idea of such a reform strategy is seductively simple, there are a number of limitations. First, even brief reflection ought to make clear that the aims of U.S. public education extend far beyond mere academic learning, much less merely raising scores on a small number of tests of academic subjects.

Second, to base high school graduation decisions on standardized-test results in isolation, irrespective of other evidence about student performance in high school, is contrary to recognized professional standards regarding appropriate use of test results (e.g., the statement of the American Educational Research Association[4]). A simple way of communicating this point is to note how college admissions test results are used. There is not a single college anywhere in the nation that accepts all applicants who score above a particular point on the SAT (say a combined score of 1000) and rejects all applicants who score below that point. Instead, colleges make admissions decisions flexibly, using test scores, grades, and other information, rather than making decisions based on test scores alone.

Third, documentation of widespread errors in test scoring, scaling, and reporting in the testing industry should make clear how unwise it is to make important decisions mechanically based on test scores in isolation (Henriques & Steinberg, 2001; Rhoades & Madaus, 2003; Steinberg & Henriques, 2001). Indeed, in Minnesota, one large testing company was forced into a $10 million settlement after it was shown that hundreds of students had been wrongfully denied high school diplomas.

Fourth, recent research has demonstrated conclusively that "low-tech" tests like those being used in all the states (i.e., paper-and-pencil tests in which students answer multiple-choice questions or write answers on paper longhand) seriously underestimate the skills of students used to writing with computers (Haney & Russell, 2000; Russell & Plati, 2001). A number of states are beginning to experiment with ways of administering tests via computer, but it will be a long time before 21st-century testing (e.g., allowing use of keyboards rather than just longhand composition, and rapid feedback of results) becomes available in most schools. And in any case, the aims of education in our society extend way beyond what can be measured via computer, much less via paper and pencil.

Finally, it is clear that when the same fallible technology—and all bureaucratic accountability systems and high-stakes testing systems are such fallible technologies (Madaus, 1990)—is used to make decisions about children and social institutions, the latter will always be in a better position to protect their interests than the former. For example, when schools are under intense pressure to increase test-score averages and are not given the resources or tools for doing so in an educationally sound manner, the easiest way to make test pass rates (or score averages) appear to increase in the grade at which high-stakes tests are administered is to exclude low-achieving students from being tested. One way to exclude them, at least temporarily, is to hold them back to repeat the grade before the grade tested.

CONCLUSIONS

Using cohort grade progression analyses based on grade-level enrollment data, we have traced student progress through the public school education pipeline from kindergarten to graduation nationally (1968–2000) and for all 50 states (1984–2000). These analyses have allowed us to identify grade 9 as a key valve in the education pipeline, one that is closing for many students. This chapter has presented two lines of evidence that when considered together clearly suggest that the grade 9 to 10 transition is becoming increasingly difficult, particularly in states that have adopted high-stakes testing policies. The rates at which students are failing to progress from grade 9 to grade 10 are increasing. Grade 9 to 10 attrition rates have tripled over the last 30 years, indicating that students are getting held back in grade 9 at increasing rates. These trends do not bode well for the future of students and have clear implications for further decline in graduation rates.

Research has consistently shown that retaining students in grade yields little to no academic advantage and in fact increases the likelihood that students will drop out of high school (Jimerson, 2001; Nagaoka & Roderick, 2004; Shepard & Smith, 1989). Unfortunately, in the absence of resources and support services, educators all too often have few options other than retaining unsuccessful students in grade or promoting them without the necessary skills for continued academic success—practices that both ultimately further disadvantage students. In the current climate of school and student accountability, high-stakes testing, and increased demands for improved test performance, the need for programs that provide additional supports and encourage the promotion rather than the retention of students has never been more pressing. Increasing rates of grade retention and attrition further exacerbate decreases in high school graduation rates. Curbing these trends is no longer just an educational issue, but one of great societal concern. High-stakes testing policies that establish promotional gates in elementary and secondary grades and determine high school graduation must be critically examined to evaluate if the human costs are outweighed by the intended educational benefits.

NOTES

1. Iowa has not developed state content standards; instead, each district is responsible for developing its own content standards and benchmarks (Quality Counts, 2001). Local district content standards rather than state standards were also included as part of Iowa's accountability plan submitted to the U.S. Department of Education in 2003 (www.state.ia.us/educate).
2. This discussion is based on the National Center for Health Statistics, National Vital Statistics Report, "Death: Final Report for 2002," available online at http://www.cdc.gov/nchs/products/pubs/pubd/nrsr/50/50-16.
3. Available at http://www.hslda.org/research/faq.asp#1, retrieved November 14, 2003.
4. See http://www.aera.net/about/policy/stakes.htm.

REFERENCES

Amrein, A. L., & Berliner, D. C. (2002a, March 28). High-stakes testing, uncertainty, and student learning. *Education Policy Analysis Archives, 10*(18). Retrieved September 17, 2002, from http://epaa.asu.edu/epaa/v10n18/.

Amrein, A. L., & Berliner, D. C. (2002b, December). *An analysis of some unintended and negative consequences of high stakes testing.* Report of the Education Policy Studies Laboratory, Arizona State University. Retrieved January 30, 2003, from http://edpolicylab.org.

Amrein, A. L., & Berliner, D. C. (2002c, December). *The impact of high-stakes tests on student performance: An analysis of NAEP results in states with high-stakes tests and ACT, SAT and AP results in states with high school graduation exams* (Report of the Education Policy Studies Laboratory, Arizona State University). Retrieved January 30, 2003, from http://edpolicylab.org.

Ayres, L. P. (1909). *Laggards in our schools: A study of retardation and elimination in city school systems.* New York: Charities Publication Committee.

Associated Press. (2003, September 10). *Are Texas schools nudging out low performing students?* Retrieved September 16, 2003, from http://www.khou.com/news/local/education/stories/khou030905_mh_dropouts.77b521f2.html.

Bainbridge, W. L. (2003, April 16) Texas model for school achievement doesn't hold up. *Columbus Dispatch.*

Bielick, S., Chandler, K., & Broughman, S. P. (2001). *Homeschooling in the United States: 1999* (NCES Report 2001-033) Washington, DC: National Center for Education Statistics.

Bauman, K. J. (2002, May 16). Home schooling in the United States: Trends and characteristics. *Education Policy Analysis Archives, 10*(26). Retrieved November 12, 2003, from http://epaa.asu.edu/epaa/v10n26.html.

Chudowsky, N., Kober, N., Gayler, K., & Hamilton, M. (2002). *State high school exit exams: A baseline report.* Washington, DC: Center on Education Policy.

Clarke, M., Shore, A., Rhoades, K., Abrams, L., Miao, J., & Li, J. (2003). *Perceived effects of state-mandated testing programs on teaching and learning: Findings from interviews with ed-*

ucators in low-, medium- and high-stakes states. Chestnut Hill, MA: Boston College, National Board on Educational Testing and Public Policy.

Edwards, V. (Ed.). (2001, January 11). *Quality counts 2001: A better balance: Standards, tests, and the tools to succeed (Education Week Special Report).* Bethesda, MD: Editorial Projects in Education.

Edwards, V. (Ed.). (2002, January 10). *Quality counts 2002: Building blocks for success (Education Week Special Report).* Bethesda, MD: Editorial Projects in Education.

Edwards, V. (Ed.). (2003, January 9). *Quality counts 2003: If I can't learn from you (Education Week Special Report).* Bethesda, MD: Editorial Projects in Education.

Edwards, V. (Ed.) (2004, January 8). *Quality counts 2004: Special education in an era of standards: Count me in (Education Week Special Report).* Bethesda, MD: Editorial Projects in Education.

Gotbaum, B. (2002, November 21). *Pushing out at-risk students: An analysis of high school discharge figures* (Report by the Public Advocate for the City of New York and Advocates for Children). New York: Advocates for Children. Retrieved April 5, 2003, from http://www.advocatesforchildren.org/.

Greene, J. P., & Forster, G. (2003, September 17). *Public high school graduation and college readiness rates in the United States* (Working Paper No. 3). New York: Manhattan Institute. Available online at http://www.manhattan-institute.org/ewp_03_embargoed.pdf, accessed 9/15/2003.

Haney, W. (2001, January 13). *Revisiting "The Myth of the Texas Miracle in Education": Lessons about dropout research and dropout prevention.* Paper prepared for the Dropout Research: Accurate Counts and Positive Interventions conference sponsored by Achieve, Inc., and The Civil Rights Project at Harvard University, Cambridge MA. Available online at http://www.civilrightsproject.harvard.edu/research/dropouts/calldropoutpapers.php.

Haney, W. (2000, August 19). The myth of the Texas miracle in education. *Education Policy Analysis Archives, 8*(41). Available online at http://epaa.asu.edu/epaa/v8n41/ (a printed version of this monograph is distributed by the Harvard Education Publishing Group).

Haney, W., & Madaus, G. (1978). Making sense of the minimum competency testing movement. *Harvard Educational Review, 48,* 462–484.

Harlow, C. W. (2003). *Education and correctional populations* (Bureau of Justice Statistics Special Report). Washington, DC: U.S. Department of Justice Statistics, Office of Justice Programs.

Hartocallis, A. (2001, June 30). Math test needed for high school graduation had confusing errors, state officials say. *New York Times,* p. B2.

Henke, R., Kaufman, P., & Broughman, S. P. (2000). *Issues related to estimating the home-schooled population in the United States with household survey data* (NCES Report 2000-311) Washington, DC: National Center for Education Statistics.

Henriques, D., & Steinberg, J. (2001, May 20). Right answer, wrong score: Test flaws take toll. *New York Times,* p. 1. Available online at http://www.nytimes.com/2001/05/20/business/20EXAM.html.

Heubert, J., & Hauser, R. (Eds.). (1999). *High stakes: Testing for tracking, promotion, and graduation* (Report of the National Research Council). Washington, DC: National Academy Press.

Home School Legal Defense Association. Retrieved November 14, 2003, from http://www.hslda.org/research/faq.asp#1.

Jackson, G. (1975). The research evidence on the effects of grade retention. *Review of Educational Research, 45,* 613–635.

Jimerson, S. (2001). Meta-analysis of grade retention research: Implications for practice in the 21st century. *School Psychology Review, 30,* 420–437.

Kreitzer, A., Madaus, G., & Haney, W. (1989). Competency testing and dropouts. In L. Weis & H. Petrie (Eds.). *Dropouts from school: Issues, dilemmas and solutions* (pp. 129–152). Albany: State University of New York Press.

Madaus, G. (1990, December 6). *Testing as a social technology* (Boisi Lecture in Education and Public Policy). Chestnut Hill, MA: Boston College.

Madaus, G., & Greaney, V. (1985). The Irish experience in competency testing. *American Journal of Education, 93,* 268–294.

Nagaoka, J., & Roderick, M. (2004). *Ending social promotion: The effects of retention.* Chicago: Consortium on Chicago School Research.

National Center for Health Statistics. (2002, September 16). Death: Final Data for 2000. *National Vital Statistics Reports, 50*(15).

National Commission on Excellence in Education. (1983a). *A nation at risk.* Washington, DC: U.S. Government Printing Office.

National Commission on Excellence in Education. (1983b). *Meeting the challenge: Recent efforts to improve education across the nation.* Washington, DC: U.S. Government Printing Office.

Orel, S. (2003). Left behind in Birmingham: 522 pushed out students. In R. C. Lent & G. Pipkin (Eds.), *Silent no more: Voices of courage in American schools* (pp. 1–14). Portsmouth, NH: Heinemann.

Owings, W., & Magliaro, S. (1998). Grade retention: A history of failure. *Educational Leadership, 56*(1), 86–89.

Pedulla, J., Abrams, L., Madaus, G., Russell, M., Ramos, M., & Miao, J. (2003). *Perceived effects of state-mandated testing programs on teaching and learning: Findings from a national survey of teachers.* Chestnut Hill, MA: Boston College, National Board on Educational Testing and Public Policy.

Rapple, B. (1994). Payment by results: An example of assessment in elementary education from nineteenth century Britain. *Education Policy Analysis Archives, 2*(1). Retrieved September 21, 2003, from http://epaa.asu.edu/epaa/v2n1.

Rhoades, K., & Madaus, G. (2003, May). *Errors in standardized tests: A systemic problem* (Report of the National Board on Educational Testing and Public Policy). Chestnut Hill, MA: Boston College Center for the Study of Testing. Available online at http://www.bc.edu/research/nbetpp/reports.html#monographs.

Roderick, M. (1994). Grade retention and school dropout: Investigating the association. *American Educational Research Journal, 31,* 729–759.

Rudner, L. (1999). Scholastic achievement and demographic characteristics of home school students in 1998. *Education Policy Analysis Archives, 10*(26). Retrieved November 12, 2003, from http://epaa.asu.edu/epaa/v10n26.html.

Rumberger, R. (1987). High school dropouts: A review of issues and evidence. *Review of Educational Research, 57*(196), 101–121.

Russell, M., & Haney, W. (2000, March 28). Bridging the gap between technology and testing. *Education Policy Analysis Archives, 8*(41). Available online at http://epaa.asu.edu/epaa/v8n41/.

Russell, M., & Plati, T. (2001). Effects of computer versus paper administration of a state-mandated writing assessment. *Teachers College Record On-line.* Available online at http://www.tcrecord.org/Content.asp?ContentID=10709.

Shepard, L. (2002, January 24–25). *The contest between large-scale accountability testing and assessment in the service of learning.* Paper prepared for the Spencer Foundation's 30th anniversary conference, Chicago.

Shepard, L. A., & Smith, M. L. (1989). *Flunking grades: Research and policies on retention.* New York: Falmer Press.

Wright, J. (Ed.). (2002). *New York Times almanac.* New York: Penguin.

U. S. Census Bureau. (2000). Migration by sex and age for the population 5 years and over for the United States, regions, states, and Puerto Rico: 2000 (PHC-T-23). Available online at http://www.census.gov/population/cen2000/phc-t23/tab03.xls.

The research reported in this chapter was supported with a generous grant from the Ford Foundation; however, the views expressed here are not necessarily those of anyone other than the authors. This chapter examines findings from a larger research report on the education pipeline study, which can be found along with the data files at the National Board on Educational Testing and Public Policy website at http://www.bc.edu/nbetpp.

CHAPTER 9

Whatever Happened to the Class of 2000?
The Timing of Dropout in Philadelphia's Schools

RUTH CURRAN NEILD

ELIZABETH FARLEY

It is notoriously difficult to pinpoint the national high school dropout rate for a given cohort of students. Administrative data on individual students, which would provide an official accounting of their whereabouts, tend to remain at the district or state level, and tracking the educational careers of students who move from one school district to another is an almost impossible task (see ch. 5). As a result, some researchers have turned to other sources of data—such as the High School and Beyond study, the National Longitudinal Survey of Youth, and the Current Population Survey—to estimate how often dropping out occurs, when it occurs, and who is most at risk. Others have made creative use of the Common Core of Data (CCD) to estimate which schools and districts experience the highest rates of dropout (see ch. 3). Without a good answer we might focus dropout-prevention efforts at the wrong grade levels.

Analysis of school district administrative data on students rounds out the picture of the dropout problem by allowing us to create a detailed educational history of a cohort of students in a single geographical area. Although there are problems associated with district data on dropouts, including district variation in reporting standards and incentives for falsely coding dropouts as having departed for other schools (Hammack, 1996; LeCompte & Goebel, 1987; Texas Education Agency, 2000), district data is valuable for its insights on the timing of dropping out as well as its incidence. Further, analysis of administrative data for large urban districts provides a check for other estimates of dropout rates in central cities that rely on national data.

In this chapter, we use school district administrative data from Philadelphia to examine dropout rates for the cohort of first-time ninth graders who entered high school in September 1996 and whose four-year graduation date was

June 2000. While we report data on the incidence of urban dropouts, a particular focus of this chapter is the timing of dropping out of school. We argue that determining the "when" of dropping out is almost as important as knowing the "whether," since the *when* provides clues about the *why* and suggests particular points for intervention and policy attention. If, for example, most dropouts leave high school in twelfth grade, when they can be assumed to be just a few credits away from graduation, particular attention should be paid to why students are leaving when they appear to be so close to the finish line. Are exit exams dimming their hopes of graduating, as some scholars have argued (Amrein & Berliner, 2002; Jacob, 2001)? Or do responsibilities outside of school, perhaps a need to support or care for a family, outweigh the benefits of remaining in high school? On the other hand, if most dropouts leave as ninth or tenth graders, having earned few credits toward graduation, then policymakers and practitioners would do well to monitor what is happening to students in the early grades of high school.

Philadelphia's public school system, now ninth-largest in the United States, is one of the school districts that—along with New York, Chicago, Baltimore, and Detroit—have a substantial concentration of schools with very high dropout rates, according to cross-sectional national data (see ch. 3). As is the case in many of the largest city school districts in the United States, Philadelphia's public school students are mostly minority and overwhelmingly poor. The district reports on its website that 80 percent of its students are eligible for free or reduced-price lunch. Sixty-five percent of the students in the city's public schools are African American, 15 percent are Latino/Hispanic, 5 percent are Asian, and 15 percent are white. In fact, in 1990, the majority of white students and 30 percent of all schoolchildren living in Philadelphia attended private or parochial schools (Saporito, 1998).

THE TIMING OF DROPPING OUT

The timing of dropping out of school can be characterized in a number of ways, including students' grade when they dropped out; the number of credits earned toward graduation at the time of dropping out; and how long they had been enrolled in high school before leaving. Each of these ways of characterizing the timing of when students leave school reveals a different facet of dropping out of high school.

Grade of Dropping Out

A useful way to report the timing of dropping out is the grade during which it occurred, or, alternatively, the last grade completed before leaving. Estimating the grade at which students drop out, however, is not as straightforward as it may seem initially. Estimates vary, depending on whether researchers draw on official school district data such as transcripts or administrative records, or rely on self-reports.

Surveys such as the Current Population Survey (CPS) and National Longitudinal Survey of Youth (NLSY) allow for estimates of the grade of dropping out using self-reported data. Drawing on CPS data, Kominski (1990) and Hauser and colleagues (see ch. 4) use reports by household members about school enrollment and last grade completed to determine the dropout grade for target individuals who have left school in the preceding year. Both Kominski's and Hauser et al.'s analyses of CPS data suggest that the odds of dropping out increase across the high school grade levels, with twelfth graders at greatest risk of leaving school without graduating. This increased risk holds across racial/ethnic groups. While the CPS data are cross-sectional and thus do not track the education careers of a single group of students, longitudinal data from the NLSY tell a similar story about when the risk of dropping out is greatest. Detailed, month-by-month school attendance calendars constructed from annual interview data suggest that, among high school students, ninth graders are at lowest risk of dropping out and twelfth graders at highest risk (Anderson, 1999). At the same time, ninth graders who are over age for their grade—likely a result of grade repetition—are more likely to drop out of school than over-age twelfth graders.

One of the difficulties with self-reports on the grade in which students drop out is the lack of clarity about whether "dropout grade" refers to the number of years spent enrolled in a high school or to actual progress toward graduation—that is, whether a student has earned enough credits to be promoted to the next grade. Estimates of the grade of dropping out based on self-reports from surveys and interviews may be biased upward, since respondents may take a less technical approach to reporting grades than would be the case with administrative data. Many respondents may think of year one in high school as ninth grade, year two as tenth grade, and so on, regardless of whether the student has made any progress in passing courses required for graduation. But having been enrolled in high school for four years does not necessarily imply that a student is nearing graduation, especially in central-city schools where course failure is rampant and large percentages of students spend more than one year as ninth graders (Neild & Balfanz, 2001; Roderick & Camburn, 1999; Weiss, 2001).

Transcripts or other administrative data from school districts provide the most accurate reports on the actual dropout grade, which is usually determined by the number of required credits earned toward graduation. An examination of school district records for four cohorts of students in the Chicago Public

Schools indicates that the majority of those who dropped out by age 19 left school when they were ninth or tenth graders (Allensworth & Easton, 2001). In the group of students who were at least 19 years old in the year 2000, 40 percent of the dropouts had not completed ninth grade. Only a very small proportion of dropouts—about 10 percent—were in the twelfth grade when they left school.

There may be several reasons for the difference in dropout grade between the CPS and the NLSY on the one hand, and the Chicago study on the other. It is possible that dropout patterns for students in large urban school districts like Chicago differ substantially from patterns in data aggregated at the national level. It may also be that, with the introduction of stiffer promotion require-ments across the country, fewer students are moving from ninth to tenth grade (Haney et al., 2004), a development that would be reflected in studies like that for Chicago, which uses more recent data than the available studies based on CPS or NLSY. The disparity may also be a reflection of the type of data source—that is, survey data or administrative records—on which the estimates are based. Whatever the reason, we suggest that it is important for researchers and policymakers to clarify the point they are trying to make by reporting the dropout grade. Are they trying to communicate how close students are to grad-uation? Or do they want to describe how long students have been enrolled in school? As we show in the next sections, school district administrative data ren-der these questions both separable and answerable.

Number of Credits Earned

During the late 1990s, requirements for promotion from ninth to tenth grade were ratcheted up by many cities and states. In Philadelphia, for example, first-time ninth graders in 1999–2000 were required to earn five credits, rather than the four credits previously required, and three of those credits had to be in Eng-lish, Algebra 1, and science (Neild & Balfanz, 2001). As a result, after four years in high school, a student theoretically could have passed all of his or her courses except for one key required freshman class—for example, English—and still be classified as a ninth grader. In that case, the grade of record would be somewhat deceptive as an indicator of how close an individual student was to graduation. If that student were to drop out of school, an analysis of the number of credits earned would present a truer picture of when they dropped out. To our knowl-edge, there have been no published reports that use the number of credits earned as a way of exploring the timing of dropping out.

Year in High School

Another way to measure the timing of dropping out is the length of time stu-dents have been enrolled in high school before leaving. Paired with the dropout grade and/or the number of credits earned before leaving school, this variable potentially provides important insights into the circumstances of dropping out, particularly for those dropouts who left school when they were in ninth or tenth grade. An important question regarding the students who left school as ninth or tenth graders is whether they left only a short time after beginning high school, or whether they were more likely to be attached to school—however weakly—for several years before finally dropping out. The year of dropping out is affected by the age of the student when he or she enters high school, since older students reach the legal age to leave school at an earlier point in high school.

DATA AND VARIABLES

This analysis tracks the educational status of a cohort of students who were first-time freshmen in noncharter high schools in the School District of Philadelphia during the 1996–1997 school year. Data come from student administrative records maintained by the school district. We determine first-time freshman status by identifying students who were ninth graders in the Philadelphia public schools during the 1996–1997 school year and who were in eighth grade in one of the city's schools during the previous year. Across the district, 14,652 students met this definition. Ninth graders who did not attend a Philadelphia public school during the 1995–1996 school year could not be included in the analysis, since we had no way of determining whether they were first-time freshmen or were repeating ninth grade.

We present data on students' educational status at a single point in time: November 2001, about five-and-a-half years after the students started high school. The variable for educational status is created by assessing two codes that students receive each year in the school district database. The first, a status code, indicates whether students were enrolled in the district, had withdrawn, or were simply unaccounted for. The second is a drop code that students receive when they withdraw from the district. There are about 20 drop codes—including leaving for another school or school district, transfer to a correctional institution, employment, enrollment in the Job Corps, graduation, and being dropped from the school rolls because of non-attendance—but each departing student is assigned only one.

Using administrative data from a single school district to characterize the educational status of a cohort of students implies several caveats and consequences. First, the data do not permit the tracking of students after they leave the school district. We cannot tell, for example, whether a student who is listed in school district data as having dropped out of school or as going directly from school to incarceration subsequently re-enrolled in another educational institution and obtained a high school diploma or a GED. As a consequence, we emphasize that this is an analysis of dropping out from a large urban school system rather than a full characterization of the educational status of a cohort of students who happened to start high school together in 1996. Second, the dropout codes from district files have not been independently verified for accuracy. Districts vary in the standards of evidence they require to count students as dropouts, and even within a district, some schools make greater efforts than others to discover the true story of students' whereabouts. However, patterns in which kinds of codes were used most frequently during different years suggest that the data from Philadelphia has some trustworthiness. The code that has the greatest potential to be misused—that of transferring to another school or district—was given most often during the students' first year in high school (1996-1997), likely reflecting the school switching that often occurs at the beginning of a new level of schooling. Sixty-eight percent of the occasions when the school switching code was assigned occurred during the cohort's first year in high school.

A larger difficulty, in our opinion, is presented by those instances in which drop codes are missing entirely or students are "lost" in the system. In district data, 14 percent of the cohort is either missing a drop code or is coded as being lost. That many of these students whose status became unclear during the third and fourth year of high school were still ninth and tenth graders makes us suspicious that these may have been dropouts who were not coded as such. We handle the missing codes by presenting several sets of estimates that reflect our varying levels of certainty about whether students were dropouts.

We also use administrative record data on students' grades (9–12) during each academic year and the number of credits earned each year. By examining changes in enrollment from year to year, as well as the date of withdrawal from school, we were able to determine how many years the student had been enrolled in the district.

OVERALL FIGURES ON DROPOUTS

Table 1 shows our estimates for fall 2001 of the educational status of the Philadelphia students who entered high school in September 1996. Five-and-a-half years after entering high school, fewer than half of the students had earned a high school diploma from the Philadelphia public schools. A number had left the system for other schools, for jail, or through illness or accident. District data indicate that 21 percent of the cohort had dropped out; if the students with missing drop codes or whose status was unclear are included as dropouts, the dropout rate rises to 36 percent, which is in line with cohort dropout estimates

TABLE 1

Dropout, Graduation, and Enrollment Status for 1996–1997
First-Time Freshmen as of November 2001

Educational Status	Entire Cohort	African American	Asian	Latino	White
Graduated	48.9%	49.9%	60.4%	38.6%	48.6%
Still in Philadelphia public schools	4.4	5.7	2.3	3.6	1.6
Left district for another school	7.6	5.6	7.1	9.1	12.7
Nonvoluntary reasons for leaving*	1.8	2	0.8	2.4	0.77
Incarcerated	1.8	1.2	1.5	0.74	4.3
Dropouts or possible dropouts					
Dropped out	21.3	20.1	19.2	30.7	20.3
Left district, reason unknown	9.8	10.1	6.4	10.9	9.5
Status unknown**	4.4	5.4	2.4	4	2.3
Total potential dropouts	35.5%	35.6%	28%	45.6%	32.1%
Total	100%	100%	100%	100%	100%
N	14,652	9,245	750	1,628	2,977

*Primarily death and illness.
**Have not been withdrawn officially, but do not have active status.

from other urban districts (Allensworth & Easton, 2001; New York City Department of Education, 2004).

If students who are coded as having left the district for other schools are removed from the denominator so that we take into account just those whose high school experiences were likely limited to those available in the School District of Philadelphia, the graduation and dropout rates both rise slightly, with 52 percent graduating and 38 percent dropping out or potentially dropping out.

A breakdown of dropout rates by race and ethnicity reveals several noteworthy features of educational status. First, the differences in dropout rates mirror patterns found nationally: Asians have lower dropout rates relative to whites, blacks, and Latinos, while Latino students have exceedingly high dropout rates (Kaufman, Alt, & Chapman, 2001). Thirty-one percent of the Latino students in the cohort were listed as dropouts in district data, and if possible dropouts are included—that is, those who left the district but have no drop code and those whose status in the district is uncertain—the dropout rate rises to 46 percent. While the Asian dropout rate is lower than that of other groups, it is clear that there were many students of Asian descent in this cohort who embarked on adult life without a high school diploma. Nineteen percent of Asians are coded as having dropped out, a rate that could rise to 28 percent if all the questionable cases were, in fact, dropouts.

Second, white students are much more likely than other groups to have exited the system by leaving for another school or, notably, by going directly from school into the juvenile justice system. Thirteen percent of the white students are coded as having left the system for another school, while the last information we have about 4.3 percent of the white students is that they had been incarcerated and had not returned to the public school system. In comparison, 1.2 percent of the African American students, 1.5 percent of the Asian students, and .74 percent of the Latino students were incarcerated. To understand why white students received a drop code of "incarcerated" more frequently than other racial and ethnic groups, particularly when minority youth are more likely to be involved in the criminal justice system (Poe-Yamagata & Jones, 2000), it is important to realize that these codes represent the *last* information we have about students. They are not an indication of whether a student was ever incarcerated. Indeed, it appears that one reason why white students have the disposition of incarcerated more often is that they are less likely than incarcerated students of other racial/ethnic backgrounds to return to the school system. For example, by November 2001, 93 percent of the white students who had been incarcerated during their second year in high school still had that code, compared to just 72 percent of the incarcerated African American students, who were more likely to have graduated or still to be enrolled in the system. We do not know whether the incarcerated students who did not return to the Philadelphia public schools had longer sentences, never enrolled in any school after release from incarceration, or enrolled in private school or in another district. But the fact that white students are more likely to leave the district for another school and less likely to return to the public schools after incarceration may suggest a greater inclination to use other educational options—such as private schools and schools in other districts— than students from other racial/ethnic backgrounds.

Research has consistently shown that males have a higher risk of dropping out than females (Rumberger, 1983), a pattern that held in these data. Among the cohort that entered high school in September 1996 and that did not leave for another school or district, more than one-quarter of the males (26%) were listed as having dropped out; 44 percent were either listed as dropouts in district

TABLE 2

Grade at School Leaving, for Students Listed as Dropouts
and Potential Dropouts

Grade	Percentage Listed as Dropouts	Percentage Listed and Potential Dropouts
9th	45.8	41.7
10th	33.5	31.7
11th	15.7	15.8
12th	5.0	10.8
TOTAL	100	100
n	3,115	5,205

data or were possible dropouts; and only 46 percent had graduated from the Philadelphia public schools by fall 2001. In comparison, 20 percent of the females had dropped out; 33 percent were either listed or possible dropouts; and 60 percent had graduated.

Dropout Grade

Figures derived from national data suggest that the incidence of dropping out increases across the high school grades: sophomores are more at risk of leaving than freshmen, juniors than sophomores, and so on. The data from Philadelphia, however, indicate an opposite pattern, with dropouts most likely to be in ninth grade and least likely to be in twelfth (Table 2). Close to half of the students (45.8%) who are listed as dropouts were still in ninth grade when they dropped out of school. If both listed dropouts and possible dropouts are included, the percentage leaving in ninth grade is slightly lower (41.7%), but ninth grade remains by far the most common grade for dropping out. An additional third of the dropouts left when they were tenth graders. In sum, then, about three-quarters of the dropouts were in the early high school grades when they left school.

The predominance of ninth graders among the dropouts holds across racial and ethnic groups, although dropouts in some groups were especially inclined to leave before being promoted to tenth grade. Latino students were especially at risk of dropping out as freshmen, with 55 percent of the dropouts still in ninth grade. Almost half of the Asian dropouts (47%) and African American dropouts (45%) left as ninth graders, while a somewhat lower percentage of whites left school when they were freshmen (41%). There were no statistically or substantively significant differences between males and females in the drop-out grade, either across the entire cohort or within racial/ethnic groups.

Credits toward Graduation

A finer-grained way of determining how close dropouts are to graduation is to examine how many course credits they have earned during high school. Of particular interest is whether students who were ninth graders when they dropped out of high school were quite short on credits, or whether they were missing just a key class or two. We examined credit files for 1996–1997, 1997–1998, and 1998–1999—the first year in which the cohort was enrolled in high school and the two subsequent years—for patterns in the accumulation of credits toward graduation. We were able to construct credit histories for 85 percent of the students who were listed in the district data as having dropped out by the end of their third year in high school. We focus on these dropouts because our available credit data extend only through the end of 1998–1999, but these students account for most of the listed dropouts.

The vast majority of these dropouts from the Philadelphia public schools were seriously behind on their credits when they left school. Among all students listed as having dropped out by the end of their third year in high school, 46.9 percent had earned no more than three credits, and more than 60 percent had earned no more than five credits, in a school system where the average ninth-grade student carried a course load of six credits during the 1996–1997 school year. Among those who dropped out as ninth graders, the vast majority had earned no more than three credits, when at least five credits were necessary for promotion to tenth grade. Almost no ninth-grade dropouts had earned more than five credits. Students who were listed as ninth graders but had been en-rolled in high school for three years before they dropped out showed a similar pattern: with no more than three credits toward graduation, the vast majority had been spinning their wheels for the three years they had been enrolled in high school.

Dropout Year

It would be a mistake to conclude on the basis of the numerical predominance of ninth graders among dropouts and the relatively few credits they had earned that most of those leaving school early departed during their first year of high school. On the contrary, fewer than 2 percent of those listed as dropouts in district data—and fewer than 5 percent of the combined group of listed and possible dropouts—left during their first year in high school. Among those who are listed as dropouts, the modal year for leaving school was by far the third year.

An additional one-third dropped out during the second year of high school. When we consider those students who were listed in district data as dropping out in ninth grade, the story is much the same. Close to half of the ninth-grade dropouts left during the third year of high school.

Many of the students who experienced severe academic difficulty during the transition into high school may have been biding their time until they finally were able to reach the legal age to leave school (17) and then could either withdraw or be withdrawn by the school on the basis of non-attendance. For some of these students, the actual date of dropping out is just the final step in a long process of disengaging from school, as evidenced in part by declining attendance. We recognize that the timing of disenrollment from school is something of a crude measure of when a dropout effectively occurred. However, we suggest that the year of actually dropping out remains an important way to characterize the timing of when students left school, since students who continue to be enrolled in school and even show up in class occasionally are more likely to receive communication from the school in the form of mailings, calls from teachers, and visits from the school attendance officer. The official time of dropping out means that, without going through a process of reinstatement, students no longer have even a casual attachment to school or the chance to earn credits toward graduation.

CONCLUSION:
A PORTRAIT OF DROPOUTS IN A LARGE URBAN SYSTEM

The portrait of the timing of dropping out that emerges from an analysis of administrative records kept by a large urban school system is both more detailed and, on some measures, dramatically at odds with statistics about dropouts derived from national datasets. In sum, the data reveal that just a bare majority of the students who entered a Philadelphia public high school in September 1996 and who did not depart the district for another school had graduated five-and-a-half years later. In a school system that serves as many students as Philadelphia's, a potential dropout rate of between 35 and 40 percent means that thousands of students in an entering cohort enter adult life without being close to earning a high school diploma. In addition, while the typical dropout has been enrolled in high school for several years, it is common for them to have made little progress toward graduation. In contrast to statistics available from the Current Population Survey and the National Longitudinal Survey of Youth, these data indicate that most Philadelphia dropouts are in either ninth or tenth grade when they leave school and have accumulated only a few credits toward graduation. Whether this disparity exists because students in cities like Philadelphia differ significantly from the national norm, or because different types of data sources give different results, or a combination of both, is unclear.

These data suggest that policies and practices designed to keep students in school should pay particular attention to the rocky transition into high school experienced by many urban adolescents (Legters, Balfanz, Jordan, & McPartland, 2002; Neild & Balfanz, 2001; Roderick & Camburn, 1999). The dearth of course credits among those who drop out of school indicates that many of the dropouts experience severe academic difficulty during their first year in high school. In fact, 33 percent of this cohort spent more than one year in ninth grade. Among those who repeated ninth grade, 45 percent were listed as dropouts in district data, and an enormous 69 percent were either identified as dropouts or were possible dropouts. In contrast, just 11 percent of those who managed to be promoted to tenth grade after their first year in high school were listed as dropouts in district data, and 20 percent would be classified as dropouts under a more generous definition that includes those who had left the system but for whom no information about their whereabouts was available.

The large percentage of dropouts in this and other urban school systems and the predominance of dropouts among ninth graders suggest that policymakers and practitioners need to consider substantial changes in how early high school experiences are structured. While researchers have shown that the seeds of dropping out often are planted quite early, even as far back as elementary school (Alexander, Entwisle, & Horsey, 1997), these early dispositions interact with subsequent experiences that allow those seeds to flourish. There is abundant evidence that ninth grade represents an enormous stumbling block for urban students (Roderick & Camburn, 1999) and that ninth-grade course failure is a substantial predictor of dropping out, even controlling for a multitude of demographic, attitudinal, and achievement factors prior to high school (Neild, Stoner-Eby, & Furstenberg, 2001).

Ultimately, the best dropout-prevention programs may be those designed to help students make the transition into the high school environment, with its more demanding curriculum, new social opportunities and pressures, and comparatively greater freedom. Some school districts have implemented summer "bridge programs" designed to introduce students to the expectations of high school and acquaint them with teachers and fellow students (MacIver & Epstein, 1991; Reyes, Gillock, & Kobus, 1994); others have introduced new organizational structures, such as "charters" or teams within high schools (Fine, 1994), or have advocated for doing away with large high schools altogether. The Talent Development model (sse ch. 13) works within large comprehensive high schools to restructure the ninth-grade experience completely. Ninth graders are taught by teams of teachers whose course rosters include only freshmen, enabling teachers to give sustained attention to how their students are experiencing the transition to high school. The ninth graders occupy a physically separate space in the building, a feature that is intended to allow students to become well known by school staff. They have a core academic curriculum, complete with materials and coaching, that helps students adjust to high school academic content and expectations, and abundant opportunities are available for students who fall behind to catch up on credits (Legters, Balfanz, Jordan, & McPartland, 2002).

The characteristics of dropouts that we describe—their sheer numbers, their lack of credits, and their enrollment for several years in high school (and, as a consequence, their likelihood of being at least 18 years old)—should bring some urgency to the need to implement a redesign of the high school experience. If Philadelphia is representative of other large urban districts (and we suggest that it is), trying to reengage current dropouts into a high school experience that allows credits to be accumulated only slowly when the students have so far to go is unlikely to produce many additional graduates. These data make clear that the critical time for dropout prevention is during the very first months of the freshman year.

REFERENCES

Alexander, K., Entwisle, D., & Horsey, C. (1997). From first grade forward: Early foundations of high school dropout. *Sociology of Education, 70,* 87–107.

Allensworth, E., & Easton, J. (2001). *Calculating a cohort dropout rate for the Chicago public schools.* Chicago: Consortium on Chicago School Reform.

Amrein, A. L., & Berliner, D. C. (2002). *An analysis of some unintended and negative consequences of high-stakes testing.* Tempe: Arizona State University, Education Policy Studies Laboratory.

Anderson, D. K. (1999). *The timing of high school dropout.* Paper presented at the annual meeting of the American Sociological Association.

Fine, M. (1994). Chartering urban school reform. In M. Fine (Ed.), *Chartering urban school reform* (pp. 5–30). New York: Teachers College Press.

Hammack, F. (1996). Large school systems' dropout reports: An analysis of definitions, procedures, and findings. *Teachers College Record, 87,* 324–341.

Haney, W., Madaus, G., Abrams, L., Wheelock, A., Maio, J., & Gruia, I. (2004). *The education pipeline in the United States, 1970–2000.* Chestnut Hill, MA: Boston College, Center for the Study of Testing, Evaluation, and Educational Policy.

Jacob, B. A. (2001). Getting tough? The impact of high school graduation exams. *Educational Evaluation and Policy Analysis, 23,* 99–122.

Kaufman, P., Alt, M. N., & Chapman, C. (2001). *Dropout rates in the United States: 2000.* Washington, DC: National Center for Education Statistics, Statistical Analysis Report.

Kominski, R. (1990). Estimating the national high school dropout rate. *Demography, 27,* 303–311.

LeCompte, M., & Goebel, S. (1987). Can bad data produce good program planning? An analysis of record-keeping on school dropouts. *Education and Urban Society, 19,* 250–268.

Legters, N., Balfanz, R., Jordan, W., & McPartland, J. (2002). *Comprehensive reform for urban high schools: A talent development approach.* New York: Teachers College Press.

Mac Iver, D., & Epstein, J. (1991). Responsive practices in the middle grades: Teacher teams, advisory groups, remedial instruction, and school transition programs. *American Journal of Education, 99,* 587–622.

Neild, R. C., & Balfanz, R. (2001). *An extreme degree of difficulty: The demographics of the ninth grade in non-selective high schools in Philadelphia.* Paper presented at the annual meeting of the American Sociological Association.

Neild, R. C., Stoner-Eby, S., & Furstenberg, F. (2001). *Connecting entrance and departure: The transition to ninth grade and high school dropout.* Paper presented at the Dropouts in America Conference, Harvard University, Cambridge, MA.

New York City Department of Education. (2004). *The class of 2000 final longitudinal report: A three-year follow up study.* New York: New York City Department of Education.

Poe-Yamagata, E., & Jones, M. (2000). *And justice for some: Differential treatment of minority youth in the justice system.* Washington, DC: Building Blocks for Youth.

Reyes, O., Gillock, K., & Kobus, K. (1994). A longitudinal study of school adjustment in urban, minority adolescents: Effects of a high school transition program. *American Journal of Community Psychology, 22,* 341–369.

Roderick, M., & Camburn, E. (1999). Risk and recovery from course failure in the early years of high school. *American Educational Research Journal, 36,* 303–343.

Rumberger, R. (1983). Dropping out of high school: The influence of race, sex, and family background. *American Educational Research Journal, 20,* 199–220.

Texas Education Agency. (2000). *Dropout study: A report to the 77th Texas legislature.* Austin: Texas Education Agency, Legislative Budget Board, State Auditor's Office.

Weiss, C. C. (2001). Difficult starts: Turbulence in the school year and its impact on urban students' achievement. *American Journal of Education, 109,* 196–227.

CHAPTER 10

Preventing Dropout:
Use and Impact of Organizational Reforms
Designed to Ease the Transition
to High School

KERRI A. KERR

NETTIE E. LEGTERS

The beginning of high school is a critical time for students. Research shows that making a successful transition to high school can help students form lasting attachments to school and increase their likelihood of graduating. The large, bureaucratic nature of most high schools, however, offers little support for incoming ninth graders, especially for those entering with weak social and academic preparation. The current high school reform movement has drawn attention to practices that schools might use to ease ninth graders' transition into high school. Little is known, however, about the extent to which they are being used or their impact on students' engagement and achievement in school. This study begins to address that gap by investigating the types and effects of practices aimed at promoting ninth-grade success. Using quantitative data collected from the universe of public high schools in the state of Maryland, we examine specific practices and assess their impact on student achievement, promotion, and dropout rates.

Results show that high schools in Maryland are using a wide variety of reform practices to ease the transition of ninth-grade students into high school. High-poverty, primarily minority schools have implemented reform practices to a much greater extent than more advantaged schools, particularly practices identified in the literature on communal school organization as promoting a stronger sense of school community. Cross-sectional, multivariate analyses show that the use of two practices representing a major departure from traditional school organization, small learning communities and interdisciplinary teaming of students and teachers, was found to be significantly associated with lower dropout rates. Additionally, analyses of student outcome data that considered how many years a practice had been in place and the percentage of ninth-grade students affected by it revealed associations between the use of these two practices in a widespread and sustained manner and dramatic improvements in schoolwide dropout rates and ninth-grade promotion and achievement rates.

BACKGROUND

Over the past two decades, research on adolescent development, secondary school organization, and school transitions has emphasized the critical nature of the ninth-grade year (see Kerr, 2002b). Researchers have argued that adolescence is an especially difficult time for virtually all children, characterized by rapid social, emotional, physical, and cognitive development. On the cusp of adulthood, children in their early teens begin the quest for independence, yet they continue to need adult guidance and support. Adolescents tend to place great importance on autonomy and a sense of personal self-worth, but also experience a need for personal relationships with both peers and adults and a sense of belonging (Alexander & George, 1981).

As a place where students are expected to spend many of their waking hours, high school is a primary context in which the often confusing, tension-filled dynamics of early adolescence are enacted (Fine, 1994; Simmons & Blyth, 1987). However, most contemporary high schools are not structured to meet the developmental needs of adolescents (National Association of Secondary School Principals, 1985, 1996). The large, bureaucratic nature of most high schools challenges students to adjust to new rules, new expectations, and a new social system, while offering little personal attention or adult support (Lee, Bryk, & Smith, 1993). As students struggle to fit in socially, they also face more demanding academic requirements that can be daunting for those with poor prior preparation in core subjects. For too many students, these conditions can lead to feelings of alienation and self-doubt, and ultimately to disengagement from school (Epstein & MacIver, 1990; Zane, 1994). Many students who are not successfully integrated into the school community make the decision to drop out early in their high school career, often during or immediately following the ninth grade (Bryk, 1994).

The literature on school transitions also offers insight into the myriad difficulties facing ninth graders. Research shows that times of school transition can be problematic for students as they face a new, more anonymous environment and greater social and academic demands (Roderick, 1993). For ninth graders, the pressure of making a school transition is amplified by the developmental struggles they are facing as adolescents, leading to a greater chance for negative outcomes. In her review, Legters (2000) reports that many ninth graders have a difficult time adjusting to the demands of high school, resulting in lower grades, more disciplinary problems, higher failure rates, and feelings that they don't "fit in" to the high school community. Furthermore, students from disadvantaged backgrounds face even greater challenges as they make the transition to high school and may lack the motivation, interest, and support needed to become successfully integrated into the new school environment (Braddock & McPartland, 1993; Bryk & Thum, 1989; Legters, 2000; Roderick, 1993). Finally, academic failure during the transition to high school is directly linked to the probability of dropping out. Roderick (1993) reports that more than 60 percent of students who eventually dropped out of high school failed at least 25 percent of their credits in the ninth grade, while only 8 percent of their peers who eventually graduated had similar difficulty.

Recent literature on the social organization of secondary schools and on high school restructuring provides insight into practices that may increase student engagement and achievement. By focusing on the distinction between bureaucratic and communal school organization, researchers have identified practices that may help create a sense of community within a school, leading to less student alienation and lower dropout rates (Lee & Smith, 1995; Lee, Bryk, & Smith, 1993; Johnston, 1992; Bryk & Driscoll, 1988). Organizational reforms such as small learning communities, detracking in favor of a common core curriculum, and interdisciplinary teaming have been promoted as key reforms in the movement to create more personalized and responsive learning environments at the high school level. Current research fails to address, however, whether and how schools are using these ideas to meet the specific needs of ninth graders and what the impact of those efforts might be. The present study addresses these gaps by examining the types of school reform practices aimed at ninth graders and their impact on students.

DATA AND METHODS

This study draws on two data sources. Primary data were collected in the form of a survey administered to public high school administrators in Maryland. With the support of the Maryland State Department of Education, a survey was administered at all 174 high schools in spring 2000. The survey invited principals or designated administrators to describe the kinds of programs and practices they use to help ease the transition of ninth graders into their school. The 79 percent response rate yielded a sample of 138 schools.

A secondary source of data for this study is information about Maryland high schools collected by the Maryland State Department of Education. Measures of student participation, achievement, and background characteristics are collected from each school and reported annually in the Maryland School Performance Report (MSPAP). This source provides contextual information about each high school surveyed (school size, average student socioeconomic status, and race/ethnicity composition), as well as student outcome measures used in this study. MSPAP reports were first published in 1992, and data from this source are available for all schools in the sample.

Student outcome data for schoolwide dropout rates, ninth-grade math achievement, and ninth-grade promotion rates were drawn from MSPAP. Schoolwide dropout rates are reported annually by the state and measure the percentage of students withdrawing before graduation or before completing a Maryland-approved educational program during a given school year. Math achievement is measured by the percentage of ninth graders who passed the Maryland Functional Math Test (MFMT) by the end of their ninth-grade year.[1] Ninth-grade promotion rates were calculated using MSPAP annual enrollment data. For example, to construct a proximate school-level measure of ninth-grade promotion rates for the 1996–1997 school year, we subtracted the number of tenth graders in 1997–1998 from the number of ninth graders in 1996–1997, then divided by the number of ninth graders in 1996–1997 to create a rough accounting of the percentage of students in a given school moving from ninth to tenth grade on time. This calculation is used to approximate a school's record of promoting ninth graders to tenth grade in those years. Similarly, the same calculation can be done for many consecutive pairs of years using the school enrollment data provided in this data source, allowing for comparisons of this promotion proxy variable over time.[2]

Analysis Plan

We first use the Maryland survey data to investigate the extent to which a subset of nine reform practices aimed at improving ninth-grade success are being used across the entire sample of Maryland high schools.[3] Next we examine the extent to which use of the practices varies with school demographics, such as student socioeconomic status (as measured by percentage of students participating in a free or reduced-price lunch program) and minority student composition. We then examine variations in the use of selected practices identified most commonly in the literature on communal school organization as being likely to produce a strong sense of school community, looking at variation in implementation by school demographic characteristics. In these analyses and others presented in this chapter, survey questions designed to determine the number of years a practice has been in place and the percentage of ninth graders affected by the practice allow us to qualify practices in terms of their level of implementation, a characteristic not available in previous studies. Finally, we use multivariate regression techniques and analysis of longitudinal data to investigate whether and how the use of reform practices with ninth-grade students is associated with schoolwide dropout rates and with ninth-grade promotion and achievement rates.

FINDINGS

Distribution of Practices across Maryland Sample

Survey results reveal that Maryland high schools currently are using a diverse set of practices with their ninth graders. Especially noteworthy is the high rate of use of practices identified by researchers as key organizational reforms to increase student membership in the high school community.

A full 25 percent of high schools currently have a school-within-a-school, academy, or other small learning community (SLC) for ninth graders, while a third of schools provide students with an extra subject period of instruction, or double dose, of a core academic class when extra help is needed. Over one-quarter of high schools employ interdisciplinary teams of ninth-grade teachers who share the same students, of which half meet at least once a week. Just over half of Maryland high schools report that ninth graders meet in extended class periods, and one-third group students in a homeroom or advisory group that meets regularly throughout the school year. Finally, nearly one in five Maryland high schools report that they use ability tracking with ninth graders in one or fewer of the four core academic classes, indicating a significant effort to abandon the use of ability tracking in these schools. Nearly 30 percent of schools in the sample report the use of ability tracking in no more than two of the four core academic subjects, while two-thirds of schools continue to group by ability in all four core subjects.

Maryland schools also are using more traditional approaches to help ninth graders make the transition to high school, as well as practices not widely recognized by educational researchers. Once considered an innovative instructional strategy and now seemingly commonplace, nearly 80 percent of schools report that teachers use student-centered instructional practices such as cooperative learning or student-directed projects or activities an average of once a week or more. Similarly, nearly all Maryland high schools (94%) conduct orientation programs or assemblies for ninth-grade students upon their arrival at high school. Other noteworthy practices aimed at easing the transition to high school include a special curriculum or class for ninth graders to help them learn appropriate study skills and/or social skills, used by nearly half of the schools surveyed, and a summer enrichment program for entering ninth graders, used by a quarter of Maryland high schools.

Distribution of Ninth-Grade Practices by School Characteristics

Survey results from the entire sample of Maryland high schools reveal the use of a wide array of practices to help ninth graders make the transition to high school. We next asked whether certain types of schools were more or less likely to use these practices.

Socioeconomic Status and Minority Composition

Based on the distribution of characteristics in the sample, schools were categorized by the percentage of minority students (defined as nonwhite) and the percentage of students eligible to receive free or reduced-price meals. Schools with a minority population of less than 20 percent and with fewer than 10 percent of students eligible for free or reduced-price meals were categorized as "Low Poverty, Low Minority," while schools with a minority population greater than 50 percent and more than 25 percent of students eligible for free or reduced-price meals were categorized as "High Poverty, Majority Minority." Of the 25 schools labeled high poverty and majority minority, all are located in or near a big city. The 31 schools labeled low poverty and low minority are located exclusively in suburban and rural or small-town settings.

In general, high-poverty, majority-minority schools are overwhelmingly using practices to help ninth graders make the transition to high school more than their low-poverty, low-minority counterparts, and more than the sample as a whole. With the exception of "student-centered instructional practices," high-poverty, majority-minority schools report a greater use of every other practice reported in Table 1. Specifically, practices aimed at creating a more inclusive, personalized learning community and at leveling the playing field in terms of instruction and ability are being used by less advantaged schools at much greater rates. Nearly all schools in this category use extended class periods, while close to half have homeroom or advisory groups for ninth graders, as compared to 42 percent and 32 percent, respectively, of low-poverty, low-minority schools. Similarly, high-poverty, majority-minority schools are nearly four times as likely as more advantaged schools to use interdisciplinary teams and twice as likely to have a school-within-a-school for ninth graders.

High-poverty, majority-minority schools also are implementing practices that may indicate the desire to provide a common educational experience for ninth graders and provide instruction that will bring all students to a common

TABLE 1

Use of Practices and Outcomes by School Demographic Characteristics

Practice	Whole Sample (N=138)	Low-Poverty, Low-Minority Schools (N=31)	High-Poverty, Majority-Minority Schools (N=25)
Student-centered instructional practices	79.7%	83.9%	84.0%
Extended class periods	50.7%	41.9%	88.0%
Special curriculum or classes for 9th graders	45.7%	45.2%	56.0%
Homeroom or advisory groups for 9th graders	33.3%	32.3%	44.0%
Extra subject period, or double dose, of a core academic class	33.3%	19.4%	56.0%
Interdisciplinary teams of 9th-grade teachers who share the same students	26.1%	9.7%	36.0%
Summer program for entering 9th graders for enrichment purposes	26.1%	12.9%	56.0%
School-within-a-school, academy, or other small learning community for 9th graders	24.6%	19.4%	40.0%
One or fewer core academic classes tracked by ability	18.1%	6.5%	44.0%

ability level, thereby leveling the playing field for ninth graders as they begin their high school experiences. While only 7 percent of advantaged schools have abandoned the use of ability tracking in all or nearly all core academic classes, nearly half of high-poverty, majority-minority schools have made similar efforts to detrack the core curriculum. Over half of disadvantaged schools offer a double dose of a core academic class, while the same percentage offer a summer enrichment program for ninth graders before they enter high school.

Implementation Level of Communal Reform Practices

To further investigate the use of reform practices with ninth-grade students, we next focused on practices identified in the literature on communal school organization as likely to promote a strong sense of school community among students. Table 2 explores the depth with which different types of schools have implemented five communal practices—school-within-a-school organization, interdisciplinary teaming of teachers and students, extended class periods, homeroom or advisory groups, and detracking the core curriculum—with their

TABLE 2

Use of Selected Communal Practices by Level of Implementation
and School Demographic Characteristics

Practice	Non–High-Poverty, Majority-Minority Schools (N=113)		High-Poverty, Majority-Minority Schools (N=25)	
	Percentage using practice	Percentage using practice for at least 3 years and with at least 75% of 9th graders	Percentage using practice	Percentage using practice for at least 3 years and with at least 75% of 9th graders
Extended class periods	42.5%	25.7%	88.0%	64.0%
Homeroom or advisory groups for 9th graders	31.0%	16.8%	44.0%	28.0%
One or fewer core academic classes tracked by ability	12.4%	N/A[1]	44.0%	N/A
Interdisciplinary teams of 9th-grade teachers who share the same students	23.9%	5.3%	36.0%	24.0%
School-within-a-school, academy, or other small learning community for 9th graders	21.2%	2.7%	40.0%	24.0%

[1] N/A = implementation data not available

ninth graders. In the statewide survey, principals were asked to disclose the number of years that these selected practices had been in place and the percentage of ninth graders affected by each practice. Results shown in Table 2 reveal that high-poverty, majority-minority schools are much more likely to be implementing the practices in a widespread and sustained manner. For the communal practices where implementation data are available, a majority of high-poverty, majority-minority schools using each practice has been using the practice for at least three years and with at least 75 percent of their ninth graders, demonstrating a more widespread and sustained implementation of communal reform practices in these schools than in more advantaged schools.

Relationship between Ninth-Grade Practices and Student Outcomes

The foregoing analyses show that high-poverty, majority-minority schools are using many of the reform practices designed to ease ninth graders' transition into high school and promote ninth-grade success at greater rates and with a more widespread and sustained level of implementation than other schools in the sample. The question remains whether implementation of the practices enabled these schools to improve student engagement and achievement.

We next present analyses that link two reform practices—school-within-a-school organization and interdisciplinary teaming of teachers and students—to student achievement, promotion, and dropout rates. Small learning communities and interdisciplinary teaming stand out as two practices researchers consider key to encouraging the kinds of shared experiences and caring relationships indicative of a strong school community. They represent a major departure from traditional high school organization and require a redefining of teacher responsibilities and student-teacher interactions. High schools are turning to these practices, rooted in middle school reform efforts, to create more supportive and successful environments, especially for entering ninth graders as they make the transition to high school.

Small learning communities typically entail creation of a smaller unit within the school for a subgroup of students (such as ninth graders). Some high schools are moving away entirely from a traditional organization around subject-area departments and restructuring the entire school around multiple SLCs (sometimes called academies or houses). SLCs often involve a separate location within the school building, a dedicated group of faculty members and administration, and a schedule that keeps SLC members together for many or all of their classes. Interdisciplinary teaming of students and teachers is a practice designed to allow for better communication among a student's many teachers, as well as collaboration across subject areas. Teams are made up of teachers from different disciplines who share a common group of students and are responsible for monitoring the progress of those students and providing needed support. Ideally, teams share a common planning time and meet frequently to discuss the progress of their students. They may also share other responsibilities, such as meeting with parents when necessary, changing student schedules, or arranging for extra instruction in a given subject when needed.

We first assess the effect of the use of these practices, both individually and in conjunction with other reform practices, on student outcomes using multivariate regression techniques. We then examine trends in student outcomes over time based on the level of implementation of the practices.

Results of Cross-Sectional Regression Analysis

To evaluate the relationship between the use of these practices and ninth-grade promotion, ninth-grade math achievement, and schoolwide dropout rates, we applied ordinary least squares regression models, statistically controlling for school size, location, racial/ethnic composition, average percentage of students qualifying for free or reduced-price meals, average prior achievement, and the

TABLE 3

Standardized Beta Coefficients for Baseline Models Predicting Schoolwide
Dropout Rates, Ninth-Grade Promotion Rates, and Ninth-Grade Achievement

	Outcome:		
			Percentage of
	Schoolwide	*Ninth-Grade*	*Ninth Graders*
Control Variable	*Dropout Rates*	*Promotion Rates*	*Passing MFMT*
Percentage minority students	−.186	−.047	−.214***
Percentage of students eligible for free or reduced-price meals	−.005	−.091	.038
Enrollment	−.029	−.042	.007
Poverty rate	.083	.151†	.025
Average percentage passing the MFMT, 1993–1999	−.008	−.065	.786***
Average prior outcome, 1994–1999	.672***	.762***	
Adjusted R²	.444	.521	.803

† p ≤ .10
*** p ≤ .001

average value of the outcome variable over all prior years where data are available. For each practice, we also constructed dummy variables to identify schools using the practice in combination with a given number of the other key practices (described in Table 1). Independent variables measuring practice use were then entered into the regression models one at a time; each variable was entered, tested, then removed before the next independent variable was entered in the model.

Table 3 presents the results of baseline models testing the effects of student background, prior achievement, and prior outcome measures on all three outcomes.[4] As expected, the average prior outcome measure is the strongest predictor of each outcome in the baseline models. For the case of ninth-grade math achievement, while the strongest predictor of current math achievement is prior math achievement, the percentage of minority students in the student body is also a strong predictor of math achievement. Notably, the model including student background variables and prior math achievement has an adjusted R² statistic of .803. This model therefore explains 80 percent of the variance in passing rates for the MFMT. This high rate of explained variance highlights the overwhelming stability in passing rates on this math test over

TABLE 4

Standardized Beta Coefficients for Ordinary Least Squares Regression Model Testing Influence of the Use of Small Learning Communities and Interdisciplinary Teaming on Schoolwide Dropout Rates, Ninth-Grade Promotion Rates, and Ninth-Grade Achievement[1]

| Independent Variable | Outcome: | | |
	Schoolwide Dropout Rates	Ninth-Grade Promotion Rates	Percentage of Ninth Graders Passing MFMT
Uses small learning community (SLC)	–.171*	.067	–.022
Uses SLC plus at least 2 other practices	–.171*	.067	–.022
Uses SLC plus at least 3 other practices	–.182**	.043	–.040
Uses SLC plus at least 4 other practices	–.227***	.122†	.000
Uses interdisciplinary teaming	–.167**	.058	.023
Uses teams plus at least 2 other practices	–.162*	.041	.018
Uses teams plus at least 3 other practices	–.151*	.020	.005
Uses teams plus at least 4 other practices	–.161*	.073	.046
Uses SLC and teams	–.160*	.005	.008

† $p \leq .10$
* $p \leq .05$
** $p \leq .01$
*** $p \leq .001$

[1] Each model holds constant the percentage of minority students, percentage of students eligible for free or reduced-price lunch, enrollment, poverty rate, average prior achievement, and average prior outcome for each school. See Table 3 for standardized beta coefficients and adjusted R^2 statistic for baseline model.

time and makes it unlikely that reform practices may be another determinant of this outcome.

Table 4 presents results of regression models testing the effect of the use of small learning communities and interdisciplinary teams, independently and in conjunction with other reform practices. Each standardized coefficient listed in the table represents the results of a separate model, where the impact of the independent variable is tested independently while controlling for student background, prior achievement, and prior outcome levels.

Results show that the use of small learning communities and interdisciplinary teams for ninth graders, either independently or together, is significantly associated with lower schoolwide dropout rates when controlling for student background characteristics, prior achievement, and prior outcome values. We also find that the influence of using small learning communities on dropout rates increases in size and significance with the use of additional reform practices. Using a small learning community with ninth graders in combination with four of the remaining eight practices produces the strongest association with reduced dropout rates. The use of additional practices in conjunction with interdisciplinary teaming does not strengthen its association with dropout rates. Finally, the use of both a small learning community and interdisciplinary teaming with ninth graders offers no greater explanatory power than that seen with each individual practice. In sum, significant associations are seen between the use of small learning communities and/or interdisciplinary teams and reduced dropout rates, with the strongest relationship appearing when small learning communities are used in conjunction with several additional reform practices.

These analyses do not show a significant relationship between the use of small learning communities or interdisciplinary teaming for ninth graders and ninth-grade promotion rates or math achievement. The use of a small learning community combined with at least four other reform practices approaches significance, but the coefficients of other measures of the use of these practices, independently or with other practices, are at or near zero, showing little or no effect of using these practices on ninth-grade promotion and math achievement.

Trends in Student Outcomes over Time Based on the Use of a Small Learning Community or Interdisciplinary Teaming

To further investigate the link between organizational reforms for ninth-grade students and student outcomes, we next examined trends in student outcomes over time based on the level of implementation of small learning communities and interdisciplinary teams. Researchers agree that creating a strong sense of community is not a task that can be easily mandated or achieved, especially in troubled or underachieving high schools (Legters et al., 2002). Strong program implementation must be coupled with teachers' and students' willingness to create a more inclusive environment. While school administrators cannot control the feelings of students and teachers, they can control the ways in which programs and reform practices are implemented. Therefore, it is necessary to consider the scope of implementation of reform practices when assessing their potential impact on students, factors rarely considered in previous research. In this paper we consider two aspects of implementation, the number of years a

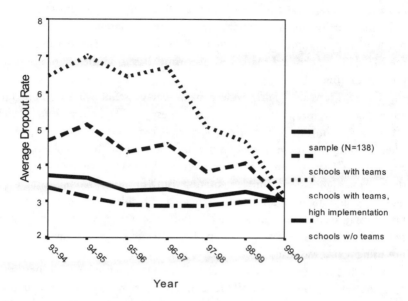

FIGURE 1

Average Schoolwide Dropout Rate over Time Based on the Use of
Interdisciplinary Teaming with Ninth-Grade Students

practice has been in place and the percentage of ninth graders affected by the
practice, when evaluating the relationship between practice use and student
outcomes. Together, these measures allow us to identify schools using these two
key practices in a manner that suggests widespread (involving at least 75% of
ninth graders) and sustained (used for at least three years) implementation.

In the following analyses, for both practices and each student outcome,
outcome levels are graphed over time for schools using the given practice at a
high level of implementation, defined as using the practice for three or more
years and with at least 75 percent of ninth graders, and for those using the practice but not meeting the criteria for high implementation. These trajectories are
compared to the outcome over the same years in both the sample as a whole and
the schools in the sample not using the given practice.

Interdisciplinary Teaming

Figure 1 presents the average schoolwide dropout rate for each year in which
dropout data are available for various groups of schools, based on the use of interdisciplinary teams in the 1999–2000 school year. Each graph includes four
lines that represent 1) use of teams with a high level of implementation; 2) use

of interdisciplinary teams in a way that does not meet our criteria for a high level of implementation; 3) schools not using interdisciplinary teaming; and 4) the sample as a whole. Comparisons across the various trajectories suggest patterns in dropout rates that may be related to the use and scope of implementation of interdisciplinary teaming. Figure 2 contains similar graphical data for ninth-grade promotion rates and Figure 3 displays the average passing rates on the Maryland Functional Math Test over time, based on the use of interdisciplinary teaming.

Figure 1 reveals a fairly wide gap in average schoolwide dropout rates among the four groups of schools in the earliest year data are available, 1993–1994. At this time, the schools that had already or would eventually implement interdisciplinary teams at a high level of implementation had the highest average dropout rate, followed by the schools implementing teams but not using them at the higher level of implementation. Both groups of schools using teams had somewhat higher rates than the sample as a whole and than those schools not electing to use teams in the 1999–2000 school year. Overall, the gap between schools using teams in a more widespread and sustained way and schools not using teams was just over three percentage points.

The graph shows an overall pattern of decline in schoolwide dropout rates over the seven school years. While dropout rates for the sample and those schools not using teams remained relatively stable or dropped slightly, those schools using teams had a more dramatic decrease in dropout rates. Schools using teams with a high level of implementation cut their average dropout rate by more than 50 percent. Overall, the gap between the groups closed almost completely, leaving only a one-tenth of one percent difference in dropout rates from the highest-performing to the lowest-performing group. In fact, the schoolwide dropout rate in 1999–2000 for schools using teams was slightly lower than that of the sample as a whole and those schools not using teams.

Similar patterns are seen across the four groups of schools for both ninth-grade promotion rates and passing rates on the Maryland Functional Math Test. Figure 2 shows fairly stable rates of ninth-grade promotion for the schools in the sample and those schools not using interdisciplinary teams. These groups maintain a consistent promotion rate of around 90 percent. As is seen with dropout rates, schools implementing teams at the highest level of implementation have the lowest earlier promotion rates, while schools using teams but not meeting the criteria for high implementation have promotion rates between that of the high implementers and the rest of the sample. Again, we see a closing of the gap between the initial rates and rates in the 1999–2000 school year among the highest- and lowest-performing groups. In 1993–1994, a nearly 10

FIGURE 2

Average Ninth-Grade Promotion Rate over Time Based on the
Use of Interdisciplinary Teaming with Ninth-Grade Students

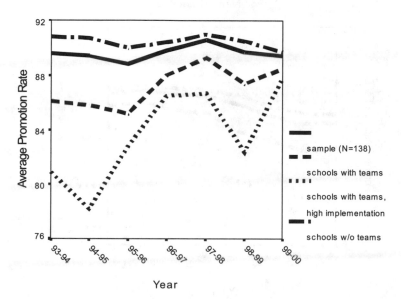

percent gap existed, compared to only a 2 percent gap in 1999–2000, a reduction of 81 percent. While both groups of schools using teams experienced setbacks, or drops, along the way, both had a net gain in promotion rates, with substantial net gains seen in the high implementers.

Figure 3 shows a pattern of improvement in passing rates on the MFMT for all groups. Schools in the sample as whole and those not using teams each gained around five percentage points, while both groups of schools using teams had a slightly steeper increase. Schools using teams in a sustained and widespread manner had the greatest upward trajectory, improving over 14 percentage points. In general, the gap between the highest- and lowest-performing schools was more than cut in half over the eight-year period, going from over 16 percent to just under 7 percent.

Small Learning Community

Similar analyses examining average outcomes over time based on the use and scope of implementation of a small learning community for ninth graders suggest a relationship between the use of a small learning community and improved outcomes. As Figure 4 indicates, large differences existed in schoolwide dropout

FIGURE 3

Average Percentage of Ninth Graders Passing the Maryland Functional
Math Test over Time Based on the Use of Interdisciplinary Teaming
with Ninth-Grade Students

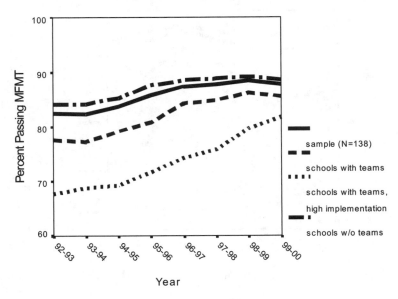

rates at the earliest time point, 1993–1994, between those schools implementing a small learning community in the 1999–2000 school year and schools not using the practice. Overall, an 8.8 percentage point gap existed between the lowest-performing schools, those eventually deciding to implement a small learning community in a widespread and sustained manner, and schools not using a small learning community. While the averages in the sample as a whole and schools not using the practice stayed relatively stable over time, both groups of schools using a small learning community reported decreasing dropout rates. Dropout rates in schools using a small learning community at a high level of implementation dropped by nearly two-thirds, while the gap between the lowest- and highest-performing schools dropped to just 1.4 percentage points.

Similar patterns exist in the trajectory of ninth-grade promotion rates and passing rates on the MFMT across the four groups of schools. Promotion rates in the sample and in schools not using a small learning community stayed the same over the seven-year period. While schools using a small learning community but not meeting the criteria for a high scope of implementation showed a slight increase of just over four percentage points, the most dramatic change was seen in schools using the practice with a high level of implementation.

FIGURE 4

Average Schoolwide Dropout Rate over Time Based on the Use of a
Small Learning Community with Ninth-Grade Students

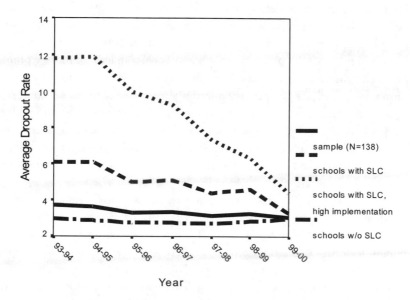

These schools increased promotion rates by 16 percentage points, closing the gap to just over ten percentage points overall.

Analysis of trends in student math achievement again shows great gains in schools using a small learning community at a higher level of implementation and a closing of the performance gap between the highest- and lowest-performing schools over the time period from 1992–1993 to 1999–2000. Schools using a small learning community at a higher level of implementation improved their passing rates by 19 percentage points, as compared to gains of approximately five percentage points for schools in the sample as a whole and for schools not using a small learning community. Overall, the gap between the highest-performing schools, those not using the practice, and the lowest-performing schools, those using the practice with a higher level of implementation, was cut dramatically, in this case by nearly 40 percent.

DISCUSSION AND POLICY IMPLICATIONS

The foregoing analyses show that public high schools in Maryland are using a number of different reform practices to support ninth graders' transition to high school. While reform practices are being used across the board, they are most prevalent in high-poverty, majority-minority schools. In addition, we found that high-poverty, majority-minority schools were most likely to have implemented practices identified in the literature on communal school organization and were most likely to have implemented these practices in a widespread and sustained manner. The overrepresentation of reform practices in high-poverty, majority-minority schools makes sense in light of the low promotion and achievement rates that likely motivate those schools to try a greater number of innovative or new organizational practices. The policy context in Maryland in the 1990s, where low-performing schools were threatened with reconstitution if they failed to develop a reform plan and make rapid improvements, also helps explain this finding. It is likely that a combination of both internal conditions and external pressure to reform led to the adoption of these practices in these schools.

Multivariate analyses reveal that two practices that have received a great deal of attention in the research literature and represent major departures from traditional high school organization—small learning communities and interdisciplinary teaming—are significantly associated with lower schoolwide dropout rates net of other school characteristics. These findings lend support to arguments that creating smaller, more personalized learning environments in schools can enhance students' attachment to school. Influence on dropout rates is especially strong in schools that combine the use of small learning communities for ninth graders with other reform practices, suggesting that high schools that demonstrate a more comprehensive commitment to reform may produce stronger results in terms of student engagement reflected by lower dropout rates.

Our multivariate analyses did not reveal, however, significant relationships between use of small learning communities or interdisciplinary teaming and ninth-grade promotion or math achievement. This may be explained in part by weak theoretical and practical links between these organizational practices and instructional outcomes. Research shows that, when well implemented, organizational reforms designed to create more communal environments in high schools can have immediate positive effects on a school's overall climate and sense of student and adult membership in a community (Legters, Balfanz, Jordan, & McPartland, 2002). These practices do not directly target curriculum and instruction, however, and may, at least initially, have little impact on what students or teachers do in the classroom. That the model that combines small learning community organization with other reform practices approaches a significant influence on ninth-grade promotion suggests that a more comprehensive approach is needed to generate academic success for ninth graders.

The multivariate analyses are limited both by the cross-sectional nature of the data and by the lack of information about the level of implementation of the practices across the schools. In those analyses, a small learning community in its first year that includes only a small group of students was given weight equal to an academy that had existed for several years and included all ninth graders. This also may partially explain the weak relationship between the practices and ninth-grade promotion and math achievement. Recent studies of small learning community and interdisciplinary teaming strategies suggest that, while schools may experience relatively quick improvements in overall climate, it takes time for adults to develop the systems and relationships and incorporate the additional practices necessary to have a meaningful impact on student learning (Gunn & King, 2003; Legters et al., 2002). Sample size restricted our ability to conduct more sophisticated modeling of the relationship between level of implementation and gains in dropout, promotion, and math achievement. The longitudinal analysis presented in Figures 1–4, however, suggests that widespread and sustained implementation of organizational reform practices aimed at ninth graders is more likely to produce both engagement and achievement gains for students. High schools that implemented small learning communities and interdisciplinary teams for more than 75 percent of their ninth graders and sustained the reforms for three or more years showed significant and dramatic improvement on all three of the outcomes considered in this study.

Though far from definitive, these findings suggest that organizational reform practices may have positive effects on reducing dropout rates and improving ninth-grade promotion and achievement, especially when they are implemented as part of a more comprehensive reform approach with a majority of ninth graders and sustained over time. It would be going beyond the data to suggest that the gains reported here can be attributed solely to the introduction or presence of a small learning community, interdisciplinary teams, or other reform practices investigated in this chapter. The question remains how the implementation of these two practices weighs against the myriad other factors that remain unmeasured in our sample, including additional resources, official and public scrutiny, data tampering to stave off sanctions, influence of state monitors and local reform partners, or general reform momentum experienced by low-performing high schools during this period.

A study addressing the actual impact of a school-within-a-school approach, interdisciplinary teaming, or any of the other practices would certainly benefit from more extensive implementation data. While we measure the extent of implementation in terms of how widespread and sustained these practices are in a given school, these measures reveal little about the quality of implementation of a given practice. For example, a school-within-a-school or other small learning community for ninth graders can range from a purely nominal change, such as renaming the ninth-grade class the "Ninth-Grade Academy," to technical changes such as changing course schedules or requirements, to instituting deep structural and cultural changes that support the creation of a more personalized, supportive learning environment where feelings of trust and belonging are nurtured among students, faculty, and administrators. The differences in these levels of implementation, though not apparent in our measures, are an essential part of determining what impact these practices have on student outcomes. A more complete understanding of how schools are implementing practices would require visiting schools, talking to members of the school community, and comparing different modes of implementation in different contexts across a number of schools. Any argument to promote or scale up school-within-a-school organization or other reform practices should be based on a richer understanding of what is needed to achieve high-quality implementation than we offer here.

CONCLUSION

This study shows that reform practices are being used by high schools in Maryland to promote ninth-grade success, and that high-poverty, majority-minority schools are most likely to have adopted these practices. Moreover, the schools that reported using a school-within-a-school approach or interdisciplinary teams with ninth graders in spring of 2000, especially those that report using it in a widespread and sustained way, showed substantial improvements on promotion, dropout, and achievement outcomes between 1993–1994 and 1999–2000. We believe these findings warrant further investigation of the potential of school-within-a-school, interdisciplinary teams, and other reform practices to improve student outcomes, especially in low-performing high schools.

As educational researchers and practitioners work to find the best ways to organize high schools for the benefit of teachers and students alike, more attention must be given to the unique needs of ninth graders as they make the transition to a new school environment while also facing the challenges of adolescence. Identifying specific organizational practices that may increase students' sense of belonging to the educational community, as shown by positive effects on their chance of graduating from high school and promising links to improved test scores and promotion rates, is an important and necessary step on the path to improving the conditions of today's public high schools.

NOTES

1. The class of 2004 is the last class for which passing the Functional Math Test and its counterparts in Reading and Citizenship is required for graduation. These tests are being phased out in favor of new subject-area exams as part of the state's general effort to raise standards for high school graduation.
2. This method of calculating promotion rate follows the concept of "promoting power" used by Balfanz and Legters to estimate schoolwide dropout rates. See Chapter 3 for a discussion of the advantages and potential biases of using these types of proxy measures.
3. See Kerr (2002a) for a discussion of additional school organizational practices used with ninth-grade students.
4. The average dropout rate from years 1994–1999 is used to control for each school's dropout rate prior to the primary data collection. Similarly, the average promotion rate from years 1994–1999 is used to control for prior promotion rates at each school. For math achievement, both the prior achievement and prior outcome levels are measured by the average percentage passing the Maryland Functional Math Test, 1993–1999.

REFERENCES

Alexander, W. M., & George, P.S. (1981). *The exemplary middle school.* New York: Holt, Rinehart and Winston.

Braddock, J. H., & McPartland, J. M. (1993). Education of early adolescents. *Review of Research in Education, 19,* 135–170.

Bryk, A. S. (1994). More good news that school organization matters. In *Issues in restructuring schools* (Issues Report No. 7). Madison, WI: Center on Organization and Restructuring of Schools.

Bryk, A. S., & Driscoll, M. E. (1988). *The high school as community: Theoretical foundations, contextual influences, and consequences for students and teachers.* Madison: University of Wisconsin, National Center on Effective Secondary Schools.

Bryk, A. S., & Thum, Y. M. (1989). The effects of high school organization on dropping out: An exploratory investigation. *American Educational Research Journal, 26,* 353–383.

Epstein, J. L., & MacIver, D. J. (1990). *Education in the middle grades: National practices and trends.* Columbus, OH: National Middle Schools Association.

Fine, M. (1994). Chartering urban school reform. In M. Fine (Ed.), *Chartering urban school reform: Reflections on public high schools in the midst of change* (pp. 5–30). New York: Teachers College Press.

Gunn, J. H., & King, M. B. (2003, March). Trouble in paradise: Power, conflict, and community in an interdisciplinary teaching team. *Urban Education, 38,* 173–195.

Johnston, J. H. (1992). Climate and culture as mediators of school values and collaborative behavior. In Judith L. Irvin (Ed.), *Transforming middle level education: Perspectives and possibilities* (pp. 77–92). Boston: Allyn & Bacon.

Kerr, K. A. (2002a). An examination of approaches to promote ninth grade success in Maryland public high schools. *ERS Spectrum, 20*(3), 4–13.

Kerr, K. A. (2002b). *Easing the transition to high school: The effect of school organization on ninth grade success.* Unpublished doctoral dissertation, Johns Hopkins University, Baltimore.

Legters, N. E. (2000). Small learning communities meet school-to-work: Whole-school re-structuring for urban comprehensive high schools. In M. G. Sanders (Ed.), *Schooling students placed at risk: Research, policy, and practice in the education of poor and minority adolescents.* Mahwah, NJ: Erlbaum Associates.

Legters, N. E., Balfanz, R., Jordan, W., McPartland, J. (2002). *Comprehensive reform for urban high schools: A talent development approach.* New York: Teachers College Press.

Lee, V. E., Bryk, A. S., & Smith, J. B. (1993). The organization of effective secondary schools. *Review of Research in Education, 19,* 135–170.

Lee, V. E. & Smith, J. B. (1995, October). Effects of high school restructuring and size on early gains in achievement and engagement. *Sociology of Education, 68,* 241–270.

National Association of Secondary School Principals. (1985). *How fares the ninth grade? A day in the life of a 9th grader.* Reston, VA. Author.

National Association of Secondary School Principals. (1996). *Breaking ranks: Changing an American institution.* Reston, VA. Author.

Roderick, M. R. (1993). *The path to dropping out: Evidence for intervention.* Westport, CT: Auburn House.

Simmons, R. G. & Blyth, D. A. (1987). *Moving into adolescence: The impact of pubertal change and school context.* New York: Aldine de Gruyter.

Zane, N. (1994). When "discipline problems" recede: Democracy and intimacy in urban charters. In M. Fine (Ed.), *Chartering urban school reform: Reflections on public high schools in the midst of change* (pp. 122–135). New York: Teachers College Press.

This study was supported by grants from the Spencer Foundation and the Office of Educational Research and Improvement (OERI), U.S. Department of Education. The content or opinions expressed herein do not necessarily reflect the views of the Department of Education or any other agency of the U.S. government. The opinions expressed are solely those of the authors and do not represent those of the Spencer Foundation, OERI, RAND, or any of their sponsors.

CHAPTER 11

What Can Be Done to Reduce the Dropout Rate?[1]

RUSSELL W. RUMBERGER

What can be done to design and implement effective dropout intervention strategies? The review of the research literature in the earlier chapter, "Why Students Drop Out of School," suggests several approaches. First, because dropping out is influenced by both individual and institutional factors, intervention strategies can focus on either or both sets of factors. For example, intervention strategies can address the individual values, attitudes, and behaviors that are associated with dropping out without attempting to alter the characteristics of the families, schools, and communities that may contribute to those individual factors. Many dropout prevention programs pursue such programmatic strategies by providing would-be dropouts with additional resources and supports to help them stay in school. Alternatively, intervention strategies can focus on attempting to improve the environmental contexts of potential dropouts by providing resources and supports to strengthen or restructure their families, schools, and communities. Such systemic strategies are often part of larger efforts to improve the educational and social outcomes of at-risk students more generally. Both strategies are discussed in more detail below.

Second, because dropping out is associated with both academic and social problems, effective prevention strategies must focus on both arenas. That is, if dropout-prevention strategies are going to be effective, they must be comprehensive by providing resources and supports in all areas of students' lives. And because dropouts leave school for a variety of reasons, services provided them must be flexible and tailored to their individual needs.

Third, because the problematic attitudes and behaviors of students at risk of dropping out appear as early as elementary school, dropout-prevention strategies can and should begin early in a child's educational career. Dropout-prevention programs often target high school or middle school students who may have already experienced years of educational failure or unsolved problems.

243

Similarly, dropout-recovery programs that begin in middle or high school must attempt to overcome longstanding problems in order to get dropouts to complete school. Consequently, such programs may be costly and ineffective. Conversely, early intervention may be the most powerful and cost-effective approach to dropout prevention.

The overall conclusion is that there are a variety of potentially effective approaches and strategies for designing dropout interventions. Given that conclusion, what evidence do we have of the effectiveness of alternative approaches?

Unfortunately, the evidence on the effectiveness of dropout interventions is generally weak for two fundamental reasons. First, there have been relatively few rigorous evaluations of dropout-intervention programs. For example, the General Accounting Office surveyed more than 1,000 dropout programs in the fall of 1986, yet it found only 20 rigorous evaluations of the 479 programs that responded to the survey (U.S. GAO, 1987). Second, the evaluations that do exist often fail to demonstrate program effectiveness (see ch. 12). Similarly, Slavin and Fashola (1998) conducted a literature search of dropout-prevention programs with rigorous, experimental evaluations and found only two that were effective.

Despite the dearth of research evidence, case studies of proven or at least promising approaches do exist. These case studies not only provide examples of both programmatic and systemic approaches to dropout prevention, but have also identified some of the features that have contributed to their effectiveness.

PROGRAMMATIC APPROACHES

There are two programmatic approaches to dropout prevention. One approach is to provide supplemental services to students within an existing school program. The second approach is to provide an alternative school program either within an existing school (school within a school) or in a separate facility (alternative school). Neither approach attempts to change existing institutions serving most students; instead they create alternative programs or institutions to target students who are somehow identified as being at risk of dropping out.

Supplemental Programs

One example of a supplemental yet comprehensive programmatic approach to dropout prevention is the Achievement for Latinos through Academic Success or ALAS program (Gándara, Larson, Mehan, & Rumberger, 1998). ALAS was developed, implemented, and evaluated as a pilot intervention program to serve the most at-risk students in a poor, predominantly Latino middle school in the Los Angeles area from 1990 to 1995.

The program specifically targeted two groups of high-risk students: special education students and other students who, because of poor academic performance, misbehavior, and low income, were at greatest risk of school failure. The pilot program served two cohorts of special education students (77 total) and one cohort of 46 high-risk students. Participating students received the intervention program in conjunction with the regular school program for all three years they remained in the target school.

ALAS was founded on the premise that youths and their school, family, and community contexts must all be addressed simultaneously for dropout-prevention efforts to succeed. Thus, ALAS consisted of a series of specific intervention strategies focused on individual adolescents and on these three contexts of influence on achievement: the family, the school, and the community. The intervention strategies were designed to increase the effectiveness of factors in each context and increase collaboration between them. ALAS provided the following specific interventions:

1. Remediation of students' ineffective problem-solving skills regarding social interactions and task performance through ten weeks of problem-solving instruction and two years of follow-up problem-solving training and counseling.
2. Personal recognition and bonding activities, such as praise, outings, recognition ceremonies, certificates, and positive home calls to parents to discuss meeting goals or improving student behavior to increase self-esteem, affiliation, and a sense of belonging with the school organization.
3. Intensive attendance monitoring, including period-by-period attendance records and daily follow-ups with parents, to communicate a personal interest in students' attendance.
4. Frequent teacher feedback to parents and students regarding classroom comportment, missed assignments, and missing homework.
5. Direct instruction and modeling for parents on how to reduce their child's inappropriate or undesirable behavior and how to increase desirable behavior.
6. Integration of school and home needs with community services.

The program was evaluated using an experimental design in which high-risk students were randomly assigned to the treatment or a control group, and participating special education students were compared to a previous year's cohort of special education students. The evaluation examined enrollment status and credits earned in ninth grade, the final year of the program, and in the remaining years of high school after the program ended. Evaluation data on mobility, attendance, failed classes, and graduation credits indicate that the ALAS program had a substantial and practical impact on students who received the intervention (Gándara et al., 1998). By the end of ninth grade, students in the comparison group had twice the number of failed classes, were four times more likely to have excessive absences, and were twice as likely to be seriously behind in high school graduation credits. These results appear even more remarkable when noting that the participants in this study represent the most difficult-to-teach students within a pool generally viewed as high risk. Nonetheless, these dramatic effects were not sustained. By the end of twelfth grade, only 32 percent of the ALAS participants and 27 percent of the comparison students had completed high school. This clearly suggests that in order to increase graduation rates, an ALAS-type intervention must be provided throughout the high school years.

Is there any evidence that interventions in elementary school or preschool could have long-term, sustained effects in reducing dropout rates in secondary school? For example, since grade retention is a powerful predictor of dropping out of school, programs that reduce the incidence of retention should help reduce the dropout rate. Recent reviews based on rigorous, experimental evaluations identified several preschool programs that have been shown to reduce high school dropout rates (Currie, 2001; Karoly et al., 1998).

One such preschool program is the High/Scope Perry Pre-School program (Barnett, 1995). The program targeted 123 African Americans born in poverty who were at high risk of failing in school. At ages 3 and 4, the children were randomly divided into a program group who received a high-quality preschool program based on High/Scope's active learning approach, and a comparison group who received no preschool program. In the study's most recent phase, 95 percent of the original study participants were interviewed at age 27. Additional data were gathered from the subjects' school, social services, and arrest records.

The program evaluation found a wide range of social and economic benefits, including reduced crime rates, higher earnings, and reduced welfare dependency. In terms of education, those who received the preschool program were a third more likely than those who received no preschool education to graduate from regular or adult high school or to receive General Education Development (GED) certification (71 percent versus 54 percent). These outcomes are quite remarkable, considering that they occurred 13 years or more after the intervention ended. They suggest that early interventions for students at risk of dropping out can be effective.

Alternative Programs

The other programmatic approach to dropout prevention is to create alternative school programs that target only students at risk of dropping out. These programs can either operate within regular schools or as separate, alternative schools. They generally provide a complete education program, but one that represents an alternative to that offered in regular, comprehensive schools. In addition, they typically provide many of the other support services that are found in supplemental programs.

There have been several evaluations of effective alternative programs: Stern and colleagues (Stern, Dayton, Paik, Weisberg, & Evans, 1988) evaluated eleven within-school academy programs in California high schools; Wehlage et al. (Wehlage, Rutter, Smith, Lesko, & Fernandez, 1989) evaluated twelve alternative and two comprehensive schools; and Dynarski and Gleason (1998) evaluated three within-school programs and six alternative schools. Although the programs differed in the types of students they enrolled, the curricula and services they provided, and the ways they were structured, there appear to be several common features among effective programs:

- a nonthreatening environment for learning
- a caring and committed staff who accept a personal responsibility for student success
- a school culture that encourages staff risk-taking, self-governance, and professional collegiality
- a school structure that provides for a low student-teacher ratio and a small class size to promote student engagement

These reviews clearly illustrate that it is possible to create effective alternative programs to address the needs and promote the learning of students at risk of dropping out. Yet creating successful alternative programs presents a number of challenges. First, programs can have difficulty in attracting students because of negative perceptions by students, parents, and educators that such schools are a dumping ground for "bad" students and that they symbolize the failure of the regular system (Dynarski & Gleason, 1998). Some programs have responded to this problem by restricting entry to more motivated at-risk students, which raises questions about the purpose of such schools. Second, because of their low regard, such programs often have a hard time competing for resources with regular school programs.

SYSTEMIC SOLUTIONS

Systemic solutions have the potential to reduce the risk of dropping out for a much larger number of students by improving some of the environmental factors in families, schools, and communities that contribute to dropout behavior. That was the position taken by the National Research Council Panel on High-Risk Youth (1993), which argued:

The primary institutions that serve youth—health, schools, employment, training—are crucial and we must begin with helping them respond more effectively to contemporary adolescent needs. Effective responses will involve pushing the boundaries of these systems, encouraging collaborations between them and reducing the number of adolescents whose specialized problems cannot be met through primary institutions. (p. 193)

Although the promise of systemic solutions to the dropout problem is great, the reality is sobering. The reason is simply that systemic changes are extremely difficult to achieve because they involve making fundamental changes in the way institutions work, both individually and within the system of which they are a part. Despite the difficulty of making such changes, there are examples of effective institutional changes, particularly in schools that have been successful in improving the graduation rates of high-risk students.

One well-known example is Central Park East Secondary School (CPESS) in New York City (van Heusden Hale, 2000). The school enrolls 450 public school students in grades 7 through 12, most of whom are from low-income families and many of whom have a history of average or below-average academic achievement. No selection criteria, tests, or interviews are required to attend the school, which is supported by public education funds. Costs per student are the same as other public high schools.

The school offers an intellectually rigorous and creative education normally associated with elite private schools. Classes are small, averaging 20 students, and the day is organized into two-hour periods, allowing teachers and students enough time to engage in concentrated work in specific areas. Students take two main subject groups: mathematics and science, and social studies and the humanities. The school offers both interdisciplinary college-preparatory courses and career-oriented apprenticeships. It has established high standards and clear expectations for its students. Student performance is regularly assessed through a process in which students explain their work and hear it criticized. To graduate, they must present seven academic projects in specified subjects over two years and defend them before committees of students, teachers, and other adults, much as a Ph.D. candidate defends a thesis.

The school has developed beneficial relationships with parents and the community, and has worked overtime to connect with and involve parents in the school and in their own child's schooling. School leaders have also formed a number of partnerships with community agencies. In addition, the school has a community service requirement where students spend one morning a week working in community service jobs.

According to CPESS codirector Brigette Belletiere, four specific practices support the school's success:

- articulation and maintenance of a clear vision and mission that the staff carries out
- goal-setting in line with the vision
- allocation of instructional resources to keep class size small
- providing time for ongoing, job-embedded professional development

The school maintains its progress and continually improves itself through an internal democratic process. The staff develops curricula, assessments, and the criteria for earning a CPESS diploma. They are also held accountable for maintaining school standards.

Student achievement data documents the school's success. Only 5 percent of the students drop out during their high school years, and more than 90 percent of Central Park East's graduates go on to college. Students have high attendance rates and a low incidence of violence.

Case studies of other schools have been able to identify effective schools and describe the salient features that enable them to keep students enrolled and eventually graduate. These features are similar to those that have been identified for "effective" schools more generally (e.g., Newman, 1993; Purkey & Smith, 1985). While the list of specific features varies from one author to another (e.g., Newman, 1993; Purkey & Smith, 1985; Wehlage et al., 1989),[2] they essentially address two basic features of schools: the commitment and competencies of the people (teachers, administrators, and staff) and the organizational structure (size, staffing ratio, curriculum design, services, etc.). While it remains unclear whether one feature must change before the other, both appear to be necessary. For example, simply adopting "progressive" structural changes, such as site-based management or team teaching, may do little if teachers do not have the requisite commitment and competencies (Newman, 1993). At the same time, certain organizational features, such as smaller school size and shared decision-making, may be necessary to develop and support teachers' commitment to the institution and to the students it serves (Wehlage et al., 1989). What also remains unclear is the extent to which it may be necessary to recruit teachers and staff with the necessary commitment and competencies before creating a supportive structure.[3]

Research has been able to identify the features of effective secondary schools. Yet while identifying such features is the first step in the school reform process (Purkey & Smith, 1985), the next step is much harder and thus far has eluded school reformers: *Identifying the resources, technical support, and incentives to transform or restructure existing schools in order to create those ineffective features.*[4] Although a number of programs and policies have been instituted by local districts and state and federal governments to support school restructuring at the secondary level, these efforts have generally not had much success, especially in reducing dropout rates.

One study (Dynarksi & Gleason, 1998) suggests that it may be more difficult to transform existing institutions than to create new ones. This may be especially true when it comes to reducing dropout rates in urban high schools. In their study of 207 urban high schools that were attempting major school reform programs based on the effective schools literature, Louis and Miles (1990) found widespread improvement in a number of areas, such as student behavior and student and staff morale. But even among programs that had implemented their programs for several years and enjoyed improvements in student achievement, improvement in dropout rates was "rarely achieved no matter how long a program had been in operation" (Louis & Miles, 1990, p. 49).

While efforts to restructure secondary schools to reduce dropout rates have proved elusive, so too have efforts to reform other institutions that serve at-risk youth. One ambitious systemic reform effort was the New Futures Initiative, promoted and funded by the Annie E. Casey foundation beginning in 1988. New Futures was an attempt to build new collaborative structures among existing public and private institutions in five cities (Dayton, Ohio; Lawrence, Massachusetts; Little Rock, Arkansas; Pittsburgh, Pennsylvania; and Savannah, Georgia) to address the problems of at-risk youth, including dropping out of school. The key strategy was to establish an oversight collaborative in each city with representation from public and private sector agencies to "identify youth problems, develop strategies, and set timelines for addressing these problems, coordinate joint agency activities, and restructure educational and social services" (White & Wehlage, 1995, p. 24). The collaboratives also included case managers who 1) brokered services among the disparate agencies serving at-risk youth and their families; 2) served as advocates for at-risk youth; and 3) served as the "eyes and ears" of the collaboratives by providing information and feedback to the group about what reforms were needed.

Evaluations of this ambitious, systemic reform effort found that it did little to reduce dropout rates and other problems of at-risk youth (Wehlage, Smith, & Lipman, 1992; White & Wehlage, 1995). White and Wehlage (1995) found several generic problems in trying to establish community collaboration:

- *Slippage between policy and action* because case mangers were generally unsuccessful in overcoming the "turf battles" among existing agencies and in getting collaboratives to address them;
- *Discord over reform policies* because of fundamental disagreements over the definitions, causes, and remedies to problems;
- *Disjuncture between policy and community conditions* because of the top-down organization of the collaboratives that resulted in an incomplete understanding of the problems and hence ineffective policies.

These problems, clearly evident in New Futures school reforms, paralleled those found in the earlier evaluation of restructured schools. In particular, "most educators in New Futures schools believed that the problems that created at-risk students were problems inside the students, not inside the school and its curriculum" (Wehlage et al., 1992, p. 73). Hence, as found in the other systemic reform efforts, there was little incentive or support for changing the fundamental functioning of schools.

CONCLUSION

The United States does seem to have the capacity to reduce school dropouts and eliminate disparities among racial and ethnic groups, or at least has the potential to do so. Capacity requires technical expertise to develop and implement effective dropout-prevention and recovery programs. A number of program models have been developed, implemented, and evaluated to demonstrate this expertise. These program models range from early intervention programs serving preschool students, to supplemental yet comprehensive middle school programs, to alternative middle and high school programs.

But to achieve widespread improvement in the dropout problem requires both systemic and programmatic solutions. And here the expertise does not yet exist. While individual effective schools and their salient features have been identified, large-school systemic solutions to the dropout problem require resources, technical expertise, and incentives to restructure existing schools (Hanushek & Jorgenson, 1996). Such solutions have been tried, but have not succeeded.[5] Research suggests why systemic reforms of schools and other agencies serving youth are problematic, but not how to address the problems. In their review of the New Futures initiative, White and Wehlage (1995) in fact conclude that institutional change is too difficult, and instead argue for a strategy of building social capital among community members:

Given the goal of building social capital, the criteria for a successful collaborative would shift from delivering services more efficiently to success in fostering community. Social capital contributes to community by fostering networks of interdependency within and among families, neighborhoods, and the larger community. In building social capital, successful collaboratives will change the role of social service institutions. Resources held by agencies will go to building networks of support that are integral to families and neighborhoods. The shift from delivering services to individual clients to investing in the social capital of whole groups of people appears to be essential if collaboratives are to ultimately improve the life changes of generations of at-risk children. (p. 35)

While this approach may appear worthwhile as a way of more effectively challenging resources and providing support to the institutions that serve at-risk youth, the approach is yet unproven. Moreover, it still requires a commitment of resources sufficient to substantially improve the lives of children and families.

This gets to the issue of political will. Does the United States have the political will to invest the resources to substantially reduce dropout rates and eliminate disparities among racial and ethnic groups? The answer appears to be no. One reason for this conclusion is that even programmatic solutions that have proved to be both effective and cost-effective have not been successful in attracting widespread funding. For example, the Perry Pre-School program has been shown to provide social benefits in excess of seven times program costs, yet the United States has yet to fully support preschool services for low-income youth (Barnett, 1995). And despite several decades of school finance reform to eliminate disparities in the funding of public schools, widespread disparities still exist (e.g., Betts, Rueben, & Danenberg, 2000; Kozol, 1991).

Without eliminating disparities in the resources of families, schools, and communities, it is also unlikely that the United States will ever eliminate disparities in dropout rates among racial and ethnic groups. And those disparities may be more difficult to eliminate in the face of increasing racial and ethnic segregation of America's schools (Orfield, Bachmeier, James, & Eitle, 1997).

NOTES

1. This chapter is the second part of Chapter 6, "Why Students Drop Out of School."
2. Purkey and Smith (1985) generated a list of 13 features of effective schools that are necessary to change the culture of the school. Newman (1993) identified a list of four commitments and competencies required of teachers, along with a list of four ideas that he describes as a "loose theory about what is needed to make substantial changes in the current

educational system" (p. 9). Wehlage et al. (1989) describes a series of qualities in the school staff, the culture, and the structure of successful dropout-prevention schools.

3. One issue that is rarely discussed in the literature on effective schools is the extent to which teachers are recruited and selected into effective schools. A private conversation with the principal of Central Park East revealed that teachers in that school are interviewed and selected based on a desired set of commitments and competencies, even though the school provides ongoing professional development for its teachers. The selection of teachers may be especially important regarding the belief that all students can and should succeed in school.

4. See Hanushek and Jorgenson (1996) for a discussion of incentives.

5. Chicago has probably come closest to achieving large-school systemic reform, although widespread variation exists in the extent of meaningful reform (see Hess, 1995).

REFERENCES

Barnett, W. S. (1995). Long-term effects of early childhood programs on cognitive and school outcomes. *Future of Children, 5,* 25–50.

Betts, J. R., Rueben, K. S., & Danenberg, A. (2000). *Equal resources, equal outcomes? The distribution of school resources and student achievement in California.* San Francisco: Public Policy Institute of California.

Currie, J. (2001). Early childhood education programs. *Journal of Economic Perspectives, 15,* 213–238.

Dynarski, M., & Gleason, P. (1998). *How can we help? What we have learned from federal dropout-prevention programs.* Princeton, NJ: Mathematica Policy Research.

Gándara, P., Larson, K., Mehan, H., & Rumberger, R. (1998). *Capturing Latino students in the academic pipeline.* Berkeley, CA: Chicano/Latino Policy Project.

Hanushek, E. A., & Jorgenson, D. W. (Eds.). (1996). *Improving America's schools: The role of incentives.* Washington, DC: National Academy Press.

Hess, G. A. Jr. (1995). *Restructuring urban schools: A Chicago perspective.* New York: Teachers College Press.

Karoly, L. A., Greenwood, P. W., Everingham, S. S., Houbé, J., Kilburn, M. R., Rydell, C. P., Sanders, M., & Chiesa, J. (1998). *Investing in our children: What we know and don't know about the costs and benefits of early childhood interventions.* Santa Monica, CA: RAND. Retrieved June 16, 2004, from http://www.rand.org/publications/MR/MR898/.

Kozol, J. (1991). *Savage inequalities: Children in American schools.* New York: Crown.

Louis, K. S., & Miles, M. B. (1990). *Improving the urban high school: What works and why.* New York: Teachers College Press.

National Education Goals Panel. (1999). *National Educational Goals report: Building a nation of learners, 1999.* Washington, DC: U.S. Government Printing Office.

National Research Council, Panel on High-Risk Youth. (1993). *Losing generations: Adolescents in high-risk settings.* Washington, DC: National Academy Press.

Newmann, F. M. (1993). Beyond common sense in educational restructuring. *Educational Researcher, 22,* 4–13, 22.

Orfield, G., Bachmeier, M., James, D. R., & Eitle, T. (1997). Deepening segregation in American public schools: A special report from the Harvard Project on School Desegregation. *Equity and Excellence in Education, 30,* 5–24.

Purkey, S. C., & Smith, M. S. (1985). School reform: The district policy implications of the effective schools literature. *Elementary School Journal, 85,* 354–389.

Slavin, R. E., & Fashola, O. S. (1998). *Show me the evidence! Proven and promising programs for America's schools.* New York: Corwin.

Stern, D., Dayton, C., Paik, I.-W., Weisberg, A., & Evans, J. (1988). Combining academic and vocational courses in an integrated program to reduce high school dropout rates: Second-year results from replications of the California Peninsula Academies. *Educational Evaluation and Policy Analysis, 10,* 161–170.

U.S. General Accounting Office. (1987). *School dropouts: Survey of local programs. GAO/HRD-87-108.* Washington, DC: U.S. Government Printing Office.

van Heusden Hale, S. (2000). *Comprehensive school reform: Research-based strategies to achieve high standards.* San Francisco: WestEd.

Wehlage, O. G., Rutter, R. A., Smith, G. A., Lesko, N., & Fernandez, R. R. (1989). *Reducing the risk: Schools as communities of support.* New York: Falmer Press.

Wehlage, G., Smith, G., & Lipman, P. (1992). Restructuring urban schools: The New Futures experience. *American Educational Research Journal, 29,* 51–93.

White, J. A., & Wehlage, G. (1995). Community collaboration: If it is such a good idea, why is it so hard to do? *Educational Evaluation and Policy Analysis, 17,* 23–38.

CHAPTER 12

Interpreting the Evidence from Recent Federal Evaluations of Dropout-Prevention Programs: The State of Scientific Research

MARK DYNARSKI

Beginning in the late 1980s, the U.S. Department of Education conducted three extensive evaluations of the effectiveness of programs to reduce high school dropout rates. The programs and the evaluations were supported by funds from the Carl Perkins Vocational Education Act and two phases of the School Dropout Demonstration Assistance Program (SDDAP), one operating from 1989 to 1991, the other from 1991 to 1996. Together, the three evaluations studied more than 100 dropout-prevention programs, and rigorous evaluation designs were used for 30 of these programs. There have been very few large-scale evaluations of solutions to the dropout problem.

Findings from the three evaluations show that most programs did not reduce dropout rates by statistically significant amounts, but some programs did improve some outcomes: three programs (funded in the second phase of the SDDAP) that prepared students who had already dropped out to get the General Education Development certificate improved GED completion rates; an alternative high school on a community college campus reduced dropout rates; and several alternative middle schools reduced dropout rates.

The three evaluations were broad-ranging studies, two of which relied on random assignment techniques to measure program effects reliably. Considering the extent and rigor of these evaluations, it is reasonable to ask whether their findings comprise a menu of program approaches that a policymaker or education program developer could use to select an effective dropout-prevention program for their school or district.

In this chapter, I argue that we do not yet have a menu of program options for helping students at risk of dropping out. The evaluation findings are useful as guides to further program development and testing, but they fall short of providing a scientific basis for implementing programs in new schools or districts based on the models.

Recognizing the urgency of the issue, however, I suggest an alternative approach to identify strategies for helping at-risk students that program developers can use while efforts to develop a stronger scientific basis for programs continue. The approach I suggest puts a premium on the ability of a program developer to readily see or infer the "logic model" inherent in a strategy being considered. The logic model is the statement of the pathways by which a program will achieve its objectives.

According to the approach I suggest, programs are more desirable when it is clear how they can be expected to affect teaching or learning, or to keep students in school. Doubts or confusion about how a program will achieve its objectives should be viewed as a downside to adopting the program. I note the effective elements of dropout-prevention programs, and suggest that implementing these elements—rather than "a program"—may be a useful strategy to reduce dropout rates.

A SUMMARY OF KEY EVALUATION FINDINGS

The largest-scale and longest of the three evaluations (carried out from 1991 to 1998) focused on programs funded by the second phase of the School Dropout Demonstration Assistance Program. The evaluation studied 20 programs in depth, collecting data on almost 10,000 students for up to three years. Experimental designs were used for 16 of the 20 programs (which were termed *targeted* because students meeting particular criteria were targeted for program services). Of the 16 programs, eight served middle school students and eight served high school students. The other four programs were schoolwide reform efforts that were evaluated using comparison-student designs.

Random assignment is a powerful method. It compares what happens to program participants (technically, treatment-group members) to what happens to students who are statistically equivalent to program participants (technically, control-group members). These students were eligible for the programs but were denied entry as part of the evaluation. Experiences of equivalent students are a proxy for what would have happened to program participants if they had not been able to enter the program.[1]

Summary results for the 16 programs are presented in Tables 1 and 2.[2] Among the eight middle school dropout-prevention programs, half provided

TABLE 1

Impact of Middle School Dropout-Prevention Programs

	Average Treatment Group Mean	Average Control Group Mean	Number of Sites	Number of Sites with Significant Impact[a]
SUPPLEMENTAL PROGRAMS				
Dropout Rate (Percentage)				
End of Year 2	7.8	7.0	4	0
End of Year 3	11.5	15.0	4	0
Days Absent				
During Year 2	10.5	10.0	4	0
During Year 3	14.3	14.3	4	0
Math Grade				
Year 2	69.5	68.3	4	1(+)
Year 3	67.5	67.0	4	0
Reading Score (Percentile)				
Year 2	36.0	35.5	2	0
Year 3	37.0	34.0	1	0
ALTERNATIVE MIDDLE SCHOOL PROGRAMS				
Dropout Rate (Percentage)				
Year 2	4.7	9.3	3	1(–)
Year 3	9.0	18.0	2	1(–)
Highest Grade Completed				
Year 2	7.9	7.4	3	3(+)
Year 3	8.6	8.1	2	2(+)
Days Absent				
During Year 2	18.3	15.3	4	3(+)
During Year 3	18.0	17.0	2	0
Math Grade				
Year 2	65.0	66.3	3	0
Year 3	62.0	64.0	2	0
Reading Score (Percentile)				
Year 2	16.3	16.7	3	0
Year 3	28.0	31.0	1	0

Source: Dynarski et al. (1998)

[a] Plus and minus signs indicate whether impact was positive or negative.

low-intensity supplemental services such as tutoring or occasional classes to promote self-esteem or leadership.[3] Four middle school programs in the evaluation took a more intensive approach to serving at-risk students. Two of these programs, the Griffin-Spaulding Middle School Academy near Atlanta, Georgia, and the Accelerated Academics Academy in Flint, Michigan, were alternative middle schools with facilities that were physically separate from the regular district middle schools. The other two programs—Project COMET in Miami, Florida, and Project ACCEL in Newark, New Jersey—were located within regular schools but separated their students from other students within the school for much of the day. These four programs typically taught students in smaller classes than regular middle school classes and provided more intensive counseling services (than other students received). Three of the four programs primarily served students who were over-age for their grade level, and these programs attempted to accelerate students' academic progress to allow them to "catch up" with their age peers.

Supplemental programs had almost no impact on student outcomes. None of the programs affected the dropout rate, and average student grades, test scores, and attendance were similar among treatment- and control-group students (Table 1).[4] The alternative middle school programs in the evaluation were more successful in keeping young people in school and accelerating their academic progress. Treatment-group students admitted to these programs were half as likely to drop out as control-group students and completed on average a half grade more of school (Table 1). On the other hand, alternative middle schools did not seem to help students learn more in school. The alternative middle schools in the study did not improve grades or test scores, and they had an impact on attendance in the wrong direction (treatment-group students were absent more often than control-group students). Although students were promoted at a faster rate than students in regular middle schools, student learning did not seem to improve in these programs.

The effects of alternative middle schools were concentrated primarily in the Atlanta and Flint programs (see box). Evidence from these cities suggests that something positive happened for their students. On the sobering side, however, is the lack of effect on attendance and academic performance.

The high school programs were all more intensive than the middle school programs. Five of the high school dropout-prevention programs in the evaluation offered high school diplomas; four were alternative high schools, one was a school within a school.[5] None of the five programs significantly lowered dropout rates (Table 2). However, alternative high schools seemed to influence whether students earned a diploma or a GED. In four of the five alternative high school programs, more students earned high school diplomas and fewer

TABLE 2

Impact of High School Dropout Prevention

	Treatment-Group Mean	Control-Group Mean	Number of Sites	Number of Sites with Significant Impact[a]
ALTERNATIVE HIGH SCHOOL PROGRAMS				
Dropout Rate				
End of Year 2	35	30	5	1(+)
End of Year 3	39	40	3	0
Completion Rate				
HS Diploma	21	15	4	0
GED	13	19	4	1(–)
Either	33	34	4	0
GED PROGRAMS				
Dropout Rate				
End of Year 2	56	58	3	0
End of Year 3	57	60	3	0
Completion Rate				
HS Diploma	9	3	3	0
GED	30	20	3	0
Either	39	24	3	1(+)

Source: Dynarski et al. (1998).

Note: For alternative high schools, completion rates refer to the second follow-up year for two programs and the third follow-up year for two programs. For GED programs, completion rates refer to the third follow-up year.

[a] Plus and minus signs indicate whether impact was positive or negative.

earned GED certificates compared to control-group students. The differences were not statistically significant in any of the four sites, but the pattern is consistent across sites. Control-group students were less likely to earn a high school degree and more likely to earn a GED.

A closer look at Seattle's Middle College High School provides insight into how alternative high schools can affect high school completion. Middle College High School had higher high school completion rates and lower GED completion rates (see box) for students whose characteristics suggested that they were least likely to drop out (termed "low-risk" students in the box, though most were at some risk of dropping out). The school also reduced dropout rates for high-risk students.

Impact in Atlanta and Flint

	ATLANTA		FLINT	
	Treatment Group	Control Group	Treatment Group	Control Group
Dropout Rate (Percentage)	6	14	2	9
Highest Grade Completed	8.6*	7.9	8.5*	7.8
Math Grade	59	63	67	66
Reading Score (Percentile)	—	—	12	12

Note: All outcomes are measured at the end of the second follow-up year, except for highest grade completed, which is measured at the end of the third follow-up year in Flint.

* Significantly different from the control group at the 10 percent level, two-tailed test.

Source: Dynarski et al. (1998).

Impact of Seattle's Middle College High School

Seattle's Middle College High School is an alternative high school on a community college campus. The program served dropouts or students on the verge of dropping out of regular high schools and screened students to ensure that they were motivated to succeed.

	LOW-RISK STUDENTS		HIGH-RISK STUDENTS	
	Treatment Group	Control Group	Treatment Group	Control Group
Dropout Rate	33	33	27*	42
Completion Rate	53	56	59	58
HS Diploma	33	24	27	25
GED	20	32	32	33
In High School	13	11	13	0

Note: Outcomes are measured at the end of the third follow-up year. Percentages may not add to 100 because of rounding.

* Significantly different from the control group at the 10 percent level, two-tailed test.

Source: Dynarski et al. (1998)

One key feature of Middle College High School is that its staff and current students interviewed prospective students to ensure that they were adequately motivated for the challenge of completing high school. The positive impact of the school suggests that alternative high schools possibly can be successful when they serve students who want to succeed. Of course, some caution needs to be exercised in linking program effects to any one program feature.

Three other programs offered GED certificates. Each program was structured as a small alternative high school. Two programs in the evaluation, the Queens, New York, Flowers with Care Program and the St. Louis, Missouri,

Impacts of the St. Louis Metropolitan Youth Academy

St. Louis' Metropolitan Youth Academy is a GED program for highly at-risk students. Nearly all of the students served were dropouts and had, on average, the most risk factors of any program in the evaluation. The program was more successful at helping students earn GEDs than other programs in the St. Louis area.

	ST. LOUIS	
	Treatment Group	*Control Group*
Dropout Rate	60	66
Completion Rate	39	22
HS Diploma	11	3
GED	28	19
Attending HS or GED program	2	11

Note: All outcomes are measured at the end of the third follow-up year.

Source: Dynarski et al. (1998)

Metropolitan Youth Academy, were designed to help students prepare for the GED. A third program, the Student Training and Re-entry Program in Tulsa, Oklahoma, was a transition program for high school dropouts to help them determine and achieve an appropriate educational goal, which usually turned out to be a GED certificate. Table 2 shows that participants in the three GED programs were more likely to earn their GED certificates than control-group students, and even somewhat more likely to complete their diplomas than control-group students (this result arises because students who start in GED programs can leave the program and go to other programs or back to high school). The total effect is that GED programs improved the overall high school completion rate from 24 to 39 percent, a relative increase of more than 60 percent.

Among the three GED programs, the Metropolitan Youth Academy in St. Louis had the largest effects (see box), with 39 percent of treatment-group students earning a GED certificate or a high school diploma within three years, compared to 22 percent of control-group students. This is a substantial effect, and it is especially notable since the academy served students who were more at risk than any other program in the evaluation.

LEARNING FROM EVALUATIONS

Knowing that some programs have beneficial effects is a good start. From a scientific standpoint, the logical and careful next step would be to replicate an effective program in a variety of circumstances and possibly with a variety of different "tweaks."

Two reasons to replicate a program are the contextual nature of program effects and the difficulty of implementing a program exactly to specification. The contextual nature of the effects arises because measured effects of the program depend on the experiences of the control or comparison group. A program impact is a relative concept, a difference in outcomes between two groups. The weakness of evaluation findings based on only a few sites is that the same effects may not arise when a program is implemented in a different site with a different context for the control or comparison group (for example, the control group may have more or fewer services available). The value of testing the model in a range of settings is precisely so that the control or comparison group contexts can vary and the impact of the program can be measured against the varied contexts.

The second reason to replicate is to test the robustness of the model to changes in its services or approaches. A program may be successful because a constellation of intangible elements comes together in its favor, but whether the constellation can be replicated elsewhere is a key issue. The program may have had a particularly effective leader or staff, or outstanding support from district administrators. It may be possible to specify generally how a program should be implemented, but it is more challenging to "have an effective leader" or "ensure that district administrators support the program." Replication is useful for testing whether the unseen elements of a program are the crucial ingredient to its success. If they are, replicating the program's success is unlikely.

Implementing a program exactly as a model or the program's designers would specify is rarely possible (perhaps *adaptation* is a better term than replication). Programs serving young people typically consist of interrelated services and activities whose composition depends on infrastructure, skills, and resources in the local area. A school-within-a-school program, for example, consists of a physical space, a targeting strategy for whom should be served, and possibly smaller class sizes, a different curriculum, training for teachers, social services or counseling, and a modified governance or administrative structure. A school district wanting to implement a school-within-a-school may have a board with diverse views on serving at-risk students, a collective-bargaining agreement that governs how the program can be staffed, and physical or regulatory constraints on the particular space to be used for the program.

With local circumstances possibly requiring modifications or compromises to the model, policymakers face the task of identifying priorities in what they implement with little guidance about the relative importance of the elements of a program's success. It would not be surprising if programs often were implemented that were flawed copies or were otherwise less effective than their models. The task is somewhat like trying to follow a recipe that lists only the ingredients to be combined but does not provide quantities.

Referring to the impact findings above, a strict interpretation of the findings is that the results for alternative middle schools are promising for program contexts similar to what the control groups experienced in Flint and Atlanta. To assess the ultimate promise of the programs, however, alternative middle schools based on the Flint and Atlanta models would need to be replicated in other districts and possibly with some variations in services or students served. A middle school model that was effective when implemented in a range of school districts, and probably with deviations from its initial model, would be a promising approach for helping at-risk middle school students. Evidence from replications sets a high standard and programs meeting the standard merit special attention. Studies of replications of successful programs, such as the U.S. Department of Labor's study of the Quantum Opportunities Program, suggest why studying replications is valuable (Maxfield, Schirm, & Rodriguez-Planas, 2003). The study found that the replication programs were far less effective than the model program based on Philadelphia. The Department of Labor's replication of the Center for Employment Training and Career Academies likewise has found less positive evidence for replications than was found for the initial model program (see Kemple, 2004).

By its nature, replication involves multiple units—schools, districts, or perhaps states—implementing a program. Considering how decentralized education is, however, higher-level government agencies, foundations, or partnerships need to assume responsibility for conducting replication research. At the federal level, which arguably has the most resources to devote to research, evaluations of education programs are increasingly common as a tool for understanding and developing better programs and for accountability.

However, federally funded education programs generally are not highly prescriptive about what states or districts need to do to operate the program, and in response, local programs can attain a wide variety of shapes and sizes, even when being funded from the same federal source. In this context, evaluations of federal programs typically focus on the question of whether the *federal* program is effective rather than on whether *local* programs are effective. For example, the federal evaluation of the Title I program (Puma, Jones, Rock, & Fernandez, 1993) was based on nationally representative samples of students in about 100 school districts and about 400 schools, and results are not reported at the district or school level. The national evaluation of the Upward Bound program (Myers & Schirm, 1999) is based on a random sample of local programs, which means the findings can be generalized to the program as a whole, but the sample sizes for any one program are small (averaging about 50 students) and not designed to support inferences about which local program approaches are most effective.

Federal evaluations also have not often tested various models relative to each other. The value of doing so is that the tests yield evidence about winners and losers. However, testing models against other models would mean exercising far more control of the types of programs that are funded, and possibly even controlling the allocation of programs (such as by random assignment) to school districts or schools that carry them out. This more scientific funding strategy—in which programs are funded consistent with a strategy for replicating models—is consistent with the view expressed by Nobel Laureate James Heckman, who, with Jeffrey Smith, wrote,

> The end result of a research program based on experiments is just a list of programs that "work" or "don't work," but no understanding of why they succeed or fail. The long-run value of cumulative knowledge is high, but is neglected by advocates of "short-run" evaluations conducted outside of coherent social-science frameworks. (Heckman & Smith, 1995)

Addressing Heckman and Smith's criticism is difficult in a context in which the criteria for granting funds to implement programs are not created with scientific learning in mind. For discretionary grant programs, reviewers rate grant applications based on specified criteria, resulting in a list of applicants who have the highest ratings and who, subject to agency discretion to ensure geographic or other types of balance, receive the grants. Only by happenstance would funded applicants fit within a scientific strategy (a planned variation, for example) that would support testing particular models. Formula-funded grant programs, which generally direct money to states based on some count of individuals or students in a state, offer even less discretion and therefore are less likely to meet scientific criteria.

Ensuring that applicants fit within a scientific strategy would mean identifying scientific criteria in advance and picking applicants to fit within these (and presumably other) criteria. Recent federal initiatives—such as programs supported by Reading First, 21st Century Community Learning Centers, and the small learning communities initiative—have awarded grants in competitions that did not employ scientific criteria in making decisions. As such, any evaluation of these programs necessarily must try to learn what they can within constraints that may or may not give the needed balance to enable the evaluation to study particular hypotheses or models. Recent efforts by the U.S. Department of Education's Institute of Education Sciences to develop and test education program models show strong promise for enabling researchers to study replications as planned variations. Results from these efforts will not be available for at least several years.

MAKING DO WITH LESS

In the end, policymakers and program operators have to make decisions about programs and funding with less information, perhaps much less information, than the scientific ideal would suggest. Rather than a well-tested model of an alternative middle school, for example, the policymaker is presented with evidence of one or two alternative middle schools or GED programs that were found to be effective. Is this a basis for implementing these programs?

Borrowing a principle from investment planning, I suggest that a program developer or funder considering a new program (a risky investment) should strive to understand how a program's structure or approach will yield the expected results. However, I am not suggesting that policymakers should implement versions of alternative middle schools based on the Flint and Atlanta programs or GED programs based on the Metropolitan Youth Academy in St. Louis. These programs might be good starts for replication efforts, but one or two examples of effective programs provide too narrow a base to stand on.

However, we can identify features of the programs that contributed to their effectiveness. For the Flint and Atlanta schools, the program logic was: "The alternative middle school programs in Flint and Atlanta helped keep students in school by creating small schools, with smaller class sizes, that helped teachers know students better and provide more help, and a focus on helping students address personal and family issues through counseling and access to social services." Programs oriented to get students GED certificates had the largest impact on high school completion (albeit through completing the GED). For example, the St. Louis program raised GED completion rates from 22 to 39 percent. For GED programs, the program logic was: "The GED programs in St. Louis, Queens, and Tulsa helped students complete the GED by providing individualized instruction in a small setting with access to counseling and social services."

What is evident is that all these effective programs operated in small settings and paid attention to students' needs inside and outside the classroom. Students had more access to adults who could help them with issues and problems. Moreover, site visitors frequently interviewed program staff members who described how they wanted to help and went out of their way to provide help. The programs recognized that students often had family or personal problems that hindered their ability to attend or succeed in school, and tried through counseling or other means to help students deal with these problems. And the programs recognized that students needed a measure of academic challenge, that even students with undistinguished academic records could respond to teachers pushing them to learn, especially when learning somehow was connected to their personal experiences. Indeed, reviews of other dropout-prevention programs have noted that successful programs generally have this characteristic of personalization (Fashola & Slavin, 1998).

However, it is also true that other programs in the evaluation tried to create small settings and pay attention to student needs but were not effective. These results illustrate why replication is valuable. If the results in the effective programs were due to other factors that were more difficult to observe than small settings and personal attention, a replication would likely show less positive findings. In the meanwhile, the findings here suggest that a high degree of personalization—a strategy of focusing intensively on why students are having difficulty and actively working to address the sources of the difficulties—is worth considering.

NOTES

1. Two features of the evaluation's design affect interpretation of the results. First, students in the treatment group did not always enter or stay long in the dropout-prevention program being studied. By using the full treatment group and control group, instead of just program participants, the evaluation measured the impact of *access to* dropout-prevention programs (known as "intent to treat" estimates), which may underestimate the impact of *participation in* dropout prevention programs. Data collected for the evaluation were not sufficient to distinguish the two different impact estimates. Second, students in the control groups were able to receive other dropout-prevention services. Thus, the measure of program impact reveals how the program affects students relative to other programs in the area.

2. Dynarski and Gleason (1998) present the highlights of the results and findings from the evaluation. Dynarski, Gleason, Rangarajan, and Wood (1998) present the complete findings from the evaluation.

3. These programs included the Albuquerque, New Mexico, Middle School Leadership Program, the Chula Vista, California, Twelve Together Program, the Long Beach, California, Up With Literacy Program, and the Rockford, Illinois, Early Identification and Intervention Program.

4. Table 1 shows average student outcome levels among treatment-group and control-group students across the supplemental middle school and alternative middle school programs in the evaluation. Since data were not always available from every site, the table also shows the number of sites on which the treatment and control averages for a particular outcome are based. The table also shows the number of sites for which the impact was

statistically significant at the 10 percent level. In reporting the results, we focused on cases in which there were statistically significant effects in a large number of sites.

5. The four sites operating alternative high schools were Boston (JFY High School and University High), Las Vegas (Horizon High Schools), Miami (Corporate Academy), and Seattle (Middle College High School). The school-within-a-school approach was used in Chicago (Wells Academy).

REFERENCES

Dynarski, M., Gleason, P., Rangarajan, A., & Wood, R. (1998). *Impacts of dropout prevention programs.* Princeton, NJ: Mathematica Policy Research.

Dynarski, M., & Gleason, P. (1998). *How can we help? What we have learned from evaluations of federal dropout prevention programs.* Princeton, NJ: Mathematica Policy Research.

Fashola, O., & Slavin, R. (1998). Effective dropout prevention and college attendance programs for students placed at risk. *Journal of Education for Students Placed at Risk, 3,* 159–183.

Kemple, J. (2004). *Career academies: Impacts on labor market outcomes and educational attainment.* New York: Manpower Demonstration Research Corporation.

Maxfield, M., Schirm, A., & Rodriguez-Planas, N. (2003). *The Quantum Opportunities Program demonstration: Implementation and short-term impacts.* Washington, DC: Mathematica Policy Research.

Myers, D., & Schirm, A. (1999). *The impacts of Upward Bound: Final report from phase one of the national evaluation.* Washington, DC: Mathematica Policy Research.

Puma, M., Jones, C., Rock, D., & Fernandez, R. (1993). *Prospects: The congressionally mandated study of educational growth and opportunity.* Washington, DC: Abt Associates.

CHAPTER 13

Essential Components of High School Dropout-Prevention Reforms

JAMES M. MCPARTLAND

WILL J. JORDAN

While no single reform model is likely to emerge as the best or only way to prevent dropping out, it can be argued from research that there are at least three broad categories of change that should be present in any serious high school reform effort. These are 1) *structural, organizational, and governance changes* to establish the school norms and interpersonal relations most conducive to learning; 2) *curriculum and instructional innovations* that give individual students the necessary time and help to be successful in a high-standards program; and 3) *teacher support systems* to provide opportunities for faculty input and the continuous backing required to implement ambitious changes. This chapter reviews the arguments and evidence for why each change category must be included in any reform program that hopes to significantly reduce dropout rates. One reform model, the Talent Development High School (TDHS) with Career Academies, will illustrate specific changes in each category and the implementation issues that arise in the real world.

The case that these components are essential for an effective high school dropout-prevention approach can be made through a theory of action that explains how different reforms touch the major sources of high school student and teacher motivation, and with direct scientific evidence that ties specific school improvements to dropout reduction. A theory of action specifies how recommended reforms in manipulable variables (those aspects of a school's structure and practice that can be directly and purposively changed) will lead to intermediate improvements in the informal school learning environments (norms, expectations, and relationships among students and staff), which in turn have a direct impact on desired student outcomes (staying in school and associated successful behaviors). The scientific evidence from evaluations of the

Talent Development model and its Career Academy structure supports the theory of action. Evidence shows that the schools using the model substantially improved student attendance, promotion, and school climate, and that students in the program showed significantly greater gains in reading and mathematics performance than students in control schools.

However, the evidence also shows that putting such a comprehensive reform in place is difficult and requires a supportive reform context, school district leadership, and faculty commitment. Nevertheless, we argue that the problems in troubled urban high schools are so severe that nothing less than a comprehensive reform strategy will work.

A THEORY OF ACTION FOR HIGH SCHOOL REFORM

Figure 1 summarizes a general theory of action for high school reform. It begins on the left with three broad categories of manipulable variables. On the right side are the desired student and teacher outcomes that are the target of high school reform programs. These variables measure the changes or improvements that are the immediate goals of reform efforts. They include observable student behaviors such as improved attendance, discipline, promotion and completion rates, and upward trends in test scores and grades. These may lead to further, longer-run improvements after high school completion, such as college entrance, occupational success, and adult citizenship.

The intermediate causal mechanisms, which focus on the informal and intangible elements of the social and motivational conditions of the learning environment, causally link the purposeful manipulable changes to the desired student and teacher outcomes. The scientific and practical value of a theory of action is determined by the specificity, richness, and persuasiveness of the links in this causal chain.

There are also conditioning variables—that is, the context that can determine the strength and endurance of the causal chains at different levels of the manipulable variables. They usually include the demographics of the school and neighborhood—such as the concentration of family poverty among the students to be served—and the external resources for change—such as the funds available to move manipulable variables to new levels and the readiness for faculty innovations based on previous experiences at the school and recent involvement in the change process.

Organization, Structure, and Governance

The first category of essential high school reforms covers changes in the structure of the school building, the organization of the school schedule for teachers

FIGURE 1

Manipulable Components	Intermediate Processes	Student and Teacher Outcomes

A. SCHOOL ORGANIZATION AND GOVERNANCE

Manipulable Components	Intermediate Processes	Student and Teacher Outcomes
Smaller self-contained units (Ninth-Grade Academy and several upper-grade Career Academies chosen by students)	Improved logistics for managing student behavior (dependable rules enforcement, traffic control)	Improved school climate and relationships
		Improved teacher morale
Alternative on-site programs for students with the most serious problems (Twilight School)	Communal rather than bureaucratic solutions to student problems (teachers do attendance outreach, discipline conferences, and academic coaching)	Improved teacher attendance and energy
		Improved student attendance
		Improved student course passing
Teachers work in teams with common planning time	Positive personalized student-teacher relationship (students experience caring learning environment)	Improved student promotion and completion rates
	Adult sense of responsibility for students	

B. CURRICULUM AND INSTRUCTION

Manipulable Components	Intermediate Processes	Student and Teacher Outcomes
Extra time in core academic courses	Improved probability of student successes	Gaps in students' prior preparation are narrowed
Summer, Saturday, and after-school opportunities to make up credits		High-standards courses are passed and higher-order competencies are learned
Catch-up courses in the first term at students' current skill level		
High-interest content of classroom activities	More engaging program and class work	
Academic program has a career focus matched to student interests		
Cooperative learning with social skills training	Peer reinforcement of learning activities	

C. TEACHER SUPPORT

Manipulable Components	Intermediate Processes	Student and Teacher Outcomes
Planning process for academy and instructional reforms	Staff establishes academies that match local interests and strengths	Staff assumes ownership of school reforms
Common planning time for teacher teams	Teachers reinforce each other's work to address student problems	Teachers implement classroom innovations with fidelity and energy
Intensive workshops followed by expert in-class coaching	Teachers are prepared for classroom innovations and are monitored in their use.	Teachers work together to sustain school improvements

and students, and the governance of management decisions. These changes add up to a restructuring of the size and staffing of the traditional high school into a set of smaller, self-contained units. Each unit occupies a particular space in the building and includes an exclusive group of students and teachers under the direction of dedicated and empowered local leadership. Under the Talent Development model, this translates into (a) a separate Ninth-Grade Success Academy with teams of four to six teachers who share the same 120 to 180 students and have a common planning time to work on individual student problems; (b) several separate self-contained upper-grade Career Academies enrolling 250 to 350 students, with an adult mentor identified for each student for grades 10 through 12; and (c) an on-site after-hours alternative program called the Twilight Academy for the short-term assignment of a small number of students with the most serious discipline and attendance problems. Under this model, each academy has its own management that controls most decisions regarding student discipline and instruction, including an academy principal and a dedicated counseling staff, as well as its own teaching faculty who provide all or most instruction exclusively to students in the academy.

The reorganization into smaller units aims to produce the desired outcomes through specific improvements in school logistics, relationships and responsibilities, and faculty teamwork that largely define the learning environment.

Logistics: As any experienced administrator of a large urban high school knows, school safety and a positive climate can be destroyed if the mundane matters of managing student behavior in the halls, stairways, and cafeteria are not under control. The smaller units simplify and encourage good logistics for managing student behavior. The logistics of controlling unruly student behavior become easier when traffic flow is contained within small areas and rules are personally enforced. When all students in an academy are well known to the adults in charge, no offender can escape anonymously into the crowd. Authorities can establish credible behavior codes, so that students know that misbehavior will bring certain consequences.

Other aspects of the academy structure and schedule also improve the logistics of managing good student behavior. The climate of the upper-grade Career Academies becomes easier to control because the more problematic students in the ninth grade have been located in their own academy, and the most serious discipline cases have been assigned to Twilight Academy. The 4x4 schedule of extended class periods, described more fully later, reduces the number of class changes during the day so less time is lost between periods when control of traffic flow and student behavior is an issue. The ninth-grade schedule also contributes to logistics of good management when all teachers on a ninth-grade team are located close to one another, so students move directly next door or across the hall for the next class.

Relationships and Responsibilities: In the smaller units, all students and adults should know one another by name. This familiarity is an essential building block for a safer and more controlled school climate and for respectful and caring relationships among teachers and students.

The positive student-adult relationships that develop within the academy structure also strongly contribute to improved learning. Teachers are more likely to care about and feel responsible for students in an academy structure. In Career Academies, both students and teachers have chosen their school based on personal interests, so they share a common commitment to their own unit. Teachers in Career Academies are likely to have the same students for two or more years, so they realize they are more responsible for what students will achieve in their subject. There is a shift in both the ninth-grade and upper-grade academies, from a bureaucratic approach that uses specialists to deal with problems of attendance and discipline, to a communal orientation where teachers themselves are the first line of serious response to student problems. Instead of quickly referring problem students to an attendance officer or a discipline dean, teachers on ninth-grade teams or in Career Academy pathway groups deal directly with individual student problems. Teachers call absent students' homes, meet individually or as a team with students having discipline problems, and monitor hall traffic by teaching with their doors open and supervising class changes. Students are more likely to improve their attendance and deportment when they are treated in a caring way by a teacher they know well, rather than being confronted in an impersonal way with little chance to discuss or work out problems.

The smaller structure is also more likely to foster friendly and respectful relationships among students and teachers, which in turn contribute to students' motivation to work hard. In well-run academies, students are greeted each morning at the school entrance by an academy administrator or teacher who has a welcoming message or personal comment for each student. This friendly familiarity usually results in more caring and respectful relationships among teachers and students.

The career focus of the curriculum within each Career Academy adds to students' attachment to their school and their motivation to take their studies seriously. Students who see the curriculum's relevance to their own goals and who are studying things they have chosen to learn are more likely to come to school regularly and to put attention and effort into their schoolwork.

Faculty Teamwork: Any successful high school reform model must generate regular opportunities for faculty members to work together in small groups that share the same students so that their collective energy can create a strong, serious learning environment in each subunit. The daily schedule should provide common planning time for teacher teams in the ninth grade and the upper grades to work on issues of student attendance, discipline, and course credits. The school governance structure should empower the faculty and leadership of each academy to solve their own problems and enhance their own program.

Causal Sequences: As outlined in Figure 1A, the effects on student and faculty outcomes of the smaller units derive largely from improvements in student attendance and discipline, which have direct consequences for student success in earning promotion to the next grade and for teacher morale and energy.

Student attendance improves within a strong academy structure because school becomes a safer, more welcoming place and because teachers reach out to bring back student absentees. In addition, the career focus of the upper-grade academy structure draws better student attendance because of its relevance to students' own interests and goals. Students are more likely to attend regularly when they get along well with the adults in their school and when they feel they are expected to come to school every day and are missed when they do not. Students are more likely to work hard on class work to please a teacher they like and to value a good grade from such a teacher.

Research shows that the student attendance rate is a major correlate of the probability of passing a course, which in turn determines the chances that a student will earn promotion to the next grade. Teachers cannot pass students who miss a significant number of days, and they are also willing to find ways to help a diligent student with good attendance to pass their course. Promotion depends on passing enough courses and earning enough credits. Reforms that improve student attendance will almost surely yield significant improvements in student passing rates and promotion, and lower dropout rates will follow.

Adult control of student traffic in halls and stairways and the reduction of disciplinary incidents that results from the academy structure are noticed and appreciated by the teaching faculty. When a climate of serious academic purpose takes hold and student attendance improves, teachers' morale shifts from weary frustration with struggling to serve all the students to optimism that they can effectively do their job for a greater proportion of students. Under these circumstances, teacher attendance improves, transfers decline, and more staff are willing to do their part to monitor and enforce good student behavior throughout the building.

Impact Studies: Evaluation studies have shown that a school structured into smaller units can lead to major improvements in school climate, student attendance and promotion rates, and faculty morale and commitment. In studies that compare Talent Development High Schools to demographically matched traditional schools in the same districts, student attendance is found to improve by 10 to 15 percentage points; promotion rates from ninth to tenth grade at least double; and schools have significantly fewer disciplinary and management problems in the halls and stairways. Promotion rates from the ninth grade that relate directly to reduced dropout rates improved by 47 percent and 65 percent, respectively, at two recent Philadelphia Talent Development sites. There is also clear evidence that teachers in the Talent Development schools moved from feeling frustrated to feeling fulfilled with their jobs, and faculty members were willing to put in extra time and assume broader responsibilities to make their school work well for students (Corbett &Wilson, 2000; Jordan et al., 2000; Kemple and Herlihy, 2004; Philadelphia Education Fund, 2000; Reumann-Moore, 2000; see also Kemple & Snipes, 1999; Stern, Dayton, & Raby, 1998).

Troubled high schools often start with these organizational and governance reforms because nothing else is possible if the students do not attend regularly, if the school climate is not firmly in control of the school authorities, and if teachers are demoralized at the prospect of working together for major school improvements. When properly implemented, impressive improvements are soon experienced in all three areas, as well as in student passing and promotion rates. But test scores usually do not go up, and many students still fail because they cannot meet high course standards due to poor prior preparation in basic academic skills. To get beyond this first threshold of improvements in school climate, major changes in curriculum and instruction become the next reform priority for high school dropout prevention.

Curriculum and Instruction

One hallmark of current high school reform policies is requiring a core academic curriculum based on high standards for all students. It is based on convincing research that the opportunity to enroll in rigorous courses is a major determinant of whether students will achieve at high levels on tests of academic performance. It seems obvious that students who are deprived of instruction in algebra and other college preparatory subjects by being shunted into low-level courses have no chance of learning the more demanding material. But simply enrolling in a common core academic curriculum with high standards will not be sufficient for many students who have been poorly prepared in earlier grades for high-level high school work.

What is the solution for the many students who enter the ninth grade with poor preparation, and who are likely to be frustrated by demanding textbooks that require reading or math skills several levels higher than they have? The answer is not to lower requirements for some students and return to tracking of courses that withhold high-standards materials from them. Instead, students should be helped to close their skill gaps so they can also be successful with a high-standards curriculum. Three related strategies to accomplish this are: (a) to provide extra time during the regular schedule in core academic courses, (b) to offer carefully designed catch-up learning activities that are attractive to young adults, and (c) to provide recovery chances outside of regular school hours to enable students to make up failed credits or polish weak skills. As outlined in the action theory, when these strategies are well implemented, student motivation to learn is strengthened in several ways and their chances are improved for success in a core college preparatory curriculum.

Extra Time: The Talent Development Model provides extra time for core academic work in the regular schedule by offering a "double dose" of math and English instruction in a ninth-grade 4x4 block schedule and by elective replacement activities and tutoring in the upper grades. Each student who enters high school far below grade level in basic skills receives daily 90-minute classes in English and mathematics throughout the year, which is twice the time students receive in typical high school schedules. Older students who need extra time to close basic skill gaps get additional course work in mathematics or English (or both) in place of elective courses, or are tutored by peers or teachers.

Close Skill Gaps: The Talent Development Model not only stretches the time allocated to core courses for needy students, but also offers some catch-up courses in reading, mathematics, and study skills in extended periods during the first term, so students can be successful at high-standards course requirements in extended-period classes during the second term.

Several features of the catch-up courses are necessary to enhance student motivation. The materials must be highly interesting to young adults but at skill levels that do not frustrate their efforts. For example, in the first-term strategic reading course, which is designed to give students better skills at drawing meaning from texts, novels are at a lower-grade reading level but include characters and situations of interest to teenagers. In addition, the classroom learning activities must allow active student involvement and time for peer discussion to increase understanding. For example, the first-term "transition mathematics" course, designed to close gaps in pre-algebra skills, uses frequent manipulatives and practical problems as learning tools while encouraging students to explain how different solutions can be reached.

Also, it cannot be assumed that incoming students know how to take notes, manage their time, study for an exam, or use the appropriate social skills in cooperative learning teams. Direct instruction in study skills and social skills can be very helpful for students who later profit from the advanced learning activities of high school, such as long-term projects and cooperative learning activities that require different roles and relationships. To provide such instruction, the freshman seminar of the Talent Development Model during the first term of ninth grade has units on study and social skills, as well as an extensive section on college and careers to prepare ninth graders for their choice of an upper-grade Career Academy in their high school.

Recovery Chances: Extra time can also be provided after school, during Summer School, Saturday School, or late afternoon Credit School. Students can attend any of these to make up failed credits so they can be promoted to the next grade, or to continue to close skill gaps through interesting catch-up activities. TDHS actually requires students to make up failed courses after regular school hours as an added incentive to succeed the first time and as a strategy to preserve the regular school schedule for core courses and extra help.

Upper-Grades Instruction: Even with the exceptional achievement growth rates in English and math experienced by the average ninth grader from an effective catch-up instructional program like TDHS, many students will still remain behind in the academic skills called for in the high-standards core courses in the upper grades. So, flexible resources of time and assistance will still be needed after the ninth grade in order to continue to narrow student skill gaps. Double time in upper-grade reading and mathematics, as well as extra help after school and during the summer months, should be offered to students who still have a long way to go to catch up with age- and grade-level standards. In the Talent Development Model, first-term catch-up courses are now also available in grades 10 and 11 to prepare students for success in required high-standards English and mathematics courses during the second term.

Causal Sequences: As outlined in Figure 1B, these approaches to providing extra time and help to needy students can be powerful sources of student motivation. Curriculum and instruction reforms can increase student motivation for learning tasks and lead to higher rates of achievement through the causal mechanisms of (a) improved probability of success, (b) greater interest in the classroom materials and lessons, and (c) social support from peers.

Probability of Success: Learning theory has demonstrated that students' motivation to work hard at learning tasks depends on the level of difficulty relative to their current skills and preparation. If the tasks are too hard for their present skill level, students will feel frustrated because the probability of success is too low. On the other hand, when the tasks are too easy or cover material already learned, students will usually be bored and unwilling to work on activities where there is no real challenge (Brophy, 1998). The ideal of the Talent Development High School catch-up courses in strategic reading and transition math is to hit the happy medium for student motivation: to present learning activities where the probability of success is in reach but challenging enough to engage students. The best balance can be achieved when the learning activities require higher-order thinking skills and deeper understanding, even though the content does not assume a great deal of prior knowledge.

Content Interest: Learning materials that have more immediate interest or clear long-term benefits for students are more likely to capture their attention and to sustain their energies. The Talent Development materials in the catch-up courses use characters and situations with which an urban teenager can identify. The upper-grade lessons seek to blend career applications into core academic courses so students can appreciate the instrumental connections between their schoolwork and their occupational interests.

Social Support: The recommended classroom reforms also feature activities where students work together in learning teams and play different roles in cooperative long-term projects. Students usually enjoy the social aspects of team learning and are more likely to be engaged in lessons where they actively participate rather than passively listening to lectures or filling out work sheets. Talent Development reforms include student training in social skills and human relations so that students can profit from cooperative learning and project-based lessons.

Impact Studies: Scientific evidence shows that selected curriculum and instructional approaches can close major skill gaps for high school students, who can then succeed with common high-standards college-preparatory curricula. Recent evaluation studies in Baltimore and Philadelphia of the ninth-grade Talent Development curriculum show that achievement growth rates in reading and mathematics are double those for matched students taught with the same amount of instructional time with a traditional curriculum. The Baltimore study, which involved 456 ninth-grade students divided between participating and control schools, showed significantly greater gains in Comprehensive Test of Basic Skills reading and mathematics tests for the TDHS students. The Philadelphia study used a sample of approximately 1,500 ninth-grade students that showed similar differences favoring the ninth-grade Talent Development participants on Stanford Achievement Test Ninth Edition tests in English and mathematics, although the reading results were less impressive in terms of over-all growth than in Baltimore (Balfanz & Jordan, 2000; Philadelphia Education Fund, 2000).

Teacher Support Systems

Many reforms fail to show strong positive effects on major student outcomes such as test score averages or dropout rates because they were never implemented as intended or were discontinued after the departure of those who originated them. Thus, it is essential to include support systems so key reforms will be put in place without modifications to their core requirements and remain in force despite the inevitable turnover of school personnel. As outlined in Figure 1C, support systems are needed in the initial planning stages to inspire teachers' commitment to the reforms, and in the implementation stages so that teachers have continuing expert help with their new roles and classroom practices.

At the planning stage, successful high school reform models must strike a balance between specifying the research-based reforms that have been shown to work and providing opportunities for the school's leadership and faculty to engage in an extensive discussion and decisionmaking process on what is best for their school. Reforms that lean too far toward prescription without discussion risk the recommended changes being viewed as coming from the outside and never being embraced and faithfully implemented by local teachers and administrators. Reforms that rely on professional talk among local educators about general principles or goals of a good high school will run the risk that the needed organizational and instructional reforms will not be strong enough and that entrenched traditional practices or interests will not be forced to change.

The Talent Development High School Model recommends a full-year planning process for teachers, administrators, and other key stakeholders to put their stamp on the reform activities. While the basic structural components of an academy and the resources for a common-core curriculum are nonnegotiable, there is plenty of room for the school to draw on its own existing strengths to fashion a local model that suits their conditions. Faculty are asked to define the Career Academy themes, to assist with the building and entrance redesign, to match teacher interests with assignments, and to prepare ninth-grade faculty for team and student outreach activities. Sometimes contractual issues need to be worked out, such as changes in teachers' use of time for common planning. A retreat for the entire school community at a location away from the building can be very useful to the planning process. Other events that mark specific decisionmaking steps within the reform model can keep administrators and the faculty cognizant of their progress and charged up to see the reforms through. The goodwill established during the planning process can also be called upon to address glitches and solve unanticipated problems when the implementation of the reforms is actually under way.

Continuing support for teachers and staff after the implementation process has begun is equally important for realizing all the potential benefits of the reforms. The Talent Development Model uses a multitiered system of teacher supports. It begins with intensive professional development workshops on a few key changes to be experienced by teachers, such as using the extended-period class schedule and working in teams with a common planning period- or on teaching specific new catch-up courses, such as strategic reading, transition mathematics, or freshman seminar. Then, full-time curriculum coaches in English, mathematics, Freshman Seminar, and teaming are hired and trained. They are selected from a pool of expert teachers from the local school district. Each curriculum coach works half-time in each of two participating TDHS sites, offering confidential assistance in the classroom without any input to teacher evaluations. The coaches model-teach a lesson, check up on supplies or materials, offer suggestions, answer questions, or provide any other peer assistance that will help each classroom teacher successfully implement new course materials and approaches. There are refresher workshops every four to six weeks after school or on weekends. The workshops are provided by Instructional Facilitators from TDHS central staff to preview the next units of the new courses and to troubleshoot problems.

The Talent Development Model also arranges for teachers to continue to plan together and to work on teams throughout the school year after the reforms have been initiated. Ninth-grade teachers are members of four- to six-member interdisciplinary teams that share the same 150 to 180 students and have a common daily planning period. Each team selects a leader who is given some relief from teaching duties to work on team functions. Special training is provided on the use of teacher teams to improve student attendance, discipline, and pass rates. A local coach with teaming expertise is available to work with the teacher groups in their common planning periods. Upper-grade teachers in Career Academies are also placed in small interdisciplinary teams with common planning time to work on individual student problems.

The teacher support systems are expensive but necessary for a high probability of effective implementation of restructured roles and instructional approaches. In the Talent Development Model, four half-time curriculum coaches (two full-time positions) must be supported for each participating high school. We also provide regular contacts with TDHS central staff assigned to the school. Workshop stipends for local teachers are also needed for the initial training and the follow-up workshops. TDHS also provides technical assistance manuals and videos for most course units, which teachers can take home and refer to as needed.

Teacher support systems must be an essential element of any high school reform model, because reforms can only reach their full potential if they are accurately and energetically implemented. Planning processes that involve teachers and other local stakeholders are needed to earn strong local commitment to the anticipated changes. Workshops that introduce reforms must be followed up by regular repeated assistance in the teacher teams and in classrooms implementing the changes. Regular monitoring and refresher workshops for each reform component are also needed to keep everyone on task and to address local implementation issues.

SOME DIFFICULTIES TO OVERCOME
FOR HIGH SCHOOL REFORM

Our experience in facilitating the implementation of the Talent Development High School Model in large, high-poverty high schools in several major urban districts revealed why high school reform is so difficult and identified some barriers that regularly appear.

Reform Context: The local context for reforming large high-poverty high schools can be discouraging. Educators have tended to emphasize reform in the elementary grades, both because it makes good sense to build a strong foundation of student skills and because few educators have strong ideas about what to do to help troubled high schools. Local officials are more likely to establish elite selective units and programs at the high school level to provide for the top end of the achievement distribution than they are to be innovative with school reforms for the nonselective high schools. We need to change the prevailing views that only elementary reforms deserve emphasis, and that it's too late to help poorly prepared older students.

District Concerns: Several specific difficulties can also arise at the district level, where support or resources for external reforms may be lacking, local priorities conflict with reform model requirements, personnel policies interfere with reform sustainability, and union regulations inhibit model innovations.

Some districts may have high-ranking officials in charge of high schools who must be won over to accept partnerships with external reform models. For example, the well-intentioned policy to offer only high-standards college preparatory courses in core subjects to all students may seem at odds with a reform model's prescription of extra time with catch-up lessons that meet needy students at their current levels. Since the goal in this case is the same—to have all students succeed at common high-standards courses—a supplemental policy of flexible time and resources to reach this goal can usually be worked out. Final credit for high school improvements should be given to the local educators, so the external providers are properly seen as partners under the local leadership.

Most urban districts are strapped for funds to provide the standard staffing, textbooks, and equipment needed in a traditional high school, so the considerable extra resources for the new curriculum materials and extensive on-site technical assistance needed for most reform models are hard to come by. It doesn't make sense to adopt a reform model if the resources are not available to get it properly implemented and sustained. The costs of reform in a large high school can easily exceed $250,000 for the first year, and schools can typically pay no more than two-thirds of this amount from internal budget transfers and reallocations. The most expensive item is adding local curriculum coaches and facilitators, but districts should see the cost of such personnel as an investment that enables the district to sustain or extend the model after an external partner reduces its presence.

One way to fund reform is through grants, and sizeable grants for high school reform have been available from federal programs such as Small Learning Communities, Comprehensive School Reform Demonstrations, or Title I, and from large private high school reform projects such as those funded by the Annenberg Foundation, the Carnegie Corporation of New York, and the Bill and Melinda Gates Foundation. But the federal funds specifically aimed at comprehensive high school reforms are no longer favored by the current administration, so major political efforts will be needed to insure that such resources continue.

Reform innovations are too often interrupted or set aside to make room for district directives. Most typical is the preoccupation with state and local tests and the directive to concentrate time and instruction on drill-and-practice activities for test preparation. When that happens, everything involved with instructional innovations will be dropped for at least several weeks to prepare students for the mandated tests, often in ways that do not develop students' higher-order skills for reasoning and understanding. District officials, school authorities, and external facilitators of instructional innovations need to work together to maximize the probability of in-depth learning and test preparation.

Personnel policies can either support or get in the way of high school reforms, depending upon the district's consciousness of new roles and responsibilities called for by the reforms. To begin with, some assurance is needed that the principal, as leader of the reforms, will remain in charge of the high school for at least three years to implement the initial reforms and help institutionalize them. Equally important is the empowerment of the local school leadership to establish new roles and relationships and to make the decisions required for the particular reform model. In the case of the Talent Development Model, authority is decentralized to the academy level, with former schoolwide vice principals becoming academy principals.

The local teachers union and other bargaining agents also need to be strong partners in the reform process and outcomes. We have found that the local union representative can be a major source of positive advice and support when he or she is involved early in the reform process and kept in the loop. Efforts to engage district union officials in the reform process and to build professional, trusting relationships can pay great dividends for serious high school reforms.

School Concerns: The local school principal must have a deep understanding of the reform model to be undertaken and a personal commitment to make it happen. In addition, teachers must develop a readiness for serious changes and a willingness to personally help implement reforms. Local educators must be the source of continuing ideas and energy to make the restructuring of school organization and instruction a reality. The locals must develop "ownership" of the specific reforms and demonstrate the "buy-in" by their own actions and enthusiasm. External change agents as outside partners can facilitate the change process and provide technical assistance for new roles and instructional approaches, but they can never "do it for" local educators in terms of making the reforms work.

One serious obstacle in some high schools is that many of the local educators doubt that serious reforms are possible, given the student demographics and local politics or self-interests. In addition, many high school teachers are not used to working together across departmental boundaries, or to taking on duties beyond instructional functions. In the worst cases, some teachers see little possibility that most of their students will respond positively to reforms with good discipline, respect for authority, and strong motivation to learn. They need to come to believe that the students are not "the problem," and that the structural and incentive reforms will draw the desired responses from students. Many teachers also want to retain a strict bureaucratic operation, where they quickly refer all student problems to relevant authorities. They need to understand that a communal approach can positively change the tone and relationships in the school, so teachers can help one another with individual students to address behavior problems.

Changes in school power relationships can also be a source of difficulty, as some who will experience loss or shifts of authority may fight the changes. The traditional department chairs are a most likely source of resistance, especially when schoolwide decisions will be influenced by academy interests and officials, rather than departments. Chairs may be asked to fit into academies as instructional leaders where their expertise is most relevant, while they continue their schoolwide responsibilities with their subject-matter faculty. The person who develops the school schedule must also adjust to new challenges or be replaced at some stages of the scheduling process. It is essential that the scheduler's priority be the academy structure, where space, faculty, and students are allocated to self-contained units. A scheduler who is used to being the arbiter of assignments and having the final say on the master schedule must give way to a decisionmaking process and approval system in which the academy structure is assured.

The schoolwide principal must also be ready to delegate major authority in a decentralized academy structure. The principal of each academy must be located in the academy's space and feel responsible for running his or her own operations, especially in terms of student discipline and faculty involvement in decisions. Schools must also decentralize guidance functions to academy locations. The schoolwide principal needs to have confidence in the academy leadership's ability to make the restructured school work as several strong self-contained subunits.

There are dangers that the Career Academy structure may reproduce a hierarchy of program tracks. For example, some influential teachers at a high school may wish to establish a primarily college-prep academy, with a title such as the Arts and Sciences Academy, which signals an elite status and recruits most of the advanced students in the selection process. To avoid this, Career Academies must be structured so that *every* academy is a college preparatory program, with the same core academic courses in English, mathematics, social studies, and science. Academies should differ only in the practical applications used in each course and in the electives offered. Also, the teachers with the strongest reputations should be evenly distributed among the academies. Advanced Placement courses should also be distributed among all academies, so each one has at least one course and an equal number of such advanced courses. In general, the various academies should be promoted as being equally viable for college-bound students.

COMPREHENSIVE REFORMS

Are *all* of the three major components of school reform—organization, instruction, and teacher support—necessary to establish an effective high school for students who have been placed at risk of failure by their poverty and weak earlier schooling? What compromises in specific reforms—such as an academy structure for only part of a student's program or a curriculum schedule that does not use extended periods—are "reasonable adaptations," and when do they become "fatal mutations"? What elements of a reform model should be nonnegotiable because their absence threatens the overall chances of effective change? What is the proper balance between a "prescriptive" model (where the core elements, including an organizational blueprint and a specific curriculum of lesson plans and classroom activities, are explicitly provided) and a "process" model (where emphasis is placed on bringing together the key stakeholders to work on defining local changes that address a general set of goals, principles, or assumptions about an effective high school)?

For the most troubled high schools, we favor strict adherence to a complete comprehensive reform model of the three key components, where each component is established with no compromises that would weaken the self-contained academy structure, the extended time and extra-help courses within a high standards curriculum, or the continuous support of teachers by expert in-class coaches for instructional innovations. The master schedule must be controlled and monitored to enable the operation of separate academies and common time for teacher team collaboration. A decentralized authority structure must be used so each academy has leaders who feel responsible for successfully operating their unit. At the same time, the reform process should be open to staff influence on important decisions within the parameters of required changes. Local definitions should be sought for the title of Career Academies and course pathways that best suit local concerns, and local initiatives should be encouraged for improving student attendance through teacher team activities and incentives. The reform components can be phased in over a two- or three-year period, but an early demonstration of extensive changes is very important. One common approach is to begin with a planning year, then follow with a Ninth-Grade Academy using double-dose and catch-up curriculum, to be followed the next year by the upper-grade Career Academies.

The entire set of comprehensive reforms is required in the most troubled schools because the strength of each component is interdependent with the strength of the others. Curriculum and instruction reforms cannot influence student learning if students are not regularly attending school and taking their schoolwork seriously. Thus, organizational reforms that make the school environment more welcoming to students and the school climate more safe and serious about learning will set the stage for improved instruction. However, organizational reforms that create smaller, more personalized learning environments may improve attendance and pass rates, but they cannot be expected to raise achievement if the curriculum is poorly suited to students' current level of preparation or does not provide the extra time and intensity to help students catch up and meet high-standards learning goals.

Improved teacher planning and support systems must go hand-in-hand with organizational and instructional reforms to ensure strong commitments and proper implementation. Teacher ownership of new organizational arrangements with their energy to make them work is only earned by extensive up-front planning processes that allow teacher discussion and input for important features of the academy and team structures. The success with which teachers actually put in place new classroom learning activities and instructional approaches depends on the strength of the teacher training and in-class follow-up services they receive. The complete set of comprehensive reforms is also the basis for the sustainability of effective school improvements when school personnel change over the years, including the turnover of the leaders who initially created the reforms. Reforms that mainly concentrate on changing the attitudes and perceptions of teachers and administrators are particularly vulnerable to fade-out effects as new staff arrive who must be indoctrinated into the new vision and policies. Specific organizational and instructional reforms will more likely survive personnel changes and become institutionalized when they are imbedded in the formal arrangements of building space, master schedule, governance structures, and classroom curriculum materials that require conscious action to replace. Moreover, the decentralization of authority under the academy structure and the existence of local curriculum coaches creates a large enough cadre of committed reform leaders in key positions that the positions are unlikely to turn over in a year or two. Finally, institutionalization of a reform model at a high school will largely depend on the early successes, since replacement authorities at a school are unlikely to overturn things that are working and favored by the existing staff.

This is not to say that any comprehensive reform model is safe from unwise personnel assignments or does not need a continuing process to sustain itself. The high school principalship is a position that can make all the difference in whether a particular set of reforms is successfully implemented and sustained. To accomplish this, initial reform efforts should be led by the same principal for at least three years and that successive leaders should have the time to learn the reform model and understand its interconnections with other aspects of the school before taking over. The selection of the appropriate staff to fill key roles of Ninth-Grade Academy principal, team leaders, and school scheduler has also proven to be make-or-break decisions for creating or sustaining effective comprehensive reforms. Ninth-grade leaders need to be able to work well with early adolescents, balancing firmness with caring, and to support the faculty team approach. The scheduler needs to be adept at creating self-contained, small learning communities within the school that have common planning time and to have the judgment to incorporate Advanced Placement courses and schoolwide activities.

The dropout problem is of such alarming proportions in many large, high-poverty high schools that powerful comprehensive reforms are required to produce significant improvements. Trying harder at the same traditional practices within the existing organizational structures of high schools will rarely make permanent inroads on the problem, even with the introduction of unusual leadership personalities and energy. A strong cause for optimism is the growing evidence that a comprehensive set of specific organizational, instructional, and teacher support changes, when well implemented, can save more current potential dropouts from a dire fate, help each student value and enjoy high school, and help students succeed at a high-standards program of studies. These essential reform components should be widely understood, and the resources and time should be provided for the challenging job of implementing and sustaining them in as many high schools as possible.

REFERENCES

American Youth Policy Forum. (2000). *High school of the millennium: Report of the work group.* Washington, DC: Author.

Balfanz, R., & Jordan, W. J. (2000). *Impacts on student achievement of ninth grade transition courses in reading and mathematics* (Report No. 35). Baltimore: Johns Hopkins University Center for Research on the Education of Students Placed at Risk.

Brophy, J. (1998). *Motivating students to learn.* Boston: McGraw Hill.

Corbett, H. D., & Wilson, B. L. (2000). *Students' perspectives on the Ninth Grade Academy of the Talent Development High Schools in Philadelphia: 1999–2000.* Philadelphia: Philadelphia Education Fund.

Commission on the Restructuring of the American High School. (1996). *Breaking ranks: Changing an American institution.* Reston, VA: National Association of Secondary School Principals.

Epstein, J. L., Coates, L., Salinas, K. C., Sanders, M. G., & Simon, B. S. (1997). *School, family, and community partnerships.* Thousand Oaks, CA: Corwin Press.

Jordan, W. J., McPartland, J. M., Legters, N. E., & Balfanz, R. (2000). Creating a comprehensive school reform model: The Talent Development High School with Career Academies. *Journal of Education for Students Placed at Risk, 5,* 159–181.

Kemple J. J., & Herlihy, C. M. (2004). *The Talent Development High School model: Context, components, and initial impacts on ninth-grade student' engagement and performance.* New York: MDRC.

Kemple, J. J., & Snipes, J. C. (1999). *Career academies: Impacts on educational and youth development outcomes during high school.* New York: Manpower Demonstration Research Corporation.

Neil, R. C., & Morrison, W. (2000). *Quiero tener un futuro: A report on the Talent Development Twilight School at Edison High School* (Philadelphia Education Fund Report). Philadelphia: Philadelphia Education Fund.

Philadelphia Education Fund. (2000). *The Talent Development High School: First-year results of the Ninth Grade Success Academy in two Philadelphia schools 1999–2000.* Philadelphia: Philadelphia Education Fund.

Reumann-Moore, R. (2000). *Students begin to think they belong here: Teachers' and administrators' perspectives on the Talent Development Ninth Grade Academy experience* (Philadelphia Education Fund Report). Philadelphia: Philadelphia Education Fund.

Stern, D., Dayton, C., & Raby, M. (1998) *Career academies and high school reform.* Berkeley: University of California at Berkeley, Career Academy Support Network.

About the Contributors

Lisa Abrams is an assistant professor of education at Virginia Commonwealth University in Richmond, Virginia. Her areas of expertise include test-based accountability, high-stakes testing, and special education. She received her doctorate in educational research, measurement, and evaluation from Boston College, and was previously a research associate for the Center for the Study of Testing, Evaluation, and Educational Policy at the college's Lynch School of Education. She has coauthored several journal articles and book chapters on the impact of high-stakes testing policies on teachers, students, and classroom practice.

Elaine M. Allensworth is the associate director for statistical analysis and archives at the Consortium on Chicago School Research at the University of Chicago. Her research focuses on the structural factors that affect school development, as well as policy effects on high school student outcomes. She is currently analyzing system- and school-level factors that affect dropout rates and is beginning work that examines students' postsecondary outcomes. She holds a doctorate in sociology from Michigan State University and was previously a high school Spanish and science teacher.

Robert Balfanz is a research scientist at the Center for Social Organization of Schools at Johns Hopkins University in Baltimore. He is also associate director of the Talent Development Middle and High School Project, which is currently working with high-poverty secondary schools to develop, implement, and evaluate comprehensive whole school reforms. His work focuses on translating research findings into effective reforms for high-poverty schools. He has published widely on secondary school reform, high school dropouts, and instructional interventions in high-poverty schools.

Mark Dynarski is a senior fellow and the area leader for education at Mathematica Policy Research. His research focuses on rigorous experimental studies of programs for children and youth, and he has explored a range of policy issues about at-risk youth, child development programs, afterschool programs, education technology, and college enrollment. He earned his doctorate at Johns Hopkins University. He has published extensively on designing rigorous social and educational program evaluations, and is an associate editor of *Educational Evaluation and Policy Analysis* and *Economics of Education Review*.

Elizabeth Farley is a doctoral student at the University of Pennsylvania Graduate School of Education. Her interests include urban school reform and math policy.

Walt Haney is a professor of education at Boston College and senior research associate in the Center for the Study of Testing Evaluation and Educational Policy, which specializes in educational technology, evaluation, and assessment. He has published widely on testing and assessment issues in scholarly journals such as the *Harvard Educational Review* and *Review of Research in Education*, and in general-audience periodicals such as *Educa-*

tional Leadership and the *Chronicle of Higher Education*. He has served on the editorial boards of *Educational Measurement* and the *American Journal of Education* and on the national advisory committee of the ERIC Clearinghouse on Assessment and Evaluation.

Robert M. Hauser is the Vilas Research Professor of Sociology at the University of Wisconsin-Madison, where he directs the Center for Demography of Health and Aging and the Wisconsin Longitudinal Study. He currently serves as cochair of the National Academies Panel on Standards for Adult Literacy and as a member of the National Academies Board on Testing and Assessment. His research interests include trends in educational progression among racial and ethnic groups, policy uses of educational assessments, effects of families on social and economic inequality, and changes in socioeconomic standing, health, and well-being across the life course.

Will J. Jordan is a senior analyst at the CNA Corporation, a Washington-based nonprofit. His research focuses on explicating the underlying causes of school failure among adolescents and helping policymakers and practitioners formulate workable solutions. He has a doctorate from Columbia University. Jordan has authored or coauthored more than thirty referred journal articles, books, book chapters, and technical reports. Prior to joining CNAC, Jordan was a research scientist at the Center for Social Organization of Schools at Johns Hopkins University.

Phillip Kaufman, who died in 2004, received his doctorate in social psychology from the Claremont Colleges. He joined MPR Associates, a research and consulting firm specializing in education, in 1988 after working for the National Center for Education Statistics (NCES) for four years. He had a lifelong interest in students at risk of school failure. He authored numerous reports on at-risk students using the NCES longitudinal surveys and assisted in designing several of the surveys. Kaufman coauthored the U.S. Department of Education's annual report to Congress on high school dropout and completion rates for more than a decade, and assisted the Interagency and Household Studies Program in conducting its annual study of school crime in the United States.

Kerri A. Kerr is an associate social scientist in the education program at RAND and a former RAND/Spencer Foundation Postdoctoral Fellow in Education Policy. Kerr's research interests include educational restructuring and reform, the education of at-risk students, school choice and accountability, and teacher education and quality. She is currently coleading research on the instructional improvement efforts of three urban districts and is contributing to the National Longitudinal Study of No Child Left Behind sponsored by the U.S. Department of Education. She holds a doctorate from Johns Hopkins University. She was recently a coleader of an evaluation of a districtwide technology initiative concerning the use of laptop computers by students at home and in the classroom. She is coeditor of *Expanding the Reach of Reform: Perspectives from Leaders in the Scale-up of Educational Interventions,* which presents lessons from the field on scaling up educational reforms.

Nettie E. Legters is a research scientist at the Johns Hopkins University Center for Social Organization of Schools and associate director of the Center's Talent Development High Schools (TDHS) program. Her primary research areas include high school restructuring, teachers' work, and equity in urban education. Legters has worked actively in urban high schools to support major restructuring efforts, serving as a key developer and organizational facilitator in TDHS replication sites. She is coauthor of the "Talent Development Planning Guide" and a "Guide for Creating a Ninth Grade Success Academy" and author of the book *Comprehensive Reform for Urban High Schools: A Talent Development Approach* (2002).

Daniel J. Losen is a legal and policy research associate with The Civil Rights Project at Harvard University. His work concerns the impact of federal, state, and local education law and policy on students of color. His recent work has focused on the implementation of the No Child Left Behind Act, specifically the unfair and racially disparate impact of "zero-tolerance" discipline. He is coeditor of *Racial Inequity in Special Education* (with G. Orfield, Harvard Education Press, 2002) and has written numerous articles on racial justice and public education, including (with C. Edley) "The Role of Law in Policing Abusive Disciplinary Practices: Why School Discipline Is a Civil Rights Issue," in *Zero Tolerance: Resisting the Drive for Punishment in Our Schools* (edited by W. Ayers, R. Ayers, and B. Dohrn, 2002). Losen taught in public schools for ten years, including work as a school founder of an alternative public school. After earning his law degree, he worked as a legal services advocate in education law, serving economically disadvantaged students.

James M. McPartland is director of the Center for Social Organization of Schools and research professor of sociology at Johns Hopkins University. Beginning with his participation in the influential 1964 congressionally mandated study Equality of Educational Opportunity (the "Coleman Report"), he has written numerous publications on survey and experimental studies of variations in school effectiveness for poor and minority students. For the past ten years he has led a team in developing and evaluating the Talent Development High School, a comprehensive reform model currently being implemented by over 50 schools in 15 states. He is presently principal investigator of a study on scaling up high school reforms and supporting teachers to close adolescent literacy gaps.

Ruth Curran Neild is an assistant professor at the University of Pennsylvania Graduate School of Education. Her interests include urban school reform, school choice, and teacher quality. Her current projects include an evaluation of an accelerated teaching certification program in Pennsylvania and a study of the effects of magnet school attendance. She earned her doctorate in sociology from the University of Pennsylvania.

Gary Orfield is professor of education and social policy at the Harvard Graduate School of Education. He is interested in the study of civil rights, education policy, urban policy, and minority opportunity. He is cofounder and director of The Civil Rights Project at Harvard University, an initiative that is developing and publishing a new generation of research on multiracial civil rights issues. Orfield's central interest is the development and implementation of social policy, with a focus on the impact of policy on equal opportunity for success in American society. Orfield has also been involved with developing government policy, and has served as an expert witness in numerous court cases related to his research, including the 2003 University of Michigan Supreme Court case, which upheld the policy of affirmative action. He has been called to give testimony in civil rights suits by the U.S. Department of Justice and many civil rights, legal services, and educational organizations. In 1997, Orfield was awarded the American Political Science Association's Charles Merriam Award for his "contribution to the art of government through the application of social science research." He received his doctorate from the University of Chicago and travels annually to Latin America, where his research work is now expanding.

Devah I. Pager is an assistant professor of sociology and a faculty associate of the Office of Population Research at Princeton University. Her research focuses on institutions affecting racial stratification, including education, labor markets, and the criminal justice system. Pager's current research involves a series of field experiments studying discrimination against minorities and ex-offenders in the low-wage labor market. She earned her doctorate from the University of Wisconsin-Madison.

Russell W. Rumberger is professor of education at the University of California, Santa Barbara, and director of the University of California Linguistic Minority Research Institute. He has conducted academic and policy research in two areas of education: education and work, and the schooling of disadvantaged students. In the former area he has focused on the economic payoffs of schooling and the educational requirements of work. His research on at-risk students has focused on the causes, consequences, and solutions to the problem of school dropouts; the causes and consequences of student mobility; the schooling of English-language learners; and the impact of school segregation on student achievement. He received a doctorate in education from Stanford University.

Solon J. Simmons is a doctoral candidate in sociology at the University of Wisconsin-Madison. His research is focused at the intersection of social stratification, presidential politics, and public ideas. His interests include the history of the measurement of socioeconomic class and economic inequality, the role of third parties in presidential politics, and the changing nature of work in a global economy. He has published several articles on culture and politics and is currently completing his dissertation on the impact of class populism in American politics over the past 50 years.

Christopher B. Swanson, a quantitative sociologist, currently serves as a research associate at the Urban Institute's Education Policy Center. He is also the co-principal investigator of a five-year evaluation of a high school reform initiative in the Baltimore City Public School System. Swanson has extensive experience developing and implementing sophisticated research designs and analytic methods for the study of educational processes and program interventions that affect academic performance and social development. During the past year, much of his research has focused on issues of urban high school reform involving small school restructuring and on the implementation of the accountability provisions of the No Child Left Behind Act. Swanson's research on a variety of educational policy issues, including standards and accountability, instructional reform, and high school dropout and completion rates, has been presented at national conferences and published in scholarly journals.

Index